THE NEXT GENERATION

THE NEXT GENERATION

Young Elected Officials and
Their Impact on American
Politics

JOHN R. D. CELOCK

continuum

2011

The Continuum International Publishing Group
80 Maiden Lane, New York, NY 10038
The Tower Building, 11 York Road, London SE1 7NX

www.continuumbooks.com

Library of Congress Cataloging-in-Publication Data
Celock, John R. D.
  The next generation : young elected officials and their impact on American politics / John R.D. Celock.
    p. cm.
  Includes index.
  ISBN-13: 978-1-4411-1951-3 (hardcover : alk. paper)
  ISBN-10: 1-4411-1951-5 (hardcover : alk. paper)
  ISBN-13: 978-1-4411-9394-0 (pbk. : alk. paper)
  ISBN-10: 1-4411-9394-4 (pbk. : alk. paper) 1. Politicians—United States. 2. Legislators—United States. 3. Young adults—Political activity—United States. 4. United States—Politics and government. I. Title.

  JK1726.C38 2011
  320.973--dc22   2010018538

ISBN: 978-1-4411-1951-3 (HB)
       978-1-4411-9394-0 (PB)

Typeset by Pindar NZ, Auckland, New Zealand
Printed and bound in the United States of America

Contents

To my parents for all of their love, support,
and encouragement during the process
of writing this book.
Thank you!

Preface

In the spring of 2004, I enrolled in a class at the Columbia University Graduate School of Journalism called *Columbia News Service*. The class is a news service, where students write six feature stories that are then syndicated on a wire service to newspapers nationally. Developing stories for the class, I found some statistics on young elected officials and this piqued my interest as a hook for a story on this topic for the class.

During the research for this story, I came across something very interesting. Although one-shot stories were common about young people being elected to office, there was very little linking these stories together over the course of time. This thought stayed with me, gnawing at me, saying to me someone needs to tell these stories and see why young people are running for elective office, what challenges they are facing, and how their age impacts their views on public policy. As a journalist, I am a storyteller and I realized that if these stories were to be told, I would have to do it and so I took the plunge.

This book has been a labor of love and an incredible learning process. The stories I have heard in the research process have been interesting and the cross section of people I have had a chance to meet has been great. I have learned so much more about the various regions of the United States in the process of writing this book, since it is impossible to write a book about young elected officials across the country without learning about where they are from.

Do you know there is a debate over urban vs. rural North Dakota? Do you know that agritourism is considered a key to future economic development in Oklahoma? Do you know how interesting lumberjack competitions can be, or how spread out rural Alaska actually is? I learned all this in the process of researching and reporting out this book and although not all of this will be in this book, I am glad that I now know all of it.

The stories of many of the people I have interviewed and included in this book are incredibly interesting and fascinating and unfortunately it was not possible to include everything. Some of the stories are very inspirational. From the young African American woman who persevered to be elected a mayor in the Deep South, to the son of immigrants who left a promising career on Wall

Street to enlist in the Marines after 9/11, to the founder of a project that has rallied young people to politics throughout Oregon.

Along the way some interesting things developed. In fact, in 2008 young elected officials took the forefront of the presidential elections with three out of four of the members of the two major party tickets having been first elected while under the age of 35: Joe Biden was 28 when he was elected a county councilman in Delaware and 30 when he took his Senate seat; Barack Obama was 34 when he became a state senator in Illinois; Sarah Palin was in her 20s when she was sworn in as a city councilwoman in Wasilla, Alaska.

I set the age of 35 as the cutoff age for people in this book. I am not implying that anyone over the age of 35 is old, but I needed a place to stop. The reason for picking 35 was twofold. First off, 35 is the minimum age to run for president, thus making it the highest minimum age for an elective office in the United States; it made sense to look at people who were first elected to public office at the age of 35 or under. Second, societal conditions have transformed the age of 40 in the last two decades, and many of the social landmarks that people had thought they'd achieve at the age of 30 in past generations people are achieving in their 30s now. It made sense to stay under the age of 40 but also go over the age of 30, thus making 35 a nice middle ground.

But I didn't just want to talk with those people who are 35 and under now; I wanted to look at the historical perspective of young elected officials. This led me to seek out such figures as Dan Quayle, Michael Dukakis, Bob Menendez, Elizabeth Holtzman, and Roz Wyman, who were all young elected officials when they started their careers. They were able to share perspectives from being young elected officials in a time period when being young and in politics was a lot different than it is today. While there are many differences between Roz Wyman being a young woman on the Los Angeles City Council in the 1950s and Jane Swift being a young woman in the Massachusetts Senate in the 1990s, there are also similarities between their experiences, spread over 40 years, two coasts, and entire changes in American society. The experience of including people from many generations, I believe, made the experience and subject matter even better.

The other thing about this book is that, when I identified people to interview, I tried to find people who had bright and interesting futures ahead of them politically. Many of the people I interviewed who had started out as young elected officials moved up to higher offices as their careers progressed. From a vice president of the United States to two Massachusetts governors, to a U.S. senator and members of Congress, it is interesting to see how their careers developed. It will also be interesting to see how the careers of many of the people in this book develop and progress. Some will leave office at a young age to pursue other careers, some will be told by voters that they should look for a new line of work, others will be the future leaders of the country.

Being a reporter, I have a need for information. I tried to keep up to date with the various people I have interviewed for this book. In many cases this has meant reading articles and websites to see where their careers have taken them and to find out about the various issues they have been working on. As a key to the whole subject of young electeds, Facebook has been a great method to keep in touch with many. In some cases, such as Sean Duffy of Wisconsin launching a 2010 campaign for Congress, keeping up to date with the issues has required little in way of follow-up. In other, more dramatic, cases, such as the July 2009 indictment of Peter Cammarano III, the mayor of Hoboken, New Jersey, keeping up to date on a story that at times was changing hourly, if not more frequently, required some rewrites. This was a story that affected two individuals in this book, even though only one was arrested.

I cherish everyone I have met on this amazing journey and the memories this has given me. I have made new friends, learned new things, and, hopefully, will be able to add a quality matter of scholarship to the American debate on an important subject matter. Also I hope that this book will share insight into the next generation of political leaders in the country and allow Americans to see exactly where they are now and what motivates them to do what they do. I hope you enjoy this subject as much as I do.

John R.D. Celock
February 1, 2010

Abbreviations

BP: Bus Project

CC: City Council

CP: Communist Party

DF: Democracy Forum

DP: Democratic Party

GP: Green Party

HCDO: Hudson County Democratic Organization

HR: House of Representatives

LP: Liberal Party

RP: Republican Party

SH: State House

SJ: Sustainable Jersey

CHAPTER 1

Family Ties, Career Goals, September 11 and More: What Motivates a Young Person to Run for Elective Office?

What leads someone under the age of 35 to run for elective office? They are embarking on a lifestyle of constant work, media scrutiny, and demands from the public — a life that is not in any way normal. In some cases they sign up to take on a second job that, although classified as part time, is as demanding or more demanding than a full-time job in the private sector. In fact they are not taking on one new job, but two new jobs: the official government work and the political work needed to stay in office. They are giving up time with family and friends and time that could be spent on hobbies. They are making sacrifices in order to hold office.

There are many reasons why a young professional will step forward and decide to run for elective office. Some want to continue on a family tradition, while others are trying to forge a career in politics. Some have an idealistic streak and see politics as a way to push forward their viewpoints. Others have been pushed by a life event or some sort of desire to translate a life event, such as the attacks of September 11, 2001, into something good.

One of the most common pathways for a young elected official into politics is that politics is the family business. This is not an uncommon path, as many people continue on in a family business and do what their parents did; having been exposed to the family business all their life, they choose to continue on that familiar path. Political dynasties are nothing new in American politics. The country, and indeed every state, is dotted with dynasties that have dominated politics for several generations. Adams, Roosevelt, Kennedy, and Bush are known as dynasties at the national level and are spread across several states. On the state level, the names are not as well known, but dynasties continue, be it the Wallaces of Alabama, the Browns of California, or the Frelinghuysens of New Jersey.

Young elected officials who enter politics because their families are politically active at times try to play down the family connections in saying how much it helped get them elected. They note that the exposure of being a member of a political family helps them get interested in politics and helps them get a foot in the door, but it is not the only thing that gets them elected.

The Schneider family is the closest thing you'll find to Democratic political royalty in North Dakota. The family has had a foothold in the state's politics since the 1980s, taking on various positions with four members of the family taking on different roles in the party. The family continues to stretch to other parts of the state outside of their native Fargo. Jack Schneider started the family involvement after being elected to the state House of Representatives in the 1980s before serving as the state's U.S. attorney in the Clinton administration before his death. His brother, Mark, became the state Democratic chairman in 2009. Jack's son, Jasper, held his seat in the state House, ran unsuccessfully for insurance commissioner and was heading the state's federal rural development office under President Obama. Mark's son, Mac, is a state senator who served concurrently with his cousin for his first year in the legislature.

Jasper and Mac Schneider do not deny that Jasper's father's involvement in politics helped bring them into politics. The spark of being in a political household helped bring them forward in the political arena. "I remember coming out here with Jasper and we would run around the halls of the Capitol and it was fun and games for us," Mac Schneider said in a 2009 interview. "Then you realize that public service is a good part of life."

While Mac grew up in politics and took the plunge more willingly than his cousin, working for a congressman in Washington before law school, Jasper Schneider took a slightly different path to the ballot. While he has been involved in politics since as long as he can remember and he remembers those childhood games of tag in the hallowed halls of power in Bismarck, it was a different relationship with his father that led him to run for office. "I don't know if my path was going towards politics until my father's passing," he said. "It was a sad period and it was an empowering period."

After graduating from Jamestown College in North Dakota, Jasper had taken a path leading towards technology and journalism. He had started a company and website during college geared towards fixing computers and was hired out of college by Cisco Systems in their marketing department. He had given some thought to entering law school and going to work for the family law firm in Fargo and possibly entering politics, but it was not something he originally thought he would do. Then his father got sick with terminal brain cancer and his young life suddenly took a new perspective and a new direction. "When my father was dying I was lucky I was at a point in my life where I could take time off and spend a lot of time with him," Jasper Schneider said. "He was in pretty good shape for three to four months and it was a good time for us to share life's little feelings. It was the best and the worst six months of my life. Coming away from that experience it was a tremendous period of growth. I was 21 at the time and I had to grow up quickly."

Coming out of those conversations, Jasper decided to enter law school and started to realize that he had something he wanted to offer the state of North Dakota and a desire to pick up where his father left off. If it had not been for his father's illness and death, he could have decided on a different path in life and not have run for office. The recent history of North Dakota would be different today and Jasper Schneider could possibly be living a simple and private life in the upper Midwest and not running around North Dakota helping to provide economic stimulation in rural parts of the state as part of his role in the Obama administration.

What the Schneiders are to North Dakota Democrats does not match what the Kean name is in New Jersey. The Kean family is descended from the state's first governor, William Livingston, and is one of the few dominant Republican families in the state over the last 100–150 years. Tom Kean Jr. currently serves as the state senate minority leader, his father is a former governor, and his grandfather is a former congressman. Other Keans have held offices ranging from state legislature to U.S. Senate. Tom Kean Sr., who also chaired the 9/11 Commission, is one of the most popular governors in recent state history and whenever he's made noises about running statewide again, he generally freezes the field until he makes a final decision, which typically has been no.

Tom Kean Jr. was born in 1968 and spent much of his time after high school outside of New Jersey. He went to Dartmouth and then worked at the U.S. Environmental Protection Agency in Washington in the first Bush administration before heading to work for a New Jersey congressman. He moved from DC to Boston to attend Tufts University for a Ph.D. in international relations. It is safe to say that he had established a life outside of New Jersey. Then Governor Christie Whitman announced she wasn't running for the U.S. Senate in the 2000 election and the entire state political spectrum was shaken. Congressman Bob Franks announced his bid for the Senate seat and Kean announced, from Boston, that he intended to return to New Jersey with his wife and daughter and run for Congress.

It was an interesting race on the Republican side that year, as three of the four candidates moved into the district when they announced. One relocated from another district where he had been a candidate for Congress and another moved back from Washington to run. Only a local assemblyman had not had to move in order to make the race for Congress that year. Kean noted when he made his announcement that while he did not live in Westfield, the town he settled in when he moved back in 2000, he grew up in Livingston, which was part of the district, and was familiar with many parts of the district from his youth in New Jersey.

Kean says he announced for the congressional seat because of a desire to work on a variety of issues including international relations and the environment. He said that his father's service as governor played a role in him making the announcement as he had exposure to the political world. Kean does not know a year where his father was not in politics, with his father being an assemblyman when he was born. The elder Kean did not serve in elective office from 1978 to 1982, but spent that period running for governor and serving on an appointive board that runs the state's sports complex, thus keeping him in a political life.

Kean is quick to point out that his parents did not expose him and his siblings to the trappings of power and the role of the governorship during the 1980s when his father dominated Trenton. The family continued to live in Livingston instead of the governor's mansion in Princeton. His mother focused on non-political issues and was not active in her role as First Lady. And other perks, including the governor's box in the state's main sports arena and concert venue, were not readily given to the children. The only tangible sign of the governorship in the younger Kean's day-to-day life was the state troopers guarding his father.

Kean became an instant frontrunner when he announced for the congressional seat. With his father's name and the recognition that comes with it, Kean was able to raise money quickly, head to the front of the polls, and secure key endorsements at the beginning of the race. The race quickly turned ugly with Mike Ferguson, another young Republican, running to the right of the moderate Kean and running negative ads against the former governor's son. In the end, Ferguson captured the nomination and Kean was sent looking for a new political path.

That new path came quickly as Kean started running for a state assembly seat the following year. In Kean's part of New Jersey, the only logical advancement for a politically ambitious Republican in local government is the state legislature. Union County has trended Democratic as a whole; Democrats have a stranglehold on county government and Republicans have not won a county-wide race since 1994. Local Republicans have lined up for years waiting for the chance to run for the assembly when a seat opened up and Kean was not one of them. When Assemblyman Alan Augustine announced his resignation weeks before his death, Kean became the instant frontrunner for a seat that had been on the minds of many in the trenches. One candidate contested Kean in the special election convention for the seat, but the vote easily went for the former governor's son. The movement was just as easy a few weeks later when redistricting placed three incumbents into the same two-member assembly district and a long-time assemblyman ended up the odd man out and Kean remained in the legislature.

In 2003, Kean would make another jump when the district's senator resigned for a corporate job. This race was less smoothed by his status in a premier political family than by his seniority in the legislature. He had a few weeks' seniority over the district's other assemblyman, Eric Munoz, and the senior assembly incumbent traditionally moves to open Senate seats in New Jersey.

Kean plays down the role his name and his father had in his quick rise in New Jersey politics. He notes that his father was able to open up doors and give him some recognition but he had to work among the district's voters in order to win the elections and gain the support to serve in Trenton.

Jack Quinn III, from Buffalo, New York, has a lot in common with Kean and the Schneiders. Quinn was elected to an assembly seat in 2004 just as his father, six-term Republican congressman Jack Quinn was retiring from Congress. Running for an open seat as a 26-year-old, Quinn grew up in the heart of the district he was seeking to represent and facing a former assemblyman in the race. Quinn's father, a moderate Republican, had won his seat in an upset in the first election and then easily held it for five elections. He was popular in the district, where he rarely faced strong Democratic opposition regardless of the Democratic overlay. He had made efforts to become close to unions and Democratic leaders, delivering on constituent services in the district. The elder Quinn also had a close relationship with President Bill Clinton during his first years in office until a falling-out over the vote to impeach Clinton.

Quinn also grew up in politics, with his father serving as the Hamburg town supervisor and a congressman for much of his youth. During this time he became familiar with the routines and duties of a life in public service and intrigued by the prospect. Graduating from law school he had thoughts of a future political career, which came from his father's experience in politics. He took a job as an assistant district attorney and settled in for a wait before entering elective office.

After a few months at the district attorney's office, Quinn suddenly had to make a decision. His father announced his retirement and an assembly seat opened up. Quinn's name came up for the congressional seat, but he took himself out of the running, citing his lack of experience for the office. Republicans would nominate the Erie County comptroller for the office and lose the seat in 2004. Quinn instead entered the assembly race, which proved to be tough given the former assemblyman the Democrats ran. He faced criticism from others, including people asking who he thought he was entering politics early in life when others had toiled in the political vineyards for years. He was accused of riding in on his father's name and of not being experienced. Quinn had left the area to attend college at Siena College in Albany and then returned for law school.

Quinn readily acknowledges that he would not be an assemblyman today if he was not the son of a popular former congressman. His father's career helped interest him in politics and gave him an entry into politics at the level that he started in. But he notes that being the son of a politician is not a guaranteed free ride in the political arena. Quinn said he automatically inherited his father's political enemies and those who did not support his father in politics, who looked at him as an extension of his father (who now heads Erie Community College).

In addition, Quinn notes that while his father's name helped get him to Albany, it is up to him to stay in Albany. He said he has to forge his own path in office, creating legislation, forming alliances and doing the work of a state legislator. People are judging him on his own two feet, looking at what he is doing in the assembly, be it promoting higher education, working on criminal justice issues, or trying to stimulate the economy in the Buffalo region. If he does not do his job in Albany or attend to constituent services back home — a key duty of any member of the powerless Republican assembly minority — he can quickly find himself out of a job.

Rosalind Jones did not have to move to Monroe, Louisiana, after law school. She had grown up in Monroe, a poorer community in the central part of the state, and then moved to New Orleans with her mother after her parents divorced. Her father had a life in Monroe as a longtime state representative and senator and she continued to see that while she was also forging a new life in New Orleans. Graduating from law school, Jones started to look at what she wanted to do with her life going forward and where did she want to practice law. Did she want to be with a large firm in the state's largest city and media hub or did she want to return to Monroe to set up a law practice and give back to the community? Did she have any desire to even leave the state and enter a law practice in another city and state? Making her decision before the devastating effects of Hurricane Katrina, she decided on Monroe. "I decided to move back to Monroe," she said. "It is a small community and where I wanted to to be."

Heading back to Monroe, Jones saw the lack of other young professionals in the area. Many members of her generation grew up in the area and then moved on to attend college and graduate school elsewhere before deciding not to move back to that part of Louisiana, if they decided to stay in Louisiana. Many asked what opportunity existed for them in their hometown and decided to move on. It is a story being played out in many communities and many states around the country. The brain drain remains in full effect as high school seniors decide to go to a college outside the area or state and not return. Others are those who go to college locally and then fly the coop, seeking greener pastures elsewhere.

Having grown up the daughter of a state legislator she said that many of these debates caused her to want to look at what she could do to keep young professionals in her part of Louisiana and move Louisiana forward. How could she help create economic development strategies, tackle higher education issues and work to recruit companies to the state? Her father's service in the legislature helped promote to her the idea of running for office herself and using that to promote changes to the system and make improvements. "It was something I had always done," Jones said of growing up as the daughter of a state legislator. She believes that serving in the state legislature that she was destined to do. "We all have a special calling to serve," Jones said. "In the legislature we are able to protect those in the area."

When she announced her candidacy for the state House in 2003 at the age of 25, she was seeking her father's old House seat. With a father who had been in politics, Jones said that it was something that helped her out a lot when she decided to make a run for the House herself. Jones said her father's background as a former state legislator helps her in terms of putting her campaign together. Jones had worked on her father's campaigns and went into the race with an idea of what she needed to do in order to run for the House. When she launched her campaign she started talking with her father, who helped lay out the first steps she needed to take to be a successful candidate in her own right. Jones said her father introduced her to key community and party leaders, transferring contacts to her that he had spent years accumulating. "In learning to run a campaign it was not my first time doing this," Jones said noting her roles working for her father's campaigns. She again does not underestimate the impact her father's service as a legislator had on her first election to office. "I would not have been elected without him," she said.

While Jones was looking to return to her small town in Louisiana and get involved in politics, Eric Croft wanted out. He wanted out of where he grew up in the Spenard section of Anchorage, Alaska. He thought he could move into a new area, meet new people, and experience a new way of life. He wanted a new life that did not involve Alaska's cold and the discussions over oil and gas and fishing that are part of the way of life in Alaska. Growing up in Anchorage, Croft was not immune to the state's politics. He ended up a part of the system growing up because of his father. Croft's father spent a term in the state House of Representatives and two terms in the state senate before being the Democratic nominee for governor in 1978. Croft didn't want to be a part of that lifestyle and was not looking to one day run for governor himself, in a race that could have had him face-off with Sarah Palin. "I did a teenage rebellion thing," Croft said. "I was going to be in high technology. I was going to get out of this one-horse town."

Croft fled to northern California and the rolling hillsides of the San Francisco Bay Area. As someone who wanted to be a part of the technology industry, there was no better place than Silicon Valley, where technology companies were growing by the day and jobs in the industry were continuing to flourish during the 1980s. Croft majored in electrical engineering at Stanford University before pursuing a law degree at Hastings Law School in San Francisco. While enjoying his time in northern California he started to feel nostalgic for home and the way of life that he grew up with and thought he was escaping when he decided to enroll at Stanford. "Coming from Anchorage, the San Francisco Bay Area was cool," Croft said. "After about the 100th traffic jam and looking at the smog, I decided to go home. But there is not a lot of demand for electrical engineer lawyers here."

Back in Anchorage, Croft settled into a small law firm in the state's largest city and found that he did not like the job he had. He had started to get involved in politics, following in his father's footsteps. The move into politics also came from frustrations he had with the state's Republican establishment on several policies including energy issues, the most important in Alaska. In 1995, when an incumbent Democrat in the state House of Representatives called to let him know that she was not running for another term, Croft decided to make the race for the House, the first office his father had held. "I had not really thought of it," Croft said of running for office before he made his decision to run in the 1996 election. "I had been frustrated by the way the Republican legislature was acting and I wanted to make a difference."

On the face of things, Eric Garcetti, the president of the city council in Los Angeles, can be seen as someone who entered politics on the heels of a politically famous father. Garcetti was elected to a district seat on the city council in 2001 at the age of 30, starting his campaign at the age of 29. He ran for the council seat after his father, Gil Garcetti, concluded two terms as the district attorney of Los Angeles County, an office he was defeated for when he sought a third term. The younger Garcetti immediately downplays any influence his father's career on his own career ambitions, noting that his father had been a deputy district attorney, a career prosecutor, for most of his life. "I did not grow up in a political family," Garcetti said. "He ran the year I graduated from Columbia. I was always interested in public service."

Like Quinn, Garcetti knows that his father was not an automatic help in his race for the city council. While the Garcetti name was known, he also was saddled with the fact that his father had lost his most recent race for office, with county voters sending him packing when he wanted a third term as district attorney. He noted that his father brought more to his race by being able to speak Spanish in campaigning door-to-door than in being the county's former district attorney. While Garcetti is an Italian last name, the family has long-standing roots in Mexico, with Eric Garcetti's grandfather's grandfather emigrating from Italy to Mexico. At one point in the run-up to the election in the spring of 2000, he said he started to have a crisis of confidence in whether or not his name would be a help or a detriment on election day. "In November 2000, I asked myself what am I doing," he said. "I would not get a fair shake because my name is Garcetti."

Garcetti said that it was not the family influence that got him into a race for the city council, but rather his own desire. After graduating from Columbia he moved back to Los Angeles settling in the Silver Lake neighborhood, which is dominated by young professionals, and began to teach college and get involved in community activities. But at the same time moving into public service was part of his thought process. "Los Angeles runs through my blood," he said. When he decided to make the run for the city council, Garcetti's attention was not even on the local issues that make up the day-to-day life of a city council-man. He was teaching college, organizing and training activists, and working on human rights issues internationally; a great portfolio in a race for Congress, but not for city council. But at the same time, Garcetti was looking to do something to help his hometown and bring issues to the forefront of his young district. In addition, he wanted to fulfill what he saw as his calling to be in public service. "I went with my heart and my gut," Garcetti said. "My Dad said it was my calling and my partner [now wife] said yes."

By his own admission, Garcetti did not expect to become a city council-man; he thought he was going to get his issues out there, promote the needs of the young professionals in the district, and then head back to the private sector. He issued a 130-point campaign platform, utilized technology, sponsored bar nights, and brought in the Red Hot Chili Peppers to campaign with him.

At the same time, Garcetti was able to focus on some of the issues which he had dedicated his life to prior to the council race. During his time at Columbia University, he obtained a master's degree from the School of International and Public Affairs, where he focused on international issues. While young elected officials like New Jersey's Jennifer Credidio and Steven Fulop went to help focus on local issues in their roles as city council members, Garcetti was focusing himself more on the international track. A conversation with Garcetti today shows that mix of wanting to talk about the potholes and traffic safety issues that dominate any city councilmember's agenda and the bigger issues like global warming, the environment and human rights. During the 2001 council race, Garcetti was able to mix in his passions for issues such as human rights, civil rights, and women's rights as he met with the liberal young professional voters dominating his district, which includes such landmarks as the Hollywood sign.

The parent-child relationships are not the only family ones that move young elected officials into politics. Harry Zikas was elected mayor of the no-stop-light town of Alpha, New Jersey, in 1999 at the age of 20, following service on the local board of education. Alpha is a small town in western New Jersey, on the Delaware River just before the border with Pennsylvania. During Zikas' eight years as mayor, he had the town's first stop light installed. In 2005, Zikas' younger brother, Alex, chose to run for a seat on the borough council, winning one of the seats and working with his brother. Under Alpha's form of government, Harry Zikas as mayor had to assign departmental oversight assignments to each council member and gave his brother the department of administration, which includes oversight over the activities of the mayor's office, along with the borough administrator, borough clerk, and human resources activities. In effect, the mayor was reporting to his younger brother.

The Zikas brothers continue to have a major role in the borough of Alpha even though Harry has since stepped down as the borough's mayor (when his second term ended at the end of 2007). He instead sought a borough council seat, saying he wanted a less time-consuming post in local government in order to focus on new professional challenges and spend more time with friends. But at the same time, the duo continues to work together on a variety of issues in the town and now control one-third of the votes on the council. Under Alpha's form of government, the six council members have votes on all legislation, while the mayor sets the agenda, serves as the executive officer, and votes in case of ties.

Not all young elected officials get their start as family members. Many come into office as staffers or by having a desire to run for office. Outside of having the family connection, working as a political staffer is a common background for many of those who run for office at a young age.

Jessica Lappin dedicated almost her entire career before running for the New York City Council in 2005 as a staffer for her council predecessor, Gifford Miller. Lappin had worked briefly in public relations at a cosmetics company, finding the work not to her liking and wanting to get back the feelings she had while interning on Capitol Hill while a student at Georgetown University. She heard of the young Miller's work on the council and through a contact of her stepmother's was able to secure a spot on his staff. "It was exciting for me," Lappin said of her time on Miller's staff. "I was 23 and had the opportunity to work for someone who was 27. You don't get too many opportunities in your 20s to work for an elected official of your generation."

Lappin grew to be Miller's most trusted aide, eventually taking a post as his district chief of staff, while he was the council Speaker. In this role, Lappin was almost the councilwoman herself, overseeing district issues for Miller, attending events he could not and networking with many active voters in the district. With Miller tending to citywide duties as council Speaker and planning a race for mayor, Lappin's role took on a new importance in his district. Some could say she had the chance to take a test drive in many of the community issues that a councilperson faces on a day-to-day basis during this period on Miller's staff.

When Miller was term-limited out of office in 2005 and sought the mayor's office unsuccessfully, Lappin said she did not second-guess any decision to run for the city council seat. "It was shortly thereafter with term limits, you are forced to think about it," she said. "I loved my job and I wanted to continue to work in public service. I thought why don't I run." In running to succeed Miller, she was succeeding someone who had also gotten his start as a staffer. Miller may have risen to be the second most powerful man in New York City in his early 30s, but his political start was at the bottom, answering phones for Congresswoman Carolyn Maloney of Manhattan's Upper East Side when he was a recent college graduate. Miller quickly rose in politics, moving up the ranks of Maloney's office to take a key role in her district operation. Maloney is the undisputed leader of Democratic politics on the East Side of Manhattan and while Miller brings many family connections in business and the non-profit sector to a race, Maloney's backing helped secure many of the community activities and political volunteers that are needed to win an election. When his predecessor, Charles Millard, stepped down to head up economic development activities in Mayor Rudy Giuliani's cabinet, Miller announced in the special election for the seat winning the seat and setting himself on the path to the speakership.

Miller said that working for Maloney led him to want to run for higher office. Working in her office and on her reelection campaigns, he saw a need for more young people to run for office on the Upper East Side. "It struck me that the people working for her had joined politics during George McGovern's campaign and there were few young people," he said. No sooner than he had entered the city council, Miller started looking at how to advance himself in the council and running for the Speaker's office and becoming the city's second most powerful person. With term limits forcing out most of the council in 2001, he would suddenly be the council member with the most seniority and he wanted to tackle the citywide aspect of the job. While the Speaker's job has a citywide focus, it is still just a district council member elected by the 51-member council to serve as the top leader of the council. "If you are on the city council and want to get things done it is easy to get them done if you are running the city council," he said.

While Miller said he put thought into his decision to make a race for the city council and saw it as a process that made him want to become a candidate himself in order to put more young professionals into the process, other aides who run for city council seats see the same progression but do not see it as something they put much thought into when they make the decision to run for office. Democrat Michael Ross said he does not think he made a conscious decision to run for the Boston City Council in 1999 at the age of 27. He was already working in city government and believes the decision to seek an open seat on the city council was one that just came about as an extension of his existing work. He had been working on the city's website and then moved into a position in the mayor's office. "I decided to run for the Council because the seat was open," Ross said.

Brent Barton came to his 2008 campaign for the Oregon House of Representatives at the age of 28 with experience as a political staffer. He had worked as an aide to a county commissioner and to Congresswoman Darlene Hooley, and in 2006 was the policy director on the successful reelection campaign of Oregon governor Ted Kulongoski. This was not the only political staff experience he brought to the race. He was a longtime member of the Oregon Bus Project, a grassroots initiative to involve young professionals in the political process. Bus volunteers travel around the state helping candidates for the state legislature in the campaign cycle. Barton would later become a board member of the Bus Project, which he cites as being a reason the amount of young elected officials in Oregon has risen in recent years. Barton notes that he had his first political experience at the age of 18, when he interned for a local elected official in Oregon.

Interestingly, with all of this experience Barton did not know if he would run for office. An attorney with a law degree from Harvard who practices in the Portland office of a national law firm, Barton had not seen himself as the elected official himself one day. "I had always considered myself on the campaign side than the elected side," he said. After several close friends, people who he worked alongside with in the Bus Project, decided to make the run for the state legislature in 2008, Barton decided that he could make the race too. Policy interests and a desire to fix what he saw as wrong with policy in the state also led Barton to decide to join his friends in running for the House. He jumped into a race where he would face a Republican incumbent in the Portland suburbs. In a Republican-leaning district that had not elected a Democrat in a quarter century, Barton was in the fight of his life in his first-ever race being the candidate.

He notes that he was able to put his age and energy to use in that first race, which ended up costing a million dollars and being the third most expensive race in Oregon history. While the money he raised was spent primarily on media, including television and radio ads and direct mail sent out on his behalf, he also kept up a strong grassroots campaign in the district. "I knocked on 11,000 doors and my opponent did not," Barton said about his campaign. "That's the greatest achievement a young candidate can have." Barton notes that, while parts of his district are suburban, other parts are not. The homes are not nearby in some of the places he was knocking on doors when he got elected. "There is space between those driveways," Barton said. "It is physically demanding."

Barton's Oregon colleague Tobias Read was 31 when he first ran for the House of Representatives in 2006. He came into the job after years as a political staffer, which pushed him forward to make the race for office. He had previously served as a campaign manager for state legislative and local candidates, along with being an aide in the state legislature. During the administration of former president Bill Clinton he was an aide in the Department of the Treasury. When he launched his own campaign for a legislative seat, Read had to undergo many changes even though he brought the experience of being a political staffer in the past. Like many staffers who become candidates, no matter how old they are, his new role was a new job, not the same post he had been doing for years. "I had to get use to being the candidate and not the campaign manager," Read said.

At no point did Barton or Miller or Lappin or Read have to deal with a major issue that one young elected official in Oklahoma had to face. At no point did their families come close to conducting some sort of exorcism when they announced they were running for elective office. "They were alarmed that their good Christian son was interested in the dark arts," Oklahoma state representative Shane Jett said of his family. Jett was elected to the state House of Representatives in 2004 at the age of 29 (he turned 30 a few weeks later). The desire to run for office was not a new one. He was a former staffer who had managed campaigns for other elected officials in the area and had been involved in politics for years. He had also run once before, in 2002, when he lost the seat to a long time incumbent. "It has been in my blood since the late 1980s," Jett said. "I had decided to run around the age of 16. That's when I started looking at getting involved in politics."

Jett attributes his interest in politics to his love of reading and is influenced by the books he reads. As a child, he loved reading the Hardy Boys books and was interested in becoming a police detective following his love of the crime-fighting brothers. Moving into his teen years, Jett started to read more political biographies, which were his interest at the time. During a family vacation to Florida, he chose to read the autobiography of former president Ronald Reagan. The book made him want to run for office and when he returned to Oklahoma he decided to volunteer for a candidate for the state legislature in order to get involved. "It was the way he communicated," Jett said about the nation's fortieth president. "I read his autobiography and I thought that's how I feel."

Going to college, Jett continued his involvement in politics, which continued in his business career. Suspending it a bit when he worked in Brazil, he picked up where he left off when he got to Oklahoma. But when he first made the decision to run for office in 2002, he had to explain it to his family; the son of a mechanic and a housewife, Jett knew the decision to run for office would not be popular. "I grew up in a conservative Pentecostal family that thought that politics was for crooks and thought I would grow up to be a missionary or pastor," Jett said. "The pastor of my church is my grandfather and I asked him to call a family meeting. I wanted to tell them. I rehearsed a script and I got there and said that politics is my calling. I read the scriptures from the Bible since that would appeal to them." His reasoning to his family was that the voters did not have to put in crooks into elective office, that they could put other people into office. He said he wanted to be a non-corrupt politician and do the right thing. He insisted to his family that he would change things if he had the chance to represent Tecumseh in Oklahoma City and he would be a new kind of politician. "After that my grandfather registered to vote for the first time at the age of 74," Jett said. Jett's family even jumped into the campaign and started talking to voters. They went door-to-door for him, talking to voters and almost preaching why voters should send Shane Jett to represent them in the state House of Representatives. He said the old-school Pentecostal school of thought translated on to the campaign trail. "God love them, they are effective," Jett said of his family as campaigners.

But like Louisiana's Rosalind Jones, who came into politics as the daughter of a former state senator, the experience of working on a campaign helped Read in his competitive primary. Jones had worked on her father's campaigns prior to running herself. "The main difference was of style since I had worked in the Legislature as a staffer and in the Clinton administration," Read said, noting that he ran a more aggressive campaign during the primary season over two opponents, one of whom was chairman of the county Democratic Party.

While many enter politics as the sons and daughters of politicians or have been staffers for elected officials, some end up involved on the periphery out of interest and then end up moving more and more into it. In some cases the initial involvement causes them to be groomed over several years in order to run for office. Philip Morin III has had a long-standing interest in politics. In fact, to an extent, you can say that while he was in high school he was the student you were most likely to see end up mayor of his town. Class president his senior year of high school in Cranford, New Jersey, Morin went to college and law school in the state, majoring in political science and maintaining an involvement in local Republican affairs. With a father involved in civic activities, Morin had a foot in the door in that regards but not within the political arena except for his own volunteer work.

Graduating from college, Morin moved back to his hometown and became more involved in politics and civic affairs in his own right. At the same time, he got approached by the local Republican Party chairwoman to see if he had any interest in running. At the time, he had not given it much thought because he was busy establishing himself as an attorney. "At one point the chairwoman had spoken to me about running for office one day," Morin said. "At that point in time I was out of college and law school and had been doing the township environmental commission. She said she wanted me on the planning board and the citizens budget advisory committee because she wanted me to run someday."

With Republicans controlling the Township Committee, the party chairwoman was able to get what she wanted. Morin was quickly appointed to those posts, a common practice in many communities nationwide when a local political party wants to give a potential candidate civic experience to list on campaign literature. Taking the posts in 1996, it was only a matter of time before Morin was asked to make a run for office himself, applying his new land use and township budget experience to the campaign literature and a campaign. As luck would have it, he wouldn't wait long, as a candidate dropped out in September before the 1996 election and the party chairwoman asked Morin to make the race at the last minute. But with the national trends showing President Bill Clinton likely to beat Republican nominee Bob Dole, many local Republicans did not know if the 27-year-old fresh-faced attorney and newly appointed planning board member had any shot of winning a seat on the Township Committee. "I had in my mind planned to run for office," Morin said.

> I did not plan to run then because they had two good candidates and at that point in time I had just bought my first house and did not know if I was quite ready. It was 1996, Clinton versus Dole and at that point in time there were three sitting Republicans and most people thought this would be good for Phil to get his feet wet and then run again. I don't think people gave me much of a shot to win.

A funny thing happened on the way to Morin's defeat and second campaign: he won the election. Bill Clinton may have been Cranford's choice for president but the native son was their choice for local government.

Michael Frerichs, a Democratic state senator from Champaign County, Illinois, has plenty in common with Morin and with Eric Croft. Like Morin, he was written off in his first race for office by almost everybody — but came close to winning — like Croft he never thought he would be running in the town he grew up in. He never thought he would be living in the town he grew up in. Frerichs grew up in Gifford, a small Illinois town of 800 people, where he said he was related to half of them. "At 17 I wanted to get as far way from there as possible," he said. Frerichs would go away to college, spend summers in Europe, teach English in Taiwan and spend time in Saint Louis. After all of that time away, he started to appreciate and realize that he wanted to go back to Gifford and live his life in the same small town that he grew up in. But if he was going to live in Gifford again, he was going to do it on his terms. "I was able to appreciate it and decided that if I was going to stay here I wanted to make it a good place to live," Frerichs said.

In 1998 at the age of 24, he was encouraged by Democratic Party leaders to make a run for the state House of Representatives against a long-term incumbent. No one thought he would win the race, they just assumed he would make a good stand in that year since the party wanted to fill the spot on the ballot. But the ambitious Frerichs campaigned hard for the seat with a determination to either win or establish himself as a political force to be reckoned with. With a narrow loss he put himself in a position to win a future race.

After the state House race, Frerichs realized he wanted to run for the state legislature and pursue issues in Springfield in the Capitol hallways once walked by Abraham Lincoln. He said returning to Gifford with a college degree and seeing how many people he had grown up with did not go to college impacted him to want to focus on the education and economic development issues that only a state government can effectively discuss. "I see a lot of kids from my town go to work in a factory or work on a farm," he said. Education is my big issue."

At the same time, Frerichs wanted to run for the state legislature again, county party leaders were steering him to a race for the county board, a race he didn't want to run. Illinois counties deal with a lot of the issues that many counties across the country deal with. Issues such as maintaining county roads, running the county jail and providing policing services for rural and unincorporated communities dominate county government agendas. With a desire to work on economic development and education issues, Frerichs wasn't enthusiastic for the chance to vote on bridge repair and snow removal issues.

Still being lobbied by the party leadership, Frerichs hatched a plan. He would make the race, if the Democratic Party committed the resources to run the race to gain control on the county board, not just to gain some seats and remain in the minority. He approached the county Democratic chairman with his plan to reclaim the county. "I said to Jerry that I have a huge ego and know I can win but we can win control," he said. Frerichs was able to get the monetary resources from the party in order to run a countywide race to win control. The plan, which seemed a long shot from the beginning, ended up winning the Democrats a very slim 14–13 majority and Frerichs was named to the county board's vice chairmanship.

He was able to use the county board seat he did not want as a stepping stone, but also as a way to make changes to the county government during his tenure. Many of the changes Frerichs put into place were to make government run better and be more transparent. "County government is not that exciting," Frerichs said. "It's not like Congress where you deal with big international affairs. It is making sure that you provide basic things. We did open up the bidding process. The GOP had been in control for so long they had an old boy network to reward their cronies."

Frerichs was able to make his way to Springfield and to serve the state government he wanted to be a part of. He would serve several years on the county board and then get elected to the post of county auditor. The auditor's job, which involved being tax collector and fiscal manager for the county government, was not one that Frerichs wanted to run or hold, but he did it to work in the finance end of government. Come 2006, a state senate seat opened up and Frerichs was able to make the race, based partially on his years of playing the good party soldier and making races and holding down the county board and the county auditor's office.

In some cases, a history of activism and work in the non-profit sector is what leads a young person to run for office. It is a natural progression, getting involved in a cause to change society and make a difference in the world. Many activists continue to remain in the non-profit sector, believing that the work they are doing as an activist is what is going to lead to the change in the world. They want to focus on a handful of issues, pushing those, lobbying legislators and elected executives, holding rallies, conducting press conferences and putting together educational campaigns. But many see the elective arena as the better spot to get the change they desire.

It comes down to a question that the activist has to answer. Is it better to effect change from the outside or from the inside? Can they have a better chance to impact the change while being inside the corridors of power, inside the room where the decision is made inside the room where they cannot go as an activist? Or do they want to be on the outside, where they are free to pick and choose any issue and press it. Where they do not have to worry about the other issues facing government. Where the questions of finance and long-term budgets are not items they are wrestling with. Where they do not have to involve themselves in the compromises that any elected official needs to make in order to get something done.

Shane Brinton of Arcata, California, is an activist at heart. He cannot help it; he quite literally was born into it. His mother was involved in a variety of causes in the northern California region, primarily centered on environmental issues and non-profits helping seniors, and other social issues. During his childhood, Brinton's mother would bring him to many of these meetings, getting him involved in a variety of social causes and giving him an interest in activism and being involved in the non-profit sector. "I'd sit in the corner and draw pictures and listen to them discuss the business of the non-profits," Brinton said. "My mother jokes that she got me medically addicted to meetings."

Entering high school at the turn of the twenty-first century, Brinton had been attending environmental demonstrations along with the non-profit meetings his entire life. During his high school years, he started to think about how he could get involved in the non-profit world on his own and become an activist in his own right. President George W. Bush ended up providing him with a gift. "The Iraq War was a turning point when I was in high school and when the war started, that was a watershed moment," Brinton said. Concerned about the reasons that Bush and his aides laid out for why they were going to invade Iraq and start a war in the country, Brinton started to do his research. He wanted to know if there was a need to go to war in Iraq, was it the threat that Bush was saying, was it necessary in the aftermath of the September 11 terrorist attacks, and was it something the United States needed to be committed to. At the same time he started to research anti-war activities and groups and the cases they were making for why Bush should not have sent U.S. troops to invade Iraq.

Based on his research and his own concerns about the Bush case for entering into a war in Iraq, Brinton wanted to do more. He started to look at what his mother did for environment causes and looked at how he could apply this to war issues. Would he be able to impact change as a high school student? "Iraq is Vietnam for my generation," Brinton said. "When it came to knowing that the government was sending people my age to die on very shoddy evidence it became more personal to me." It is interesting that Brinton chose to promote his activism on the war issue and compare the Iraq War to Vietnam. Many college students and young people opposed the war and many campuses had protests and demonstrations in opposition to the war. People would protest the war in the streets and lobby the president and Congress to not go ahead. The war would help usher in a Democratic Congress in 2006 and President Barack Obama in 2008. But at the same time, it is not always the same war and same cause as Vietnam. The campus unrest and demonstrations did not compare to the levels of Vietnam. While a turning point in a generation, it was one of many turning points in a generation that will also have the September 11 terrorist attacks as part of their common memories.

Little did Brinton know that one thing would come along during his anti-war phase that would later come back to haunt him a bit when he entered politics a few years later as a candidate for the Board of Education and the city council. When he started organizing the anti-war effort he was looking for other groups that he could work with, groups that would be able to help him organize high school students against the war and also work with him in organizing other demographic groups against the war — with his goal to get the entire city of Arcata organized in opposition to the Iraq War. The group that he found most organized and most interested in helping him — the Communist Party. "When I was 15 I was known as the local Communist," Brinton said. "I was Shane the Marxist. When I got involved in anti war issues it was the Marxists who had their shit together. But I am not a Marxist. People would say that 'you're that kid who used to be a Communist.' I am not ashamed of it, but it is not me."

He defends his involvement with the Communist Party, while at the same time noting that he is not, nor has he ever been a member of the Communist Party. He said the group had a platform that interested him in terms of the anti-war issues and had gotten a good organization together in order to oppose the war. It was a natural fit for him when he was trying to put together a group and did not have a lot of experience in organizing groups of that size and scope. "They are not dummies," Brinton said. "When they were writing their platform, they do not say they will take private property. They talk about health care and housing and those are issues that appeal to me. I realize they were not right for me and gave me the fight to make the Democratic Party better." Brinton does not regret any involvement he had with the Communist Party at that point in time. He notes that while he does not agree with their beliefs and that he is not a member; he thinks it was a good move at that moment in time and based on what he was doing. "It was part of my growth," he said. "They also offered a lot of opportunities for young people. To write articles and be on conference calls, which at 15 is exciting."

Moving away from the war, Brinton started having issues with how the high school he went to operated. He felt the school district and high school administration was not working well. The school administration was too strict, while the board was not doing a good job communicating with the community and the student body. These are complaints that are common to many high school students almost out of High School 101 and Brinton agrees. He just wanted to do something more about it than complain and be an activist on education issues. "Everyone complains about high school for their whole lives and why not do something about it," he said.

In addition to the conduct of the school administration and the work of the Board of Education on communication and outreach issues, Brinton had a major policy issue he wanted to bring up with the board. He wanted to reinvent the school system's sex education curriculum. The school system at the time was focused on the traditional system of sex education. A teacher would stand in front of a classroom and lecture. Videos would be shown, statistics would be discussed, and health information would be communicated. Students were learning but Brinton wanted more. Brinton wanted the school system to move to a peer-based sex education system. He wanted to bring in outside groups to do skits on the subject matter and involve the students in the teaching process. Brinton wanted to tackle one of the most controversial — if not the most controversial — subjects that a local system handles and reinvent it.

Brinton knew that he could not just promote the peer sex education program as an activist. He would not get the support for it, given how sensitive of an issue it was. Even in liberal northern California, he could not take a chance as an activist. He decided that he wanted to run for the Board of Education in order to push his program on the inside; to be able to work within the system to get the ideas out there and the program known.

In addition, Brinton took his old anti-war advocacy to the school board race, wanting to impact military issues from within the Board of Education chambers. Under the Bush administration's signature education law, the No Child Left Behind Act, local school districts are required to send the contact information for all students to the military, unless the student and their parents chose to opt out of the program. The all volunteer military had led to decreases in the amount of military personnel and the military was using recruiting in high schools as a part of their human resources marketing program. Brinton wanted to run for the board in order to promote the fact that students have the option to opt out of having their information sent to the military, believing that it would be easier for a school board member to get this information out. He also wanted to help adopt policies to restrict access of military recruiters to the school campus. "More transparency and openness in government was the overall message," Brinton said of his successful 2005 school board campaign at the age of 18.

Jefferson Smith was 35 years old when he was elected as a Democrat to the Oregon House of Representatives in 2008. He did not seek to run for office. He was very comfortable in his life as an activist and community organizer; he wanted to continue to grow his organization and have an impact on the future of Oregon in that way. He did not need to make a race for office in order to do something. Smith shares the same name as Jimmy Stewart's iconic character in Frank Zappa's *Mr. Smith Goes to Washington*, and he did not think there was a need for him to go to Washington or Salem to effect change. He was looking to stay where he was.

Smith is the founder of the Oregon Bus Project, a non-profit organization dedicated to getting more young professionals involved in the political process. The Bus Project is discussed in depth in Chapter 8, but it will be discussed briefly here. The organization used an old school bus to transport young professionals around the state to work on campaigns over the course of the last decade. Growing in size and scope and focusing on the state legislative elections, the Bus Project has served as an incubator for the next generation of young elected officials in the state. Oregon's complement of young elected officials serving in the state legislature has grown in the 2006 and 2008 elections with many being veterans and board members of the Bus Project, including Smith.

Given his role in founding an organization dedicated to community organizing and bringing young professionals into the political process, it is not surprising that people were asking Smith to run for office. He had been approached on several occasions to run for seats on the legislature and in county government and the city council in Portland. But given his background in working on — and getting young professionals involved in the Bus Project — state legislative campaigns, the main place he was asked if he wanted to serve was Salem. In the run up to the 2006 statewide election, Smith was even asked if he wanted to challenge a one term Democratic incumbent for governor, an idea he quickly dismissed.

Smith kept declining the offers because he felt the Bus Project would suffer if he decided to run for office. He would have to focus his attention on his own campaign and not on the Bus Project. He would be deemed as partisan when he had tried to found a non-partisan group. While attending to legislative duties in Salem he would have his full attention on state government and not on the Bus Project for several months. He did not know if the group would be able to survive him being a state legislator if he chose to run for office when the group was still in its growing stages. He didn't want to end up stopping the growth of a new generation of young elected officials, political party leaders and political activists for the state of Oregon.

By the time 2008 rolled around, Smith felt he could finally make the race. He wanted to push many of the issues he had been pushing as an activist from within state government. He believed he could have a bigger impact from the inside. By this point Smith had also hired a staff for the Bus Project who could handle the day-to-day operations during his campaign and during the time he was spending in Salem. He knew the Bus Project had reached the point that it could continue to go on even if he stepped away for a period of time to pursue a political career in his own right.

Surprisingly, when Smith ran for his open seat in the state House of Representatives in 2008, he did not have the competitive race he expected to have. He raised the money and started planning for a competitive race and when the filing deadline came and went, no one else filed for the seat. Smith was elected unopposed, a rarity for his district. Of course, Smith could look at the results of the 2008 election as a good omen. The last time a state legislator ran unopposed for the seat on their first try, the candidate's name was Barbara Roberts. In 1990, Roberts became the first woman elected governor of Oregon.

While Brinton started his advocacy at a young age, Snohomish county executive Aaron Reardon in Washington State has him beat. While a fifth-grader Reardon was assigned a homework assignment in his current events class. It was an assignment that came naturally to him, given the environment in which he was raised. "I was born in the 1970s and my parents made me watch everything political," he said. "My earliest memory is my mom and grandfather debating Watergate." Going through the newspaper for the homework assignment, Reardon gravitated to a story about President Reagan looking to classify ketchup as a vegetable for the purposes of school-lunch funding. Reardon did the homework assignment and submitted his report, but he kept following the issue as the debate developed around the country. It was something his mother picked up on. "My mother realized that I was doing more than reading and writing reports, she encouraged me to contact my congressman about it," he said. Reardon did contact his local congressman and discussed why he believed ketchup should not be a vegetable and he also sent a letter to the White House for the president. A Reagan aide contacted him by phone to discuss the issue and find out why the fifth-grader wanted the policy changed.

Reardon never lost the political itch he developed from questioning Reagan's policy. He worked on President Clinton's 1992 campaign and after college relocated to Olympia to work as a staffer in the Washington state legislature. Moving closer to Seattle to take a job with a business advocacy group, Reardon decided to run for the state House of Representatives at the age of 27 when a seat opened up in 1996. Capturing the seat, Reardon settled into Olympia, taking the chairmanship of an economic committee before winning a state senate seat in 2002. He would serve in the senate only a year before he sought the county executive's office successfully.

During those campaigns, Reardon noticed something coming through in voter reaction to him and his age: a reaction similar to what someone who got into politics from an advocacy point of view would face. "There was a perception that I was not part of the establishment and being young I would fight for them," he said. While Brinton is a Democrat who was endorsed by the Green Party during his run for the city council in Arcata, California, Jason West is a member of the Green Party who had to overcome two unsuccessful runs for public office before he made a successful race for mayor of New Paltz, New York, in 2003 at the age of 26. An activist by nature and house painter by profession, West settled in the Upstate village when he enrolled in State University of New York at New Paltz, where he was continuing to complete his degree during his term as mayor.

The two races he made for the state assembly in 2000 and 2002 were more to get his issues out there. Running against a Democratic incumbent for an office where incumbents are reelected by almost force of habit by the electorate, and running as the nominee of a minor party, West was never expected to become an assemblyman. But after making two races where he was running to bring issues forward, West was tired. He was tired of spending time campaigning in elections he did not have a shot of winning. He was tired of just running as a candidate in order to raise issues. He wanted to run for something to win. Luckily an office was coming up that he could run for: the mayoralty of New Paltz. "I had been fighting the village board for years," West said. West had become an activist representative of the changing population of the village. Many students and staff at the college had settled off campus, making the entire village younger. Many decided to stay after college and find work in the Ulster County area, continuing to make the village younger. When West announced his mayoral candidacy in 2003, 80 percent of the village population was under the age of 40 and 75 percent were renters. At the time West was a 26-year-old renter who been battling the village board on issues relating to renters. At the time the village board consisted solely of property owners. "They ignored the vast majority of the residents and the businesses," West said, noting that he did not see village board members spending enough time shopping in businesses located in New Paltz' quaint downtown business district.

West also had problems with infrastructure issues in the village. The sewer system was old and West saw a need to make upgrades. Rain storms had over-flowed the system onto residential lawns. West wanted to press for greening the town's buildings and operating the town government in an environmental friendly way. West had served several years on the environmental commission in the town of New Paltz and had served as the chairman of the commission. Under New York State law, the village of New Paltz is a government operating within the town of New Paltz. Both elect separate governments and residents of the village are also residents of the town.

In short, he saw the mayor's office as being the best way he could exact change. And while the mayor is the village's chief executive officer, the job also only has one vote on the village board. West quickly recruited running mates for the two village trustee seats that were on the ballot at the same time, hoping to gain a majority, which could change the direction of village government. "I ran because of infrastructure issues and that the village should be run for people and small businesses," West said. "We want New Paltz to have a distinct character and not become Long Island." With West being a young former student at the college and one of his running mates for village trustee being young and a student at the college, he does not like it when people say he was elected solely because of his appeal to students at the college. While the numbers of students show an influence they had on the 2003 mayor's race and the old timers in town were partially caught off guard by the candidacy of West and his two running mates, West does not want to be considered as having ridden a wave of college student activism to the top spot in village government.

When Brinton ran for the Board of Education at the age of 18 when he was leaving high school, it was a quirky decision but understandable. A graduating senior has a vested interest in the school system and a race for the Board of Education has a certain logic to it. A race for a seat in the state House of Representatives in one of the nation's largest states, on the surface does not have the same logic that the school board has.

For 18-year-old Derrick Seaver in 2000, he had not intended on running for the Ohio House of Representatives. He thought he would go on to college and then maybe pursue politics. He had been involved in the Young Democrats but did not list running for office as an immediate priority. Then he got a call from the Democratic Party explaining they were looking for someone to seek a House seat and would he be interested in making the race. Looking forward to college in the fall, Seaver had to debate whether or not he wanted to make the race, which was considered a long shot when he was first approached. While he had given some thought to running for office in the future, he did not expect that it would come up while he was still in high school. Seaver decided he would take the shot for the seat, figuring he would delay college by a semester and then enroll after his adventure on the campaign trail. "It was a circumstantial thing more than anything," Seaver said of his first run for the state House.

Seaver campaigned hard in the race; with a fundraising disadvantage, he focused mainly on grassroots campaigning in order to get his message across. At the end of the day, Seaver pulled off a victory, entering the House chamber in Columbus as an 18-year-old just months out of high school.

Seaver did end up starting college late, but as a part-time student while maintaining a full-time job as a state legislator. The whole college experience would be different for him, with it taking almost five years to gain enough credits to become a sophomore because of the amount of time he was dedicating to his duties in Columbus and to his other political duties, including a stint as the chairman of a county Democratic Party. While Seaver could have run for a fourth term during the 2006 election cycle, he declined, noting that he wanted to go to college full time.

Can a third-grader in Mrs. Ripley's third-grade class in Brookline, Massachusetts, grow up to continue in politics and become a young elected official as a reformer? Michael Dukakis likes to think so, considering that was the very first elective office he held. Dukakis of course would grow up to become a three-term governor of Massachusetts and the 1988 Democratic nominee for president, along with a potential appointee to the U.S. Senate seat held by Edward Kennedy until his 2009 death. Dukakis was not necessarily an activist like a Brinton or a Smith, but reform and activism issues were what drew him to run for office.

Dukakis was inspired by his anger in the 1950s to the anti-Communist crusade of Wisconsin senator Joe McCarthy. The anger at McCarthy led him to start seeking out new ways to get involved and change the system. The best the law student could find was to run for office. He started his time as a candidate and then member of the Representative Town Meeting in Brookline, the 240-member town legislature. Looking to grow out of the minor municipal post, which was second in power to the much smaller Board of Selectmen, which actually handled many of the day-to-day affairs of town government, Dukakis decided in 1962 to run for a seat in the state House of Representatives. "In 1962 this was one of the most corrupt states in the country," Dukakis said of Massachusetts. "The fact that one was young was a plus."

He ran for the seat on Beacon Hill in order to bring reform to the corridors of power in Massachusetts. He wanted to change the way the state legislature ran and how the state government was run. He was looking to make the changes from the inside in the state that inspired men like John Adams and John Hancock and Samuel Adams to tell King George III that the colonies were seceding and becoming the United States and starting a great international experiment in democracy.

Getting to Beacon Hill, Dukakis started to identify the other young officials and the other state legislators who wanted to reform state government. One area they targeted was the Speaker of the House, who was part of the old-time group running the show on Beacon Hill and resistant to change. Complicating things was the Speaker's alcoholism, which left members of the House not even knowing the exact start time of House sessions on each day. Change started to happen in the legislature and was pushed forward when the Speaker died.

Other measures the group pushed included combining departments and agencies, changing statewide constitutional officer terms from two years to four years and combining the general election candidates for governor and lieutenant governor to run as a team instead of as separate candidates. Many became law and help define Massachusetts politics today. Outside of the government operations reform practices, Dukakis and his group also pushed anti-corruption measures in the state legislature.

Dukakis is not the only young elected official to run for office because of a desire to be a reformer. In 2005 Jun Choi ran for mayor of Edison, New Jersey, in his early 30s. A graduate of the School of International and Public Affairs at Columbia University and an education policy expert, Choi had campaign experience from helping former New Jersey senator Bill Bradley in his 2000 race for the Democratic presidential nomination. Working on other issues and campaigns, Choi saw a need to fix New Jersey's infamously corrupt political environment.

Announcing against a longtime mayor in a Democratic primary, Choi was instantly written off by many political observers. None thought he could win a race against an entrenched incumbent who had the backing of the powerful Middlesex County Democratic machine. Choi had help from a mentor from his work in the state education department, a former Democratic state senator from the Republican bastion of Morris County who gave him pointers on how to win an upset in the face of an all-powerful party machine. He hoped to use this and the ethnic politics that were dominating New Jersey's fifth-largest city as a reason to win the chief executive's office. "I was thinking the Democrats had lost their way," Choi said. "There was a disconnect between Democratic Party politics and what the average voter was thinking." Choi notes that he had two choices when he decided to make a race for the mayor's office. "I could have worked within the system and built the relationships and trust to have the opportunity to run for office or I could run against the party as a reform Democrat and move the party and government in a major way."

Choi would win the mayor's office and enter into a rocky four-year tenure as the mayor. He would never fulfill his wish of capturing control of the local Democratic Party. He would get some people elected to county committee seats for the party but not enough to get control. Choi would continue his feud with county party leaders and end up in disputes with the police and fire unions, along with the ethnic tensions in the community. When 2009 rolled around, the party machine ran a candidate against him again and she unseated him, most likely ending the career of a reform Democrat who was mentioned as a candidate for higher office on several occasions during his tenure atop the township of Edison.

Brinton notes that the Iraq War is the defining moment of a generation — the generation that lived through the September 11 terrorist attacks, then the War on Terror and the wars being run in Afghanistan and Iraq. The culture of the first decade of the twenty-first century has been one where the concept of going to war is opposed on college campuses nationwide along with communities around the country. People are not supportive of the wars, but they are supportive of the troops. More young elected officials that are coming up in this time frame are being defined by their military experience and their need to be involved in the military. They are looking to gain the experience as they look to run for office. While it is not as widespread as in the years after World War II when being a young war veteran made you an instant frontrunner for elective office, the military connection does help, especially in Middle America.

Jason Kander of Missouri had been active in politics for several years, working with his wife, Diana, to found Heartland Democrats of America. A more partisan group than the Oregon Bus Project, the group was more of a traditional campaign organization not affiliated with a political campaign. It trained candidates, provided volunteers and raised money. Outside of this,

Kander had given thought to running for office but was not sure when or if he would make a race.

Kander had joined the Army Reserves after law school and was working in Army Intelligence at a stateside unit and found himself deployed into Afghanistan. Returning home to Missouri in 2008 at the age of 27 he found term limits pushing out state legislative incumbents, like Seaver and Lappin before him. He also was remembered what he saw during his time in Afghanistan. He decided that he wanted to make a bid for the state House of Representatives. "I saw how political ideology could drive policies that did not work," Kander said. Kander was an underdog in the Kansas City-based district, a campaign that is detailed in Chapter 2. In the end he was able to pull it off and has reported to Jefferson City pushing for ethics reform bills.

Stephen Webber was elected to the Missouri House of Representatives at the same time as Kander and has many things in common with his colleague. The 25-year-old, who won in 2008, had long been active in politics in his native Columbia. He had attended Democratic Party meetings and volunteered on campaigns in high school and continued that interest even when he left to attend Saint Louis University. At the age of 19, and a sophomore in college, Webber was sitting and watching TV and kept seeing the images of the first days of the war in Afghanistan and decided that he had to do something. So he enlisted in the Marine Corps Reserves. "I remember sitting in my dorm room as a freshman and seeing people my age going to Afghanistan," Webber said. "As a healthy, physically fit young man it was my duty."

He would head to Iraq twice: during his first tour in 2004 he was a guard at the infamous Abu Grab Prison, which would later make history, and during a 2006–2007 tour he was stationed in one of Iraq's most dangerous cities, Fallujah. "It was a time in late 2006 when the insurgents tried to take back Fallujah," Webber said. "It was one of the most violent cities in Iraq. We took casualties every day." What is more remarkable about Webber's second tour is that he volunteered to go back when the insurgency was picking up steam and the situation in Iraq becoming more unstable by the day. He said he did it because he felt a duty as a marine. "I came back in 2004 and when I was sent it was all new guys," he said. "My experience could help keep other marines alive."

Coming back the second time, Webber went to Washington and became a political staffer. He joined the staff of Missouri's new U.S. senator, Claire McCaskill, and settled in for what he thought was a career in Washington, when a state House seat back home opened up and he started thinking about making the race. He was debating, should he take another risk. He had already taken a risk when he had decided to return to Iraq. Should he take another risk and run for the state legislature? A conversation with his 21-year-old brother helped him make up his mind. "He was the best asset I had," Webber said. He was one of the first people I talked to and realized it was the right decision."

Webber is not the only person to enlist in the Marine Corps in the first months following the September 11 attacks and the country went to war in

Afghanistan. And he is not the first to become a young elected official. Steve Fulop, the downtown councilman in Jersey City, New Jersey, who was elected in 2005 at the age of 28, put himself on the path to office in the days following September 11, 2001. A bond trader at Goldman Sachs who was right near the attacks, Fulop enlisted in the Marines right after and then became one of the first troops to enter Iraq in the invasion. Returning home, a ceremony where he received a proclamation from the mayor helped introduce him to city politicos and set him on the path to running for office.

Webber and Fulop are also not alone in being young elected officials who have also launched a career in the military reserves in recent years. Garcetti is now a Naval Reserve officer in Naval Intelligence and Niagara County legislator Kyle Andrews became a commissioned officer in the Army Reserves Judge Advocate General Corps.

As you can see, there are many reasons why people under the age of 35 run for elective office. There are a few key patterns that come together on why they do this. Many are ambitious and show that ambition quickly. Politicians like Morin and Frerichs wanted to make that race early on and start looking how they can do it. In the case of Morin he gets mentored along, while Frerichs makes a race for an office he doesn't want to hold in order to get to the job that he wants to hold.

Others come up as staffers working their way up the ladder and positioning themselves to succeed their bosses one day or run for another office. It is a logical step. For a political staffer a natural course of career advancement is running for an office one day. Lappin's victory to succeed Miller almost seems like she got a promotion she had been working for instead of winning a city council seat and establishing herself as an elected official. To some extent her race was preplanned by her and Miller given her move from his citywide staff to be his district chief staff, basically making her the councilwoman in waiting.

The family connections should not be dismissed with young elected officials. Going into the family business is a major source of what causes a young person to run for office. The family connection gives them instant name recognition and instant access to those who are deciding who gets to run for office. They can get to know fundraisers and key political party activities easily. A young elected official with solid family connections can usually jump the line and easily position themselves to run quickly.

Activists have a chance as shown here. They can establish themselves in order to run by gaining credibility on an issue and gaining support and media attention. But at the same time they have to deal with any issues they developed while an activist that may not help in the political environment. Brinton and the Communist Party are a key example of this.

As the twenty-first century progresses, young elected officials who came of age in the years following September 11 and saw the progression of wars in Afghanistan and Iraq will likely see military service and homeland security experience considered by the electorate. Veterans will be considered as those you want to run for office, because of the experience they had overseas. It is very similar to what happened in the post-World War II era when many young veterans were able to run for office and be successful. While the new veterans will not win as easily as the World War II veterans, they will continue to gain and exercise power. With organizations forming to recruit and support veterans in running for office, this will only continue.

Another aspect that ties all of them together is the fact that they want to take a risk and are able to take that risk. They all have a chance to want to take a risk in running for office. It's an idea that is fraught with risks from the beginning. Candidates can easily lose, be publicly humiliated, and find any budding political career killed off with an early loss or two. They may have to quit a job in order to make the race for public office. Can they take the financial hit of not having an income for several months while they shake hands, attend festivals and recite the same stump speeches so many times that they are saying them in their sleep?

There is something else on display along with the concept of risk taking and the varied reasons why young elected officials decided to run in the first place. Where they come from helps determine when they run for office and what office they run for. In the traditional industrial states of the north east and industrial Midwest, where machine politics has thrived and the whole concept of a political ladder continues in full force, there is a hierarchy and a party boss control system in place. Morin talks about it with relation to his path, where his local party chairwoman was having him placed on town boards in order to groom him to run for office one day, and then running him as a replacement candidate to give him campaign experience.

You see it with Quinn in Buffalo where he was helped along by being the son of a former congressman. Lappin was helped along for a seat on the city council in the nation's largest city because she was an aide to her powerful predecessor. Seaver in Ohio is almost an anomaly chosen in part because of a need to fill a spot on the ballot and then he went and won the election.

Frerichs notes that he had to gain support from his party for the races he made and he had to keep running for offices he did not have a lot of interest in, in order to get to the race he wanted for state senator. While he had almost unseated an incumbent state representative, he quickly found party leaders were shuffling him to a county board race that he did not want to run for. The party leaders showed the control of the situation by moving him around to offices before he was able to finally make the run for the state senate that he had long sought.

In other parts of the country it appears almost easy for a young elected official to make a race for the state legislature as their first office, even if they do not have family connections. Many of them have gained political experience on their own, volunteering for a campaign, maybe holding a staff position on a campaign. Just busily getting the word out for their candidates, but at times it does not seem as tough for them to get on the ballot.

The lessened control of party machines is evident when the strength of who the party bosses press to run for office and what challenges they face. A state like North Dakota or Missouri or Oregon makes it easier for anyone to get on the ballot, which allows the budding young elected official to focus their time on running a campaign and not spending half of their time making sure they can even get on the ballot.

The ability to run with less control from party bosses and to get on the ballot easier helps out for young elected officials who want to run for higher office. While in all places there are exceptions to the rule, with candidates like Kean in New Jersey or Schneider in North Dakota being helped to move forward very quickly because of their fathers, it is not needed in many parts of the country. Schneider was helped by his father's name and he was helped by the circumstances of North Dakota. But Morin could not have jumped the line the way that Kean did. Young elected officials in the party boss states will continue to have to work their way up the political ladder and start as small town council members before being able to consider a run for higher office.

Young elected officials will continue to run for office and they will do so for a number of reasons and use their experiences. Some, however, continue to have to jump through hoops and get certain boxes checked off before they can even consider any race for office.

CHAPTER 2

From Bringing Baseball to Los Angeles to Taking Pictures with Voters: How Young Elected Officials are Thinking Outside the Box

It is hard to imagine Los Angeles without certain things. The beach and sweeping views of the Pacific Ocean, the entertainment industry, freeways, the Hollywood sign, Valley girls, smog, and the Dodgers are all part of the landscape of the City of Angels. But the Dodgers have not always been there. In fact, to many they don't deserve to be a part of the Los Angeles landscape at all.

The Dodgers had been a Brooklyn institution. It was a part of the time when New York was home to three professional baseball teams: the Dodgers in Brooklyn, the Yankees in the Bronx, and the Giants in Manhattan. Jackie Robinson, Gil Hodges, Roy Campanella, and Sandy Koulfax dominated baseball in Brooklyn, and Ebbets Field was packed nightly in the summer as Brooklynites gathered for a night of fun. In the post-World War II years, the Dodgers had become a fabric of life in Brooklyn, just like Nathan's, Coney Island, and the Brooklyn Bridge. But unbeknownst to Brooklynites from Bensonhurst to Brooklyn Heights, a new young elected official in Los Angeles was setting in motion the process that would steal the team from Brooklyn and bring professional athletics to Los Angeles.

Roz Wyman had been involved in politics while in college and had become involved in the Young Democrats during and after college. Following listening to Franklin Roosevelt's fireside chats as a student, she became involved with Adlai Stevenson's presidential campaign and became California's national committeewoman for the Young Democrats of America, teaming with the national committeeman, Phil Burton, who would later become a congressman and political powerhouse in San Francisco and statewide in California. In 1953, the Democrats were looking for a younger person to seek a seat on the city council and interviewed a variety of political active young Democrats interested in the seat, including Wyman. "They were pretty dull," Wyman said of her opponents for the backing. "I was pretty outspoken and they asked me to run." Filing for the race five minutes before the deadline, the 22-year-old woman was dismissed by her opponents. Living at home, because of the affordability, Wyman concentrated on grassroots campaigning, knocking on doors most of the day. In her campaign literature, she was able to include photos of her with Stevenson and Eleanor Roosevelt and was pictured in *Life* magazine. She surprised the city with her election and entered a city council that did not want to welcome the fresh-faced young woman to what had been a gentlemen's club.

Entering the council, Wyman wanted to focus on how to improve Los Angeles, which was growing in the boom post-war years and seeing the San Fernando Valley rival Levittown as veterans moved from the city for more room or moved to Los Angeles to enjoy Southern California's warmth and sunshine. With the growing suburbs in Orange County and other parts of Los Angeles County, Wyman saw a need for Los Angeles to provide more for its residents.

Looking at what was needed to help lure more people and businesses to Los Angeles, Wyman centered on the city's lack of professional sports teams, including baseball and basketball. "I could not believe that a major league city did not have a major league team," Wyman said. Wyman had wanted to make the arts the centerpiece of her tenure, along with sports, but the business community had stressed the need for a sports team and she put her weight behind the initiative. She did concentrate on the arts as well, expanding arts programs in the public schools and working to expand museums in Los Angeles, but the Dodgers and the Lakers remain her legacy to the people of Los Angeles.

Wyman did not set out specifically to bring the Dodgers to Los Angeles. Any team would do. She looks at the Dodgers as her main legacy, along with the arts programs. She proudly notes that her work on professional sports was not just a benefit to the people of Los Angeles or even the people of Southern California. "I opened baseball for the West," Wyman said. Wyman's work on professional sports is just an example of how a young elected official is an elected official who thinks outside the box and uses the opportunities given to bring something new to the policy arena. Not being tied to the old way of doing things, young elected officials are likely to think outside the box. My interviews show that many young elected officials think outside the box and look to do new things for their constituents.

Many elected officials who have been in office for a long time do not think outside the box. Those tied to existing power structures when they get into office, after having successful careers in law or business or another profession, will be tied to the old way of doing things. They will not look outside the box and think, how can I do something new? They will likely continue with the same process, and the solutions to old problems will be conventional. They will not be looking to lure a professional sports team as an economic development engine for one of the largest and fastest growing cities in the country.

While Wyman's work was unusual for many reasons. She was a young woman in the 1950s — a period when many women were not serving in elective office and those who did were usually older and had toiled for decades in the political vineyards. Many concentrated on health and education issues, not using professional athletics for economic development. Thinking outside the box for her took many levels and she continued to pursue issues that were not in the standard political sphere for a Los Angeles politician at the time. Wyman is not alone in thinking outside the box. While others may not have pursued as notable an initiative as luring the Dodgers to Los Angeles, becoming a hero to generations of Angelinos and a scrooge to millions of Brooklynites, they have thought outside the box on issues of importance to their constituents.

Garwood, New Jersey, is a small community of just over 4,000 in Union County, just over 20 miles outside of Manhattan. A working-class community sandwiched between several more affluent communities, Garwood is the total opposite of Los Angeles, but in terms of a young elected official thinking outside the box during their service in public office it is similar to Los Angeles. The chairmanship of the Garwood Borough Council's buildings and grounds committee is something of a political backwater. Traditionally assigned to a minority party member of the council, the chairmanship is one that does not impact high-power areas of policy. The buildings and grounds chair concerns him- or herself with leaky roofs, heating, ventilation, air conditioning issues, the cutting of the grass at Borough Hall, and other mundane ministerial tasks. A previous chairwoman of the committee brags that her biggest achievement was climbing a ladder to the roof to see if it needed to be replaced. The buildings and grounds chairmanship seems to exist to make sure that each of the six council members in the small town receives the chairmanship of something.

When 25-year-old Republican Anthony Sytko took his council seat in January 2008 he was given the buildings and grounds chairmanship, mainly because of its status as a political backwater. The body's only Republican, succeeding another Republican, Sytko also took his predecessor's role as buildings and grounds chairman. A politically ambitious councilman, Sytko has made little secret of his desire to run for higher office — in fact he would unsuccessfully seek one before his first term was up — and it's not surprising that he wanted to do more than make sure the roof at Borough Hall didn't leak and that the Borough Hall parking lot was cleared of snow. In fact, Sytko said he was looking for a way to make his mark in public office, not just with being the lone no vote on the council.

Coming into office in a time of rising heating oil costs and a renewed global battle against climate change, Sytko would find several things converge to give him the chance to utilize the buildings and grounds job as a way to think outside the box. Starting to look for an area to make his mark, he was looking for ways to jump on environmental issues. Garwood mayor Dennis McCarthy's announcement that he wanted to focus on ways to green borough buildings gave Sytko his opening. "I felt it was a perfect match for me, coming from a different generation, a generation that is environmentally conscientious," he said. "I felt I had a different skill set and it was a perfect fit." He started to focus the buildings and grounds committee's work on greening borough buildings including installing solar panels on the buildings. He started investigating the issue of installing solar panels and looking for ways to tackle the issues.

With New Jersey being in a fiscal crisis and rising property taxes being the top concern of voters statewide, Sytko was also put between a rock and a hard place. While solar panels would bring a newer cleaner energy form to the borough, saving money in heating oil costs during the course of the year, the costs of installing solar panels would be high, perhaps too high for the borough to afford in a tight municipal budget. At the same time, shared services is not only a big issue in New Jersey, but also a tough issue. New Jersey is a home rule state with a capital H and a capital R. State residents take pride in the tradition of home rule and while politicians talk about shared services, home rule trumps most discussions. While people talk about shared services and merging governmental department across municipalities, it is rarely done because local governments are rare to want to give up too much power. But talk of shared services in the area of procurement is an area that can be discussed. It's an area that doesn't hurt towns or take away power from local officials. It is a safe shared service for the politicians of the Garden State.

Thinking ahead in terms of the solar panels, Sytko started thinking of shared services and decided to start reaching out to neighboring towns and school districts in order to jointly purchase solar panels. In the beginning, Sytko found himself having to reach out to towns and interest their elected officials in the whole discussion of solar panels before he could get them interested in the idea of a joint cooperative between multiple towns in order to buy the panels. Coming from the small town of Garwood, Sytko was not in a position of power when it came to discussions with other towns in Union County.

Meeting with elected officials who chaired public works departments in neighboring communities, Sytko started to find interest in the solar panel concept. Putting together meetings, he found enough interest to start forming the cooperative and getting the framework together in order to start purchasing panels. By 2009, he was in a position to start discussing the idea more publically with officials in other towns talking about the discussions during their meetings on environmental issues.

At the same time, Sytko found a way to expand his role as buildings and grounds chairman into more of an environment chairmanship for his small borough. Several groups in the state, including the Board of Public Utilities and Rutgers University formed a program called Sustainable Jersey, which would allow towns to enroll in order to receive an environmental designation and the chance to qualify for environmental and energy grants. As a part of entering the Sustainable Jersey program, towns are required to create a green team, which will govern the town's work in Sustainable Jersey and plans to start programs to garner the 100 points necessary for certification. Sytko moved into the chairmanship of Garwood green team, using it to focus discussions on solar panels, energy audits of borough buildings and other issues outside the realm of the traditional work of a buildings and grounds chairman.

Sytko likes to note that while transforming the buildings and grounds chairmanship of a town of 4,000 into an environmental crusade is his top example of thinking outside the box politically, which he attests to his being younger, he notes it is not the only aspect of how he has thought outside-the-box politically. "I come from a generation that is very in touch with technology," he said. "I had brought up getting everyone a borough e-mail address." The environment continues to be a cause of the young. From the first Earth Day to the current debates over climate change and the need for an international agreement on the subject, the discussions have been fueled in large part by the young. Sytko is not and will not be the only young elected official to push environmental issues in office. Many others will also take up the cause, in a variety of ways and in a variety of formats. They will tailor it to their constituencies and their levels of government and what they can do. Sytko can push for solar panels, but he is limited by being a councilman in a small New Jersey town. There is not much he can do environmentally in local government, it is just limiting.

Earl Blumenauer is a different story. His career as a young elected official started when he was elected to the Oregon House of Representatives in 1972 as a 23-year-old. Portland, Oregon, is one of the most liberal cities in the country and one of the most environmentally friendly. Pedestrian-friendly land-use decisions, ease of mass transit, and alternative transportation resources are all big deals in Portland. While someone in Buffalo may be upset that Main Street is closed to cars to allow a light rail or when Mayor Bloomberg closed parts of Broadway in order to create a pedestrian paradise people got upset, it is expected that these ideas would be warmly embraced in Portland and other areas of environmentally friendly Oregon.

Blumenauer has been a long-time advocate for transportation alternatives in order to better the environment. While his tenure in the Oregon House is dominated by his tenure as the revenue committee chairman, when he moved on to a seat on the Portland City Council he helped put these issues at the forefront. Under Portland's commission form of government, Blumenauer and his council colleagues also took on jobs overseeing a portfolio of departments in city government and Blumenauer oversaw transportation during his tenure as a councilman. Moving on to serve in Congress, Blumenauer is now the nation's leading transportation alternatives advocate, including bicycles. He routinely discusses biking as a regular method of travel on a regular basis by those in many areas of the country. Dating back to his early days in the environmental movement as a young elected official, the congressman has made the transportation end of the environment a key issue.

Eric Garcetti, the city council president in Los Angeles has embraced the environment along with embracing the outside the box tradition for Angelino young elected officials that Wyman set. Los Angeles is not a city that comes to mind for many people when they think of an environmental capital. While the environment has been a consistent issue in California and the West Coast is an environmental leader of the country, the issues facing Los Angeles include smog and a poor public transportation system. A reliance on the car is a consistent issue for the land of the freeway. Los Angeles residents' aversion to any form of transportation not involving a car is consistently lampooned in the national entertainment. The last episode of *The West Wing* even includes the chief of staff's secretary, Margaret, joking to the chief of staff, C.J., about Los Angeles not being a pedestrian-friendly community. How can Garcetti expect to push these issues in his community? It took him a little outside-the-box thinking.

Since being elected as a district councilman in 2001, Garcetti has managed to triple the number of parks in his district, while helping to write the nation's largest clean water bond ordinance and pass the largest green building ordinance in the county. Garcetti has also embraced the concepts of transportation alternatives in his own way. He will bike to work and champion other ways for residents to commute from his residential district to the city's commercial center. The issues of the environment remain big ones for Garcetti and he continues to move them forward. Garcetti's championing of the environment is not just confined to his work as a councilman and his professional life. He and his wife have taken their Los Angeles home and turned it into a green structure and he has driven an electric car for over a decade.

At times thinking outside the box for a young elected official is not just limited to taking a new idea like bringing in a professional sports team or reinventing a political backwater: it can be bringing people together to solve a problem that has not been able to be solved.

Niagara County, New York is home to one of the most famous tourist attractions in the world — Niagara Falls. While a worldwide destination for tourists who are looking to marvel at the millions of gallons of water that cascade over the three separate falls during the course of the day, providing both majestic sights and cheap electricity, the government of the county and the American city has long been a source of confusion and sheer mismanagement from an institutional level. While the city of Niagara Falls can be its own case study in institutional mismanagement — the city has conflicting charters in place and no mayor can seem to garner a second term — the county had many issues facing it as well. Governed by a 19-member county legislature, elected from single-member districts countywide with no central executive, the county was clinging to a government structure that worked well for the rural days but not for the twenty-first century.

The county had a modified commission form of government, where the committees oversaw day-to-day operations along with broad policy decisions. Committee chairs, all majority party members, served as department heads in principle and practice if not in name. They would frequently make decisions for the departments under their control and do more than the part-time nature of the job allowed. In 2001 a charter commission proposed a new charter for the county calling for an elected county executive to set priorities and govern the day-to-day issues of the county. Voted down by the voters, the county would need to find a new way to tackle the systematic issues facing the governance of the county.

In the same 2001 election that voted down the proposed office of county executive, the voters of the largely rural fourteenth legislative district turned away the long-time Republican incumbent, Shirley Urtel, in favor of a fresh-faced 21-year-old Niagara University student, Democrat Kyle Andrews. At the same time, the county chose to install a 10–9 Democratic majority in the county legislature, based partially on Andrews' status as a Democrat representing a largely Republican district.

Coming into the Legislature, he knew he had a short time to make a mark on county government. While he had been elected through a strong grassroots campaign, he knocked on every door in his rural district; he also knew that the 2003 election could bring a strong Republican challenger and the fact that he would have to defend his record and the record of the Democratic controlled Legislature. After defeating Urtel based partially on her record as finance committee chairwoman and majority leader in a Republican-controlled legislature that had raised property taxes, Andrews knew he was in a position where he needed to do something big and fast.

Taking the chairmanship of the administration committee, Andrews found himself overseeing the managerial functions of county government. The county clerk, county historian, Board of Elections, data processing and other administrative functions were under his control. In addition, he found himself wrestling with the issue of the long-term governance of the county and how to address the issue of no chief executive officer for county government. He could have tried to punt on the issue, but he also knew that while the county executive concept had been defeated there was a demand for a chief executive officer in the county. Researching ideas on how to address the issue, he steered away from the role of county administrator, popular in other New York counties without an elected executive. The role would have made the county administrator more of a chief operating officer, carrying out the work of the legislature, rather than a CEO focused on governing the county and working with the legislature.

Andrews would focus the county instead on the creation of a county manager form of government. Bringing in a county manager as chief executive officer, the new form would still keep the elected Legislature in the top spot in county government. The appointed county manager would focus on the executive functions of government. Aware of the shifting political landscape of Niagara County, where two-year legislative terms could shift party control easily and make it hard to recruit a county manager, Andrews made sure the job was tough to dismiss and had a longer term. When the time came to recruit a county manager, Andrews started to look towards bringing in a county manager from the world of public administration. With many appointments in Niagara County government being patronage in the past, the sheer thought of hiring on merit for the top spot in county government was a new thought. In the end, he and his search committee recruited a county manager from outside the region, someone with new thoughts on how to govern the county and ways to recruit companies to the economically struggling region.

In an interesting twist, the person hired by the county at the end of the day to become the county manager, ended up thinking outside-the-box as well. The new county manager would end up streamlining county operations and the county legislature's committee structure pretty quickly, quickly implementing the outside-the-box thinking Andrews and his committee had talked about when they envisioned the job.

Andrews did not stop his outside-the-box thinking in his role as administration committee chairman — a role he would give up after a year to assume the chairmanship of the parks and environment committee. In his November 2009 announcement that he would seek the post of county treasurer to succeed an incumbent who took office in 1973, Andrews stressed thinking that in many corners would not be thought of as outside the box, but for Niagara County and for the treasurer's office it is outside the box. He vowed increased transparency and use of technology, including placing the county checkbook online. Why is this outside the box for the treasurer's office and the county? The website in 2009 only gave very basic contact information for the treasurer's office and a listing of some staff. The website didn't even list the general duties of the treasurer and his office. The idea of placing the county checkbook online is something that is almost never heard of in that environment.

Thinking outside the box from a political perspective is not just limited to local governments in towns and counties large and small. State officials who are young have been thinking outside the box as well. In Oklahoma, Shane Jett serves as a member of the state House of Representatives. Coming from a rural background, Jett wanted to grow the economy of his region of the state and started to think outside the box in terms of how to grow that aspect of the economy. Jett notes that the economy has been changing in Oklahoma over the years with the oil and gas industries retaining top billing in the economic structure of the state, but the oil industry being a downturn since the 1980s. Having seen the impact of the oil bust on the state's economy in the 1980s, Jett wanted to be able to give the state a new way to look at tourism. But at the same time, more tourists were looking to come to Oklahoma to enjoy their vacations and observe the diverse state. The state had even installed the lieutenant governor in the chairmanship of the tourism commission, making the industry a focus of the state's independently elected second in command.

Jett takes pride in noting the diverse nature of his home state. The gleaming downtown of Oklahoma City brings energy companies and commerce together in one spot while past the city's suburbs, long plains balance both agriculture and the history of the Native American culture. The farms of Oklahoma have been celebrated on Broadway in terms of "the wind goes sweeping down the plain." Now Jett wanted to celebrate those plains in new terms, he wants them to be tourist destinations. "I believe we can have an incredible tourism industry," he said. "I think we can have agritourism and tourism with Native Americans." Jett wants to open up the farms of Oklahoma to tourists who want to learn more about the nation's agriculture industry and rural past. He sees an environment where city dwellers worldwide will be interested in coming to Oklahoma to work on and visit farms during their vacations and learn more about agriculture. With a growing base of ecotourism in various areas of the country, Jett sees agritourism as a way to grow off the growing ecotourism industry and showcase the plains of Oklahoma.

With one of the nation's largest populations of Native Americans, Jett sees the culture as a way to bring in more tourists to tour reservations and learn about Native American culture. "We have the largest Native American population in the U.S., but California registered more in the Census," he said of the state with 29 Native American tribes. He even likes to note that there are other hidden treasures in the state, including the fact that one of the architects of the iconic Route 66, which runs through Oklahoma, is from the state. "We are one of the best kept secrets in the U.S.," said Jett, showcasing his pride in his native state. "We have Route 66." Jett has made tourism the centerpiece of his legislative service, expressing a desire to serve as chairman of the tourism committee down the road in order to shape tourism policy statewide. He has also expressed interest in serving as the state's lieutenant governor in the future, to be in a position to focus more on tourism policy and the economic benefits of tourism than as the state representative from Tecumseh.

Jett's interest in transforming the state's economy through tourism comes from several focuses. He notes that his age has given him the ability to focus outside the box on issues that have faced the state for generations and his choice to live outside the state and country for several years. Following college he spent two years living in Brazil working in international business. During his time in Brazil he started seeing life outside of the world of small-town rural Oklahoma and learning how to do things from that perspective. With his home town of Tecumseh having 8,000 residents, he found himself thrust into a city of 3.5 million where his wife's church has 15,000 parishioners.

At the same time, the experience of living in Brazil and being a part of a larger community played a major role in his being able to reinvent the wheel when it came to the state economy. It should be noted that his age contributed to this. Being young and unmarried and not owning his home, Jett was in a position to move for two years to Brazil and get to know the issues and see how tourism could help his native state. He was able to be in a position to learn new things and get a chance to apply what he learned to new policies in Oklahoma. He has been able to think outside the box as a young elected official because his age and family situation allowed him to make the move that has changed how he approaches his job.

Being a young elected official and thinking outside the box is not just limited to those in elective office who are new to government and politics. Even those who find themselves old hands can find themselves as outside-the-box thinkers during their service. Jessica Lappin was 30 when she was elected to the New York City Council in 2005 representing Manhattan's Upper East Side. By the time she came into office, she was already a political veteran and a veteran of her district and the city council. In fact she had spent her entire career up until that point doing every possible job in her district except being the city councilwoman.

Lappin had worked on the staff of her predecessor, Gifford Miller, for her entire career before running to succeed him in 2005. She had been his scheduler, worked on his legislative staff, ran his citywide political action committee, served on his staff when he became council Speaker and then was his district chief of staff. As district chief of staff, she served as an almost surrogate councilmember, taking care of Miller's constituent service needs while Miller was occupied with his duties as Speaker and his planned 2005 mayoral campaign. While she has the experience in the council and in the district, Lappin had been an aide for years. She gave her advice privately to Miller but at the end of the day was representing Miller's ideas in her service. At the same time she gained insight into the issues and what had been tried, what had been proposed, and what could and could not be done.

Becoming the councilwoman herself, Lappin said she was able to put that knowledge to use mixing it with her own ideas on city policy. She said she is able to approach issues and say that she is not tied to the old ways of doing things. "I don't feel tied down and hindered by how it was done in the past," Lappin said, a surprising statement from a politician with the range of experience Lappin brought to her post. As a part of this, Lappin said she is willing to explore old ideas that may have been rejected at one point for any number of reasons but can be proposed again in order to get the ideas out for discussion. She said many of her colleagues were not willing to propose rejected ideas and instead struggle looking for a new idea thinking that it will be considered at that point. She noted that this is one place where her experience with Miller mixed with the fresh perspective she brings with her youth. Her experience allows for her to think in a way that has the knowledge of what has been proposed and why it has been rejected, knowing the fact that a new mayor or council Speaker in office will allow the decision to see the light of day on the second go round.

Lappin had another reason to approach the issues differently and be willing to take a risk that was part of her being young and part of a new phenomenon in New York City politics. The advent of term limits, at the time limiting city officials to two terms — or eight years in office — has caused a changeover in the city council.[1] Not only have a lot of new faces entered the council, but the council is more apt to start trying to get attention and council members are quick to want to gain attention with certain issues, partially to help themselves in a future race for office.

Corey Ray Mock is an unusual legislator in most of the country but typical for his North Dakota district. With the University of North Dakota dominating his district, being 23 at the time of his election is almost the norm. For him campaigning in college dorms and at Greek houses was the norm. Following his 2008 election, Mock would find himself sitting in Bismarck wanting to think outside the box in a state where older politicians dominate the legislative landscape.

Top on Mock's priority list is higher education issues. Tuition caps, textbook cost reduction programs, ways to curb student fees, all of these issues are part and parcel for any politician representing a district where students and professors are the overwhelming majority of the constituency. Outside of this, Mock takes an interest in areas of government administration that involve him wanting to compare and contrast with other states and research best practices. "I try to think outside the box," Mock said. "I am willing to look at other states. I am willing to talk to others. I am not so quick to say it's my idea or it's nothing at all."

Mock tries to stay in touch with legislators from other states and has gotten involved with organizations that give him the chance to network with his colleagues from across the country. While many of the conferences he attends are considered junkets where legislators spend more time on pleasure than business, a look at some of what Mock sends out from the conferences show he spends time in the workshop sessions studying issues and talking to colleagues. During one such conference, Mock regularly sent Twitter updates to friends, colleagues, and constituents about the workshops he was sitting in and seeking ideas for discussion regarding the issues he was listening to. A follower of his Tweets would also mistake them for those of a college professor given his penchant for putting together a lively conversation and discussion on a variety of issues.

One area that Mock falls into is young politicians who utilize their age to impact issues facing those younger than them, and thinking outside the box on these issues, which they say is an approach they have not found from their older colleagues. Many issues facing public higher education are approached from a viewpoint of those who have been in college recently. In Mock's case the fact that his district is a college campus, helps out a lot in approaching higher education policy differently from others.

Andy Meisner was elected to the Michigan House of Representatives at the age of 29; he said that while he does not think his age impacted how he approached public policy in the state legislature or now in his post as a county treasurer, he agrees with Mock that higher education issues were impacted by his age. "(My age) gave me some sense to the plight of students and student loans," he said.

Sean Gatewood of Topeka, Kansas, had another issue his age brought to his approach to higher education and the need to think outside the box in those terms. The 28-year-old Democrat was elected to the state House in 2008 partially because he was spurred into running for office because of how his wife was treated by the University of Kansas. He said that when she was going for her graduate work in pharmacy, the university suggested she drop out for a year and then come back. The decision would cause problems with her student aid since the pharmacy graduate program is designed to be a continuous program. In an effort to address what he sees as management problems with the University of Kansas, Gatewood was spurred to start thinking about running for office.

Outside of this, Gatewood notes that he wanted to run for office in order to keep people in his generation in Kansas. He is quick to note that a common complaint of those in their 20s is that there is nothing to do in Kansas and he wants to be able to correct this. In order to correct this, one area he wants to build up is higher education. Gatewood believes that a strong academic sector will bring new faces into the state and keep young Kansans in the state for college and encourage them to stay later. The tendency of strong college environments bringing strong communities around them is also close to Gatewood's mind in thinking out this subject.

One way of thinking outside the box for a young elected official is the need to promote ethics reform in government. With a growing demand for ethics reform nationally many are looking for young elected officials to help push the issue and get it off the ground. Young elected officials have been quick to pick up this cause mainly because they are not tied to the political establishments. They are new to the system and are willing to push the changes that are needed to accomplish something in this area. They also have the ability to think outside the box. A politician who has been in office for a number of years is tied to the system and will continue to push the system that they are a part of, not looking to change a system where they have prospered. Young elected officials also have the courage to stand up to the entrenched interests and the ability to take that risk to their careers. Possibly losing a political career in your 20s after a term or two is a lot different than losing your political career in your 50s after you have devoted most of your professional life to the career.

Gay marriage has been one of the key issues of the first decade of the twenty-first century. There have been debates on whether or not to have a federal ban on gay marriage put into law and states have been discussing such issues on whether or not to have civil unions in place at the state level or whether to allow homosexuals to marry with all of the rights given to heterosexuals who marry. The debate continues to play out in statehouses and courtrooms from coast to coast. And young elected officials play a huge role in the debate.

New York State is known as one of the most liberal in the country, but that liberalism is also confined at times to only small parts of the state. The impact of New York City's population on state politics gives the city clout in helping to shape the agenda, but the state's conservative rural areas — along with the conservative parts of the city — play a role in shaping certain social policies, including gay marriage. While New York is home to one of the largest gay populations in the country, it has also not allowed gay marriage, with the latest bill being defeated by the state senate in late 2009.

While the state law does not allow gay marriage, this has not stopped some young elected officials from trying to find a way around the situation. New Paltz is the typical college town; dominated by the local state university, the small village in Ulster County is a liberal enclave near Woodstock. The influence of the college and college students and the influence of liberal beliefs of many who move from urban areas to the semirural New Paltz in search of clean air and a slower way of life but close to the hustle and bustle of Manhattan has helped bring gay marriage to the forefront of New Paltz politics.

In 2003, the voters of New Paltz elected 26-year-old Jason West, a house painter and member of the Green Party, to the mayor's chair. West was elected with several running mates for the village board, ushering in the Green Party as having control of the village. West was elected partially because of the support of students, who were able to dominate the voter base in the small village. This served partially to showcase some of the traditional tensions in college towns with having college students vote in local elections.

In 2004, West, who talked a lot about the humdrum issues facing a village government — including sewers and green buildings — during his campaign, put gay marriage at the forefront. West decided to use his power under state law to conduct several gay marriages on the village green in the center of town. Slight problem: the weddings were illegal. West faced criminal prosecution and worldwide media attention, at one point appearing on *Late Night with Conan O'Brien* as a part of this. West took the ultimate risk when he decided to conduct the gay marriages: he lost his reelection bid in 2007. While he was basking in national and international media attention and hobnobbing with the NBC late night star, he was considered by some in the village to be ignoring his duties as mayor, not focusing on the pothole and sewer issues that dominate village government.

Several years before West made his decision, Massachusetts acting governor Jane Swift started to think outside the box on similar issues. Swift did not legalize gay marriage but in 2002, when she started her short and aborted campaign for a full term as governor, she picked another young elected official — who was gay — as her running mate for lieutenant governor. Swift decided to think outside the box on many levels in her running mate, she was running in a Republican primary, placing a ticket of a woman with a gay running mate up against the popular and well-financed Mitt Romney. Swift said that when she was looking at running mates, Patrick Guerriero, her deputy chief of staff and a former state legislator and Melrose mayor in his early 30s, kept coming to the top of her short list. His background as a former legislator and mayor was at the forefront of her consideration and Swift ignored his sexual orientation and the fact that he was just younger than her. Unfortunately she was the only one who could. Many in the conservative Republican Party targeted Guerriero, not for his age, but for his sexual orientation.

Like West, Swift's outside the box choices contributed to her demise in the governor's race. Shortly after announcing her running mate, Swift announced her decision to not seek a full term as governor, ceding the Republican nomination to the well-financed Romney. Swift attributes it as one of the three reasons she fell out of favor with Republicans in her bid for a full term. She says the others are not commuting the prison sentence of a convicted child molester who was supported by top fundraisers and the *Wall Street Journal* and supporting a toll hike.

While gay marriage is generating controversy in statehouses and court-rooms nationwide, sex education is a controversial issue in schools and board of education meeting rooms. While some believe that sexual health should be taught in schools, along with pregnancy prevention and other health-related issues, there are many who oppose this curriculum pattern, saying that it is better taught at home or citing moral and religious objections. There are also heated debates on how sex should be taught in schools.

Shane Brinton waded into these waters in 2005 when he was elected to the Board of Education in Arcata, California, at the age of 18. In fact the sex edu-cation curriculum was one of the reasons he chose to run for the school board just months after graduating from high school. "I was a passionate supporter of a strong sex education program," Brinton said. Joining the school board, Brinton started to work on rewriting the sex education curriculum including changing over from a teacher-based curriculum to a peer education system for sex education. He believed that by having students talk to and teach other stu-dents about sex education, the program could be more effective than listening to the teacher at the front of the room. He said that, from his research and his own experience, he had seen that the peer approach would be a better way to go. To help pursue this and reinvent the sex education curriculum, Brinton also recruited a theater group, which works with Planned Parenthood to conduct lessons in the schools.

Brinton knew the issue would be controversial and knew he was taking a risk with the liberal position. While his constituency is one of the more liberal in northern California, he also knew he was playing with fire by urging changes to the sex education curriculum. But he said it was a chance he wanted to take because it was personal to him. "For me speaking out for peer sex education, I know it is more effective," Brinton said.

New Jersey has never had a history as a state that has had the cleanest eth-ics. A look at Chapter 10, which focuses on Steven Fulop and Peter Cammarano, discusses issues surrounding New Jersey's ethics history more in-depth. But it is also a state that has seen a long history of young elected officials stepping up to attempt to think outside the box in terms of ethics reform. Fulop is one of them. Elected at 28 to the Jersey City Council, he has quickly pushed a series of measures including bans to awarding redevelopment contracts to those who donate to city politicians and banning dual government jobs for city employees. While common sense thoughts to many, Fulop was proposing ideas that were near sacrilege in Jersey City, long the seat of the Hudson County Democratic machine.

Fulop is not the first Hudson County young elected official to promote eth-ics reform and he will hardly be the last. One who did promote ethics reform early in his career, and even has the death threats to prove it, is U.S. senator

Bob Menendez. Menendez surprises many though, since he has become the consummate insider in the world of Hudson County politics, many have placed him in the corner of those not seeking reform, forgetting that he cut his teeth on the reform end of the spectrum.

First elected to the Board of Education in Union City at the age of 19, Menendez had first got the town to change to an elected school board. After serving on the school board for several years, he became the board's secretary and an ally of the long time mayor, William Musto. That is when things took a turn.

In the late 1970s and early 1980s it became apparent that Musto was involved in corrupt activities with relation to construction additions to two high schools in Union City. The case centered on the fact that the original contract for the additions was for $2.2 million and the final construction costs centered on $12 million. With federal investigators looking into Musto and businessmen involved with the case, Menendez played a pivotal role. As school board secretary, Menendez, then a part-time law student, kept the fiscal records of the construction project. As he became more aware of the crimes Musto committed, Menendez decided to work with federal investigators and testified against Musto, his one-time mentor. "When I saw things went sour, I saw I could not stay quiet," Menendez said.

This was not an easy time for Menendez, going up against his mentor and other powerful interests in Union City: he saw that his political career could be in jeopardy. Not only that, but he also saw that his life could be jeopardy. He received several death threats during this period in an attempt to prevent him from testifying against Musto. He was given a bulletproof vest to wear during this period, as danger lurked behind every corner whenever he left his house. While threats became a commonplace in his life at this time, Menendez said he wanted to continue with his decision to testify, since he believed then, as he does now that it was the best decision he could make. "It was a dark period in my life, it was a lot of risk," Menendez said. "I think that it was an aspect of youth in public service. Idealism burns strongly and overcomes fear, I knew it was right."

The twists and turns of New Jersey politics come together in a variety of ways and none is more evident in this discussion of ethics reform and young elected officials. Fulop challenged Menendez for Congress in the 2004 Democratic primary and when Menendez wan for his first Senate term in 2006 he was challenged by Republican state senator Tom Kean Jr.

Kean brought to the race the most famous name in Garden State politics. His father had been a popular two-term governor who had won in a landslide in his second term, ironically helping clear the way for Menendez to become a state assemblyman. Kean had easily moved into office because of those connections rising to the state Senate, a coveted post in the New Jersey power structure, barely three years after he entered the state's political arena. As a state legislator, one who was seen as ambitious from the day he took the oath as an assemblyman, Kean had made ethics reform his issue. He started with trying to ban "pay to play," the practice of giving government contracts to those who contribute to campaigns. The legislation often stalled, partially because the Democrats in power did not want to cede a win on the issue to an up and coming Republican and partially to preserve the new spigot of money following Democratic domination of state government. Kean attributes his desire to work on the ethics reform issues because of his age and the fact that he was bringing a new perspective to government, something that puts him in the same boat as Fulop and Menendez, who indicated the same thing. "If it doesn't make any sense you can look at it," he said in an interview. "As I looked at the system in New Jersey, I saw a frustrating pattern known as pay to play."

Kean notes that it was a huge risk for him to make the take on the issue. The issue sat at the core of the Garden State's politics and was one that helped make the government function in New Jersey. The fact that Fulop entered politics several years later and wanted to tackle a form of the same issue only proves how it lies at the center of the political culture of the state. Kean also had to find that pay to play did not exist on any one side of the aisle but was on both sides at many levels of government. Would the rising star suddenly destroy his career? Hardly not — Kean would be able to continue to ride ethics reform as he moved his way through state politics. He would hit a few road blocks though, like when the assembly Speaker refused to allow him to discuss the issue on the floor on his last day in the assembly before moving to the Senate. While Kean says the Speaker, Albio Sires, did not want him to bring the issue up on the floor, Sires defended his decision at the time by noting that Kean's assembly resignation had already been processed and he could not recognize a non member on the floor, let alone a new state senator.

Kean also notes that he wanted to bring his government reform case to Washington with him if he had been a senator. Kean kept hammering at the cause of government reform for most of 2006, at one point reciting the line "Bob Menendez is under federal criminal investigation" multiple times even though no charges were ever proven or made against the senator. "I was a very strong articulator of a reform agenda in DC," Kean said of his U.S. Senate race.

Thinking outside the box does not apply just to young elected officials when they are in office, for some it applies when they are running for office. Jason Kander was 27 when he was first elected to the Missouri House of Representatives in 2008. An army man, he is a veteran of the war in Afghanistan, where he served before deciding to run for office. Active in politics in the Kansas City area for several years before and after his time in Afghanistan, Kander took the plunge for a vacant seat in the House.

Making the plunge into elective office, Kander made several decisions early on that helped shape his campaign. First he was going to adopt his army background — he's a lawyer outside of the Reserves — to the work of his campaign. Kander ran his campaign like a military operation, planning everything out to army precision and beginning the campaign earlier with a sustained ground operation at the end of the day. "We took a unique approach to it," he said. "I took a military approach to everything." Considered an underdog when he started his campaign, Kander began by looking for the lifeblood of any race — money. He started a year in advance fundraising early and focusing on raising money in his district, something unheard of in past races. At the end of the day he was able to pull into about 70 percent of his war chest from the district.

Having supplies to push his campaign forward, Kander started his ground campaign, focusing on a heavy door-to-door strategy. Focusing on his youthful energy, Kander started walking early and often. While he brought a walk list of prime voters with him, he would often walk in the middle of the street in order to dash to any potential voter he found as they entered or exited their home. At the end of the campaign, Kander said he visited the homes of prime voters at least three times each.

He anticipates he met approximately 80 percent of the prime voters during the run-up to the election. To stand out and also to emphasize his background as a veteran, Kander dug his winter army boots out of storage and wore them as he walked door-to-door. When he knocked on doors he went in for an approach of being a friendly young guy, not a prospective state legislator seeking a vote. "I went to their door with the intent of being their friend," Kander said. "I could sit with them for half an hour and I got their e-mail address each time." Building the e-mail address list was a key part of his strategy but he also started seeking early commitments from voters who would be interested in putting out a lawn sign for his campaign. In a move reminisant of the army's shock-and-awe bombing campaign in the first days of the Iraq War, Kander wanted to start his own shock-and-awe campaign just with lawn signs. By the time voters could start putting out lawn signs, he had a list of 1,000 homes willing to place his signs outside. "On Monday when they went up, every single street had a sign saying Kander," he said.

While lawn signs don't vote and many candidates and political operatives complain about them being an eyesore or a waste of money, in some cases they make a quick and important point in showing the level of support for a candidate. In the case of an underdog, it allows them to get their level of support out quickly, building a level of inevitability and showing outside-the-box thinking. No political consultant would address spending that much time putting lawn signs on lawns, preferring a shock and awe of lots of lawn signs on the sides of highways and other busy roadways. Kander didn't keep his lawn sign campaign to the beginning of the race. He put together a second lawn sign, one that debuted two weeks before the election and had his picture and name on it. Then he left a blank space on the signs, a space where he asked voters to write in why they intended to vote for Kander. Soon his district was blanketed with his picture and handwritten testimonials of support from voters.

Kander didn't just stick his picture on lawns district-wide, he wanted to make sure people remembered what he looked like, as much as possible. "On election day, every single polling place had a volunteer and a lifesize cutout of me," Kander said. In his quest to become friends with the people in his district, Kander did something that may be unheard of in most parts of the country. He bought coffee mugs for the campaign and took them on his walking trips. While walking door-to-door, his wife, Diana, would go with him and ask each voter to pose with the coffee mug and take a picture. She would then catalogue the photos and a week before the election, Kander sent the photos to voters with a note reminding them that they met and showing them proof in the coffee mug photo. With the note and photo, he was hoping to gain one more vote.

Kander credits this unorthodox strategy as being a key part of his winning. "That was the corny stuff that worked in my district," he said. Kander said being able to use outside-the-box gimmicks in his campaign helped him get his message across. By becoming friends with voters and having them take pictures with coffee mugs, he was able to also talk about his key issues of health care, education and environment. He notes that voters remembered him later on because of the outside-the-box thinking. A conversation with a politician about health care, even if it lasts a half hour in your living room may have a vague recollection when it comes time to vote. A conversation about health care complete with taking a photo with a coffee mug and being asked if the candidate can put a picture of himself on your lawn, it is rare that any voter would forget that. Kander also notes that the outside-the-box thinking on his campaign strategy also serves as a way to remind voters that once in Jefferson City he would think outside the box.

Kander also notes that his state has an outside-the-box thinking when it comes to elective office. At the time he was running, the state's retiring governor, Republican Matt Blunt was in his mid-30s, but Kander was quick to shy away from any comparison with the deeply unpopular Blunt, whose name is a toxic word to any Missouri Democrat. He is quicker to embrace President Barack Obama's victory in his district's Democratic primary and the culture of the state. "What helps younger candidates in Missouri is that we are the Show Me State," he said. "We are open to people. That is a culture here. The other part that helped me was that I was running in a Democratic primary and my district was choosing Obama over Clinton. Democrats were used to rejecting that their candidate was too young and inexperienced."

While some of Kander's campaign ideas were thinking outside the box and were different than anything someone would find in a campaign playbook, he is not the only young elected official to think outside the box when it comes to their campaign strategy. Eric Garcetti is the city council president in Los Angeles. A district councilman from an area of the City of Angels with a large amount of young professionals, Garcetti was first elected in 2001 at the age of 30. The son of the former Los Angeles county district attorney Gil Garcetti, who presided over the prosecution of O.J. Simpson, Garcetti entered the race for the open seat with some name recognition from his father. But he did not want to rest his laurels on his father's name and career or use that to get himself elected. In fact when Eric Garcetti launched his campaign for city council it was a year after countywide voters had turned his father out of the district attorney's office.

During his campaign for the city council, Garcetti made 130 promises to the voters of his district and then wrote them down and issued a bill of rights for the residents of his district. He wanted the residents in his part of Los Angeles to know what they could expect from him should he become their councilman, and know that he was laying it out there during the campaign and not hiding behind anything. "At the time it was unconventional," he said.

Coming into elective office, Garcetti is the first to say that his age has caused him to think outside the box on how he approaches his job. Like Sytko's comments about adopting government e-mail addresses, Garcetti is an early believer in utilizing technology for communicating with his constituents. While Sytko is working in an environment of a small town where a government e-mail address is a novelty, in Los Angeles the government e-mail is the norm for Garcetti and members of his staff. Instead he became one of the first in city government to utilize Facebook, Twitter and other forms of social networking to engage his constituents and allow them to communicate directly with him and his staff.

In addition to this, Garcetti recruited high school students to work on his campaign, particularly in the multi-lingual parts of the district. He was able to get the Red Hot Chili Peppers to headline a fundraiser for him and he sponsored many bar nights and fundraisers at clubs targeting young professionals in his district. With a demographically young district, and being young himself, Garcetti wanted to rally these voters to his side.

Rural Kansas is one of the least likely places you would expect unorthodox campaigning. Dotted with small towns where the church is the centerpiece of the social life and pancake breakfasts and soup suppers are common place. The social events and parades are the regular circuit for those seeking seats in the state legislature. The norm is to be expected, it is the way to campaign. Anything outside the norm is considered surprising and would almost be questioned by political professionals as whether or not it could backfire. While in some parts of the country, political professionals encourage politicians for any office to play it safe, especially in races where the candidate is the frontrunner, in rural Kansas, political consultants are not to be found on state legislative races and the culture of the region plays more into the decision to steer clear of unorthodox campaigning.

In 2002, Josh Svaty was 22 and just out of college. Returning home to the family farm, he decided to jump into a race for the state House of Representatives and quickly looked to distinguish himself from his older opponent who was wed to the old ways of doing things. In a campaign strategy similar to many other young elected officials across the country, Svaty made a strong grassroots strategy a key to his campaign. Knocking on doors district wide, Svaty started looking for new ways to get his message out.

Campaign T-shirts are nothing new. They are a pretty common site in many campaigns. Most are pretty tame, maybe a new color or design; in one extreme case for county judge in the Buffalo, New York, area, the candidate's picture was printed on the shirt. In covering Westfield, New Jersey, elections in 2009, campaign T-shirts were common for the incumbent mayor and one of his council running mates. A sea of royal-blue shirts or bright orange shirts was almost commonplace at any event where you expected either candidate to be nearby. But what Svaty ended up doing with his T-shirts wouldn't make a Westfield politician blush, but it would cause them to question why they didn't think of it.

Svaty started carrying T-shirts with him regularly in order to get his name out and to pass out to people who would march with him in the any of the numerous parades that are part and parcel with campaigning in his district. When he got to one parade he discovered something, the high school marching band had no uniforms. Eager to get the band into something matching that would make them stand out along the parade route, Svaty quickly outfitted them in T-shirts supporting his campaign. "The whole band got shirts," he said. "A high school marching band that has no business making endorsements suddenly became the Josh Svaty marching band."

Speaking of those Westfield, New Jersey, politicians who would kick themselves if they did not outfit an entire marching band in campaign shirts, the candidate behind the orange shirts in 2009 also was thinking outside the box during his successful campaign. Keith Loughlin is a 31-year-old Republican attorney who sought a seat on the Town Council facing a one-term Democratic incumbent who had won the seat by one vote. Loughlin became a force of nature in the race, running a campaign few in Westfield had ever seen.

Loughlin became known early on for two things: his willingness to raise and spend large sums for the race to represent a quarter of the 30,000-person town, and his ability to have fundraisers that were different for Westfield.[2] Loughlin suddenly had his supporters playing kickball and participating in chicken-wing-eating contests. At times his campaign began to mimic a summer camp and not a real campaign, outside-the-box thinking became the hallmark of the Loughlin campaign and their events. While the events were outside the box, many of his positions were not; Loughlin was quick to talk about policies similar to the rest of his ticket. At times Loughlin seemed like a fourth ward representative of the mayor and not his own candidate.

Loughlin suddenly became the only Westfield Council candidate to campaign at the town wide street fair on his own and his tent started popping up all over town. In July he debuted a commercial on the movie screen before movies at the Rialto.

Loughlin would even get a marching band involved in his campaign, but not in a way where he clothed them all in his signature orange shirts and marched them up and down Westfield's main drag. The Sunday before the election, he and the Republican ticket held a pep rally at Loughlin's law office, located on a main street just a block from the main retail district. At one point he camped the drum line of the local marching band on the office's front lawn to help draw attention to the pep rally. Loughlin managed to recruit cheerleaders too, with cheers being done for each of the five local Republican candidates in town. By the time election day came, Loughlin's campaign tactics had become a buzz around town, with voters wondering if he was seeking the fourth ward Council seat or was looking for something just a bit higher.

While Loughlin was busy recruiting cheerleaders and marching bands and getting the kickball out to put out alongside the tray of wings, other Jersey young elected officials were trying something else. Fulop ran into a major problem running as an insurgent in a city dominated by a political machine. He needed campaign workers for his 2005 race for the council and he needed them fast. Yes, he was able to draft many of these friends, just like he had for his 2004 congressional race. But there were only so many of them and they had other commitments than knocking on doors in Jersey City. Yes, he could try to recruit his neighbors, but again he ran into the issue of seeing many of them work demanding jobs that they could not spend all of their time campaigning for his election to the city council. While he used these, he also found a new way to bring ground workers to his crusade — he hired the homeless.

In what is a campaign tactic rarely seen, Fulop reached out to a local home-less shelter and was able to hire people to hand out literature, make phone calls and do the various other tasks associated with any political campaign. While unconventional and defiantly outside the box, it gave Fulop the campaign work-ers he needed in 2005 when he was a reform candidate without the many field workers his opponent could tap being supported by a large and well-financed political machine.

Come his 2009 reelection to the council, Fulop would not need to rely on hiring the homeless. Because of his reformist policies and reform zeal, Fulop became a magnet for the reform-minded throughout Jersey City. He has gained many supporters just from this, supporters who are willing to back him because they believe him to be the real deal in reform for Jersey City. A rally he called in 2008 to open the petition drive for his government reform referendum initiative drew a crowd that jammed a downtown Jersey City bar with Fulop supporters who seemed ready, willing and able to do just about anything for the young councilman. And this wasn't even for a campaign to elect Fulop to anything: it was for the passage of changes to the city charter, which may be just about one of the least politically exciting areas of local government.

Many candidates for office across the country find a need to bring in pro-fessional political operatives and consultants to take on many of the duties of running their races. While many local races are run by long time political volun-teers and friends of the candidate, many also involve political consultants who work full time for clients in these races. In Loughlin's race, he had a volunteer running his campaign but he also retained one of the most powerful political consulting firms in the state to design his literature. He is not alone and when races get into the state level many candidates focus on hiring consultants and professional staffs in order to run their campaigns. Many of the state legislative campaigns also raise money in large sums on a continued basis. There are many stories dotting the landscape of safe state legislative incumbents holding fundraiser after fundraiser in order to build up a war chest to ward off potential challengers.

Democrat Ben Cannon took an unconventional approach when he successfully sought a seat in the Oregon House of Representatives in 2006. A veteran of the Oregon Bus Project, a grassroots group of young professionals that helps candidates across the state, Cannon did not want to participate in the business of politics. While political consultants and professional political operatives across the country will tell you their services are needed in order to run a successful campaign, partially because it keeps them employed and in existence, Cannon thought differently. "I recognized it wasn't rocket science," he said. "I have friends who are good writers and designers." Cannon recruited a friend of his who worked in information technology for *Reuters* in New York to come to Oregon to run his campaign, knowing that the friend had limited political experience, but he thought he was the right man for the job. "I knew he would get a kick out of it," Cannon said. "He is creative and smart. Politics is not rocket science and there are skills and attributes from other professions that work in it."

For other jobs he reached out to friends who were able to design literature and write campaign material. Cannon said that he didn't want to use his campaign to help fund the permanent political infrastructure of Oregon. "I have seen those campaigns and had enough," he said. For fundraising, Cannon focused on small dollar donations, similar to the strategy that Obama would use two years later and that Howard Dean had used two years earlier. But while the two presidential candidates would also have large dollar fundraisers, Cannon was able to keep his focus on the small donors, which is unique for legislative districts in a state like Oregon. To make up for the large donors, Cannon employed an outside the box strategy in how he helped raise small dollars. While knocking on doors, he carried a coffee can with him, asking people for donations when he knocked on their doors. Using this strategy he was able to receive 500 donations. "Any moment that I was not out talking to constituents was a moment not well spent," Cannon said. "I spent little time dialing for dollars and talking to interest groups."

Cannon believes that his decision to not hire the professional political operatives to run his campaign was a turning point that helped him win the Democratic primary in the safe Democratic district. He believes he was able to connect more with voters because he did not have a political operative telling him to play it safe and pursue a tested strategy. One area he points to is the campaign literature he used in 2006, where he said he tried to put information out there for the voters. He did not want to believe the concept that flyers with few words and glossy photos of Cannon talking to voters and Cannon waving a flag and Cannon playing with children would attract voters to his upstart campaign. He wanted to think outside the box and do something different. "My mail was more detailed than others," Cannon said. "One thing that frustrated me about campaign literature was that it said little and was quite shallow. I went into details, it made my stuff more wordy but the voters responded."

What is it that makes a young elected official think outside-the-box? Why are they looking at the issues in a different regard? It is plain and simple; the age of the official is playing a major role in the young elected official choosing to look at the issues from outside the box.

An elected official who enters office at a younger age is more likely to start thinking about issues in a way that others are not. As Lappin notes, she was not tied to the old way of doing things, she did not say that just because something had always been done a certain way that it had to continue to be done the same way. At the same time she also notes, correctly, that just because something had been proposed and failed that it was not something that could never be tried again. At times her different approach was being willing to take a risk to repeat the same something that had already been written off.

Many young elected officials are willing to take a risk in terms of their careers and in terms of what they want to do while in office. Oregon state representative Brent Barton said in his interview that with his state's fiscal difficulties in 2009 — an all too common refrain from many elected officials in the last years of the decade, if he wants to get anything done to keep his state solvent, he'll need to take some risks and possibly alienate some voters in a stance of coverage. In addition, he notes that he needs to start thinking outside the box in order to address the financial issues, mainly because the situation has become so dire in the Beaver State — like it has in almost every state — that it is the only way to get anything done.

This is not to say that every young elected official is someone who is thinking outside the box or approaching it with every issue. Peter Cammarano was 27 when he was elected to the city council in Hoboken, New Jersey, and then 31 when he became mayor for a brief one-month term in 2009.[3] While he approached some issues from an outside-the-box perspective during his four years in city government, on many of the issues he was as inside the box as any other member of the city government. Cammarano was a member of the old boy's club political machine that dominated Hoboken government and he sided with the mayor on many of the issues coming before the council. He did embrace new ideas, a vital necessity in a city where young professionals and young families — the demographic Cammarano physically and socio-economically fit into — were fast becoming the key voting bloc. But at the same time he needed to embrace the born and raised component of the city's voters where he had to sound more like an old school politician and not someone looking at doing things totally in a new way.

In Ashland County, in rural northern Wisconsin, Sean Duffy is the district attorney. While at some times he does approach the job from a different perspective, he is, after all, not only a young elected official but also the first reality-show veteran to be elected to public office in American history,[4] at other times he does not. But in Duffy's case, he is not handcuffed by traditional voting blocs that need to be courted in order to win a higher office, as was Cammarano's case. It was the fact that there are so many ways a district attorney in a rural community or any district attorney can approach his job and make decisions on law and order issues.

Young elected officials can serve as a valuable resource at a time of economic crisis and a time when new ideas are needed in government. They are not tied to the same old way of doing things, as has been mentioned to me time and time again. They are willing to think of the new ideas. Maybe the same programs don't need to be continued, maybe a position can be eliminated in government, maybe something that was proposed but had no following once can be brought back and considered again.

The ability to think outside the box and take a risk is needed in government and politics. Was it easy for Roz Wyman to decide to be a risk taker and fight for professional athletics to be brought to Los Angeles? No. It was a new idea at the time and something that she determined was needed to move Los Angeles to the next level as a city. It was needed in order to help draw in new businesses and residents. While Los Angeles has had a solid background in the entertainment industry, which has only continued to grow in the five decades since Wyman pursued the Dodgers for the city, the addition of professional sports has helped the City of Angels grow to new heights and bring in new businesses and residents. The idea of thinking outside the box was needed at that moment in time for Los Angeles and Wyman was in a position to do this.

Taking a risk is a key component of any young elected official and it is clear from many of these outside-the-box examples, and others that I have heard in the course of these interviews, that young elected officials are willing to take a risk. Take Brent Barton in Oregon; he's young and clearly wants to move to higher office — he's already running for a state senate seat in 2010 — and he's willing to chance his career on the outside-the-box choices needed to solve the state's fiscal crisis. Or look towards Jason Kander in Missouri. While his unusual campaign tactics may have gotten him elected and created a buzz about his campaign — how could life-size cut outs of the candidates at polling places not cause a buzz? It was still a tremendous risk for him to think outside the box in this way. Many political operatives want to stick to the nice safe campaign choices. They do not want their clients to move outside the box and take a huge risk. They remind their clients that thinking outside the box could be costly to the campaign and could likely result in a loss for the candidate. A candidate looking to move into office will not want to take the chance of thinking outside the box when they are running because they do not want to risk losing.

And this carries over once a candidate gets into office. They continue to play it safe and look for the safe way to handle the issues, an eye on reelection. A younger elected official, who has his or her entire life ahead of them and an entire career where life could lead them into many different directions, there is a willingness to take that risk. While no one likes to lose and any politician is going to take a calculation of the impact that a decision or a vote will have on their future political ambitions, a younger elected official is going to look at things from a new angle.

This risk taking is a constant with many of the young elected officials that I have talked to and it is a key component of what brings them together, something you can see in the young elected officials who have thought outside the box. Roz Wyman could have easily lost her seat after one term because of voter backlash about focusing on recruiting a professional sports team to the city. Shane Jett could have faced a backlash from the voters of his legislative district with his focus on agritourism and diversifying the economy of his state and his district. Jessica Lappin's desire to combine her background as an insider with her desire to think outside the box could have hurt her ambitions within the city council. But they are in a stage of their lives where they could take that risk.

Many young elected officials who enter public office in their 20s are unmarried or newly married and many do not have children. They are in the beginning of their careers and have few financial obligations; they are perfectly poised to be able to take that risk because they will be able to move on to a new career should the risk fail and they are voted out of office. Pam Iorio is now the mayor of Tampa, Florida, but she started her career in the 1980s as a twentysomething woman on the Hillsborough County Commission, the youngest woman ever elected to the county commission slot. She summed up her race, which featured her quitting her job in order to campaign full-time for the commissioner post, as saying that it was the only time in her life where she could take that risk and jump into the political arena, knowing that she had that ability. Iorio's comments were in regards to why she wanted to run for political office, but they apply to anyone who is a young elected official and why they are thinking outside the box.

Younger elected officials in this day and age are more likely to think of technology as second nature. They have grown up with e-mail being a common thing, with going online as the norm. To them having the latest BlackBerry is common and being on Facebook second nature. Tweeting is a normal behavior. This helps make technology a common outside-the-box thought process of those who are young and in public office. Having technology as a part of their daily lives makes them willing to want to use technology in government and deciding how to improve government through technology. They also want to use technology in their campaigns. No longer is having a website good enough; they want the Facebook fan page and Twitter accounts and YouTube ads and interactive community-building features on their websites. Social networking and social media continues to be a part of their campaign thought process.

Whether it is bringing in a professional sports team or solar panels or utilizing Facebook or making campaigning into something more than the same old thing, young elected officials will continue to think outside the box when it comes to how they pursue their campaigns and tenures in public office. They will be running races that are different and running offices that are different. They will be thinking outside the box and making that into a new way for how they want to do their jobs. They will bring that into many parts of the job and will be doing more and more. The outside-the-box thinking will also lead many to want to reform the way government runs in their districts, communities and chambers.

Based on what has been seen in the political and governmental arenas from young elected officials in the past and based on the research conducted for this book, outside-the-box thinking will continue in terms of what young elected officials bring into the arena. They will continue to think outside the box and continue to look at ways to change government. The youth perspective will continue to change government, if government will listen.

While in some cases, government may not listen to the outside-the-box perspectives brought by the younger generation of officials elected to office, such perspectives will continue to be brought to government by young elected officials. These proposals will help bring government forward and, if not adopted when they are first brought up, they will be at the forefront of discussion. They will be in front of the public and the press. While professional baseball in Los Angeles was an outside-the-box concept when Wyman first brought it up to her colleagues on the city council, she did help bring it to fruition. She brought the idea out there for more cities to discuss and made professional sports teams a concept to upgrade the economic development of up-and-coming cities nationwide.

Notes

1   The decision of New York Mayor Michael Bloomberg and the New York City Council in 2008 officially changed term-limits. While in 2005 — when Lappin was first elected to succeed the term-limited Miller — the city charter limited municipal officials to eight years, the charter change advocated for by Bloomberg has extended the term limits to three terms. While designed primarily to aid Bloomberg and other term-limited politicians in 2009, the limits are legally still three terms. There has been talk of a citywide referendum to address term limits and decide whether to keep them at three terms or revert to the original two-term ban. Such a referendum was not held in the 2009 general election and the next referendum cannot be held until the 2010 general election.

2   Campaign finance records filed with the New Jersey Election Law Enforcement Commission and reported by me in my capacity as the editor of *Westfield Patch*, showed that Keith Loughlin spent the second highest of any ward council candidate in Westfield in the 2009 general election.

3   Cammarano was arrested on federal corruption charges in July 2009, several weeks after being sworn in to a four-year term as Mayor of Hoboken. He resigned on July 31, 2009, after he had taken office on July 1.

4   Duffy appeared on the MTV series *The Real World*, during the Boston season. He is also the first man in Real World history to marry another Real World alum, Rachel Campos of the San Francisco season.

CHAPTER 3

"I look like I'm 12": The Reaction to Young Elected Officials

"Not only am I younger, but I look like I'm 12," New York state assemblyman Andy Hevesi said of one of his challenges when he first ran in a 2005 special election at the age of 31. Hevesi is not alone in thinking how he looks or acts could play a role in how voters will perceive him as a candidate. There are many common ideas on what an elected official should look like. Many people like to think of their state legislators and city council members and mayors and members of Congress as older. Maybe some gray hairs, but older, not in their 20s and early 30s: having some life experience as they go about doing the business of the people. These elective bodies are in many ways populated by a lot of people who are over the age of 40 — having been in office for many years, working together and sharing the same point of view of a generation. In some state legislatures the joke can be that a legislator in their mid-40s or early-50s is considered young for the group.

What do young elected officials encounter when they start running for office and getting their names out there? How are the voters accepting them when someone who at times looks barely old enough to vote is knocking on their door asking for their vote? How are their colleagues accepting someone who may be young enough to be their child or grandchild suddenly ends up as their equal?

When Gifford Miller was elected to the New York City Council in a 1996 special election at the age of 26, he was at that point the youngest member ever elected to the city council. Representing the Upper East Side of Manhattan, he did not have much of a problem getting his point across to voters based on his age or youthful looking appearance. The main problem he encountered would still have been a problem for him even at twice his age. "The east side of Manhattan is a tough place to campaign," he said. "I've campaigned all over the city and it is not as friendly on the east side. East-siders are a little less open and less interested in talking to random strangers in the street. There is no question that in other parts of the city they are more friendly."

While the reception in his district had nothing to do with his age, it was when he got to city hall that he started to stand out. Although he was the youngest member of the council at that time, he had some colleagues in the youth caucus, but many started picking up on Miller's endgame for his service on the council. Term limits would likely make him the most senior member in terms of service by the end of 2001. "They thought I was overeager and overly ambitious," Miller said. They pegged him right. No sooner had Miller taken the oath as a councilman, he was launching a bid to be the council's Speaker following the 2001 election when term limits would first take effect in city government. Not that he was the only ambitious member of the council, with many of the term-limited members looking at races for higher office and his three colleagues, all of whom were in their early 30s looking at races for Congress at that point. Two, Vito Fossella and Anthony Weiner, would get there while a third, Andrew Eristoff, would lose to Miller's mentor, Carolyn Maloney.

Miller launched his bid for Speaker, which would involve an effort akin to a citywide race in which 51 people would vote at the end of the day. Miller would be in the public sphere, would be looked at like someone who was barely old enough to vote, and yet he could be the second most powerful person in city government. However, in the backrooms where speakers are made, his age was not the main issue. "There was a healthy skepticism," he said. The skepticism was from my being from Manhattan rather than from being young." In the view of New York City politics, with Manhattan dominating the city and the next mayor likely to hail from the borough, the outer borough Democratic leaders who carry much clout in picking a Speaker were concerned about entrusting the office to a Manhattanite. Getting into office though, and pursuing a mayor's race in the 2005 Democratic primary to face incumbent Michael Bloomberg, Miller's age would become an issue.

Miller's age and appearance became issues during his four-year speakership. If he brought up an issue, he would be derided as whiny. He was portrayed as a baby in a carriage. He was generally dismissed because of his age. Miller may have commanded control over approving the city budget and zoning decisions, run a large government organization and been trailed by police bodyguards citywide, but to some his age was a hindrance in taking him seriously. Miller lets the cartoons slide saying they came with the office. "As a general rule if you are in politics, you should be flattered," he said. "Cartoonists draw caricatures and they draw out the most obnoxious characteristics and take it to an absurd point. I was young. Some were funny and some were not that funny. When you are a candidate running against an incumbent mayor you will get your lumps. I knew that going in."

While Miller ended up on the leadership track because of term limits forcing out most of his legislative colleagues, another young elected official was helped on the leadership track by term limits but also being promoted by those in the leadership when he entered office. Andy Meisner was 29 when he was elected to the Michigan House of Representatives in 2002, in a time when many seats in the House would turn over because of term limits. When he was running for office, he had to deal with people questioning whether he was serious because of how young he looked. Meisner would end up compensating for his youthful appearance by throwing himself into the issues and making sure people knew he wanted the job.

Getting to Lansing, Meisner had to overcome the same original thoughts that he was not serious about his career in the legislature because of his youthful appearance. He continued to compensate by talking about his background in government and politics and studying up on the issues. During this time, he was able to make enough of an impression to find himself not having his age being taken into account when people met him. "I was on a leadership track the entire time I was there," said Meisner, who is now Oakland County treasurer. "They almost elected me Speaker at 32."

Don Ness was 25 years old when he first sought an at-large city council seat in Duluth, Minnesota, in 1999. Entering the race, Ness was not a political novice. He had been an aide to the local congressman, including heading his district operation and running his reelection campaign. He had the institutional ability and know-how to make the race, but he had to deal with the local reaction when he was talking to voters. Little did he know that the challenges he would face and how he would handle them would make him a trailblazer in northern Minnesota. Unlike Miller, Ness did not have to deal with voters more interested in rushing to the subway than talking to some politician in the morning. While the voters wanted to talk, they were not jumping to consider a youthful looking potential candidate. "I was 25 and looked 10 years younger," he said. "I had to quickly establish credibility. That I was not running as a joke or to see my name in the paper. For young candidates and young elected officials you need credibility. It is difficult to get anything accomplished without that."

Ness started to use the knowledge he gained in his day job with Congressman Jim Oberstar, along with studying up on the plethora of issues facing local government and northern Minnesota, in order to win over the voters. He could not talk in soundbites though; he would need to communicate his knowledge through in-depth answers to the voters. He needed to make sure that they knew that he knew the details of the issues and was comfortable in tackling the duties of a city councilman.

Once he got to city hall, Ness was able to translate his work on the campaign trail into credibility with his colleagues in city government. Using this knowledge and his continued work for Oberstar, he had early entrees into government, but there were still areas of personal growth he had to overcome during his early years in elective office — issues that threatened his ability to accomplish anything during his term. "For many young elected officials the ability and willingness to accept criticism is a difficult lesson to learn," he said. "Coming in you want to serve your constituents and have them appreciate your efforts and what you bring to the table."

Ness found that he was not easily deflecting the criticism early on. While Miller says that he was able to let some of the cartoons brush off him and fall by the wayside, Ness was having the problem continue. "The word went out that with a certain type of criticism against me, folks began to use it as an issue," Ness said. "Once you have that label people will do that. It took years to overcome, in some ways you had to over correct. That's the area where I grew most, to be able to take the constructive part of the criticism."

Like Miller during the 2005 election, Ness saw that the criticism started getting personal. While Miller attributes it to running for mayor in the nation's largest city, Ness attributes it to his age. "As a young elected official people will play to inexperience," he said. "They will demonstrate their dissatisfaction in a very personal manner. It is an outward display of their displeasure. They will ignore you on the sidewalk." During eight years as a councilman, Ness would work to overcome their opinions and treatment. He notes that at times he tried to over-compensate, for what people were saying about him or doing to him.

By the time 2007 rolled around, Ness was willing to take a jump for higher office, hoping to have put any criticism about his experience level and ability to accept constructive criticism to rest. That year he would be able to success-fully run for the mayor's office. By the time he made the race for mayor, Ness saw very little of the criticism that had marked his political debut eight years before. While he was running to lead the city, he would also be running in the same constituency he had represented as an at-large councilman. Ness believes his work ethic over eight years played a role in him being received a lot easier when he decided to run for the mayor's office. "Many in the community had seen me grow into adulthood in the public eye," Ness said. "When I first ran for council I was 25, single and a renter. The progression over the course of eight years I had gotten married, had two kids and bought a house. That progression of being a college student to evolving into a professional. When I first got on the council, I would show up to the Chamber of Commerce meetings in shorts and a T-shirt. I was able to earn my credibility at those meetings because I knew the legislative process. I had the advantage of people seeing me progress."

Winning the mayor's office, Ness would do one more thing during that campaign. Personally and during his eight years as a councilman he was known as Donny. When he started his bid for — and time as — Duluth's mayor, he became Don. While Jimmy Carter fought to be known as Jimmy over James and Bobby Kennedy was known as Bobby over Bob, Ness wanted to stop using the more casual nickname. He believed he would be taken more seriously as a mayoral candidate as Don. But Ness found he couldn't change his first name without generating headlines. "That can be an awkward and embarrassing task to rename yourself and being in the public eye it was a media event." Ness said. "There were editorials all about this personal transition I was making from Donny to Don. The last thing you want is people to focus on that trivial thing. However, I am glad I did it."

Ness' eight years on the council showed that a councilman in his 20s could work in Duluth and ended up helping to pave the way for younger offi-cials to run for office in Duluth. In 2007 when Ness gave up his council seat to run for mayor, 29-year-old Tony Cuneo made a race to succeed him in the at-large seat. While the city's voters were used to Ness during that time, and he had been at a younger age than Cuneo, the new candidate had to overcome similar hurdles. The policy director for a local non-profit, Cuneo would still need to prove himself in similar ways to how Ness proved himself. He needed to show that he knew the issues and was a credible candidate to be a councilman. "I remember going to one community forum and you're nervous and heard three women asking who was this 16-year-old kid getting up on stage," Cuneo said. "You have to be more prepared and know your issues better."

At the same time Ness and Cuneo won their races in 2007, 30-year-old Jeff Anderson also announced a bid for the city council in Duluth. A radio professional who had been an on-air DJ during his career, Anderson was able to build credibility with the voters before he announced his bid for the city council. It is these relationships that helped him to establish himself when he decided to run for the city council. Anderson has since moved off the air, taking jobs in the non-broadcast realm of his radio station.

Anderson attributes three things to his being able to one day win a council seat and not face challenges based on his age: the first was the name recognition his time on the radio had given him; the second is that he looks older than he is; the third was the in-roads Ness had made in the community that helped future young candidates. "I got a good reaction," Anderson said. "I think I look older than I am and I wear a suit and tie to work. I don't think I fought that much of a battle of people saying you're too young."

Starting out as a political staffer helps many young elected officials get a good reception when they start in their legislative bodies. During the time they've served as a staffer they've been able to meet many of their future colleagues one on one and have already been received in that environment. While they have to be known as the legislator and not as the staffer in some respect, it helps play down the age factor.

John McGee was 31 when he was elected to the Idaho state senate in 2004. He came to the post after working as an aide to fellow Republican Dirk Kempthorne during the latter's time in the U.S. Senate. During this time he had gotten to know many of the state senators, which helped ease his transition into the Senate. At the same time, McGee acknowledges that he had to reach out to the other senators in order to show that he was serious about the job and the issues affecting state government.

Going out and campaigning as a young elected official, the candidate talks to voters across spectrums of the community. While the particular demographics of a district could mean a disproportionate amount of young professionals or elderly or young families, most places where candidates are running remain the same at the end of the day. Candidates could start the day talking to commuters and then move to senior citizens and then to young families and empty-nesters.

One common factor that remains the same for any political candidate, young or old, is that senior citizens remain one of the largest voting blocks. With senior citizens having more free time and a large amount of institutional knowledge of the community, they will be likely to vote early in the day and will be more likely to vote at all. In some senior citizens communities, dedicated polling places are set up in the community room in order to get the vote out. It is not surprising to hear that a candidate is spending much of their time campaigning at senior citizen centers and other events that are likely to attract large amounts of senior citizens. This is done largely for two reasons. First senior citizens are most likely to be around during the daytime hours in order to attend a political event; and second the high voting block the senior citizen population presents in many communities.

One perception with young elected officials is that they will not get a good reception from senior citizens when they are campaigning. They worry that senior citizens will be concerned that they are too young and they do not have the life experience in order to run for and hold elective office and that senior voters will reward experience over youth when they get the privacy of the voting booths.

But young elected officials found that to be a surprise, noting that senior citizens turned out to be some of their biggest supporters as they campaigned. In terms of Illinois State Sen. Michael Frerichs, who was 24 when he unsuccessfully sought a seat in the state House of Representatives in 1998 and then 27 when he won a seat in the county board, he found seniors to be his biggest supporters and young voters to not be his most enthusiastic voters. "Most everyone says that young people will be excited and you'll have a tough time with senior citizens," Frerichs said. "I found that to be the opposite with the senior citizens loving me." In addition to the support he was seeing from senior citizens, Frerichs said voters younger than him also reacted well to his candidacy to represent them in Springfield. He equates the younger support to enthusiasm to the chance of having someone just older than them serving as their state representative.

The demographic where Frerichs found himself having a tough reaction was his own. He said those in the age range of 25–40 were the toughest for him to crack and make in-roads. He still doesn't know why. "They would not say why," Frerichs said of why others in his age range were not excited about the prospect of voting for a peer to represent them in Springfield. "I think there was a feeling amongst other people that I did not have enough experience.

It has been over 40 years since Democrat Roz Wyman served in elective office as a city councilwoman in Los Angeles. But she has kept many of the lessons she learned in 12 years on the city council to heart and let them guide her post-elective office career. The youngest woman elected to the Los Angeles City Council, Wyman was 22 years old when she was elected in 1953.

During her first campaign, Wyman was able to put together a strong grassroots campaigning strategy. A state officer for the California Young Democrats and a campaign staff veteran, Wyman knew how to put together a grassroots campaign and gain support. She was also prepared for the amount of work that was needed for her to be a grassroots candidate and focus on door knocking, knowing it would be one of the things she brought to the campaigning. She found that she was able to lay the groundwork for a campaign beforehand and passes on a piece of advice for young professionals looking to run for office in the future. "I think a lot of people don't realize that you need to join," Wyman said of what fledging young candidates need to do to build up a grassroots base. "I had Young Democrats coming down on weekends to do precinct work."

Wyman said one area that she needed to learn quickly when she got into office was that she could stick to her principles but she would need to work with her older colleagues closely and learn to compromise in order to get anything done. "I compromised if I thought I could get something," she said. "There are certain principles you don't compromise on."

But at the same time she noticed that fundraising was a tougher game for herself and other young elected officials and candidates. In the end though, the experience Wyman acquired in fundraising for herself in the 1950s led to her reinvention in the political world. After leaving the city council in 1965 she would become a top political fundraiser in southern California. This would include being Senator Dianne Feinstein's chief Los Angeles fundraiser and raising money for House Speaker Nancy Pelosi. In 1984, she was the chief fundraiser for the Democratic National Convention in San Francisco.

Eric Croft may have been the son of a former state senator and Democratic nominee for Alaska governor, but he knew when he ran for a seat in Alaska's House of Representatives in 1996 at the age of 31 that he had to work harder to prove himself because of his young age. He ran a strong door-to-door campaign, showing that while he was young he knew the issues and wanted to work hard for the district. He knew there were certain challenges to overcome by looking younger than he was. "For those who start young we have to prove our credentials," he said. While Croft did work hard, he noted that Alaska is different in terms of what they look for in a candidate. He said a 20-year-old lifelong resident would stand a better shot than a 50-year-old newcomer to America's forty-ninth state. "In Alaska they want to know age and how long you've been here," Croft said. "There is a carpetbagger thing. They want people with a commitment to the state. I could get around the age thing by saying I was born here."

Pam Iorio agrees with Croft that she had to work hard to prove that her age would not be a hindrance in why she should be elected to public office. The future mayor of Tampa was 26 when she was elected to the Hillsborough County Commission in 1985, the youngest person ever elected to the county commission. She made the decision to run for the commission after the county changed the make-up of the governing panel and decided to have the commissioners elected in single member districts.

During the race, her age and experience level did come up. Iorio had worked at the University of South Florida and in the political arena as a volunteer and some questioned whether she was up to being a full time county commissioner in one of Florida's largest metro areas. Looking back she sees things a bit differently than she saw them at the time. "Now that I look back I see that I had little experience," Iorio said in a 2006 interview. "When you are running you say you will be a fresh face." Most of the voters Iorio talked to in her district talked to her about needing a change in how the county was run and mentioned to her that being young was a positive to them, since she was not wedded to the way things have always been. Iorio remembers one meeting with a voter where her age did become an issue. "I had one person who said they would not vote for a young single woman," she said, noting that the person stands out more than 20 years later because of their singularity.

While Iorio saw a question raised during the campaign but not materialize when she took the oath of office, Terry Bellamy saw the opposite. During her 1999 race for the city council in Asheville, North Carolina, at the age of 27, she found voters asking her if she was too young to make the race. They wanted to know if she would be taken seriously on the council if she got elected. They wanted to know if she could get people to listen to her.

Bellamy was able to win over voters by talking about how she would look to work with the other council members if elected, and ended up finishing first in the multi-winner field. Getting to the council though, her experience was different from the Iorio with her colleagues giving her push-back early on. Bellamy would end up winning over the other members to get items accomplished and then move on to higher office. In 2005 she was elected the city's youngest — and first African American — mayor. Like Ness, she said the mayor's race was easier for her in that she was able to get more support and fewer questions because she had already used the council as a proving ground.

Brent Barton has something in common with Andy Hevesi and Don Ness: he looks younger than his age. Running for the Oregon House of Representatives in 2008 at the age of 28, he had to combat the fact that in pictures and while campaigning he looked more like a college student than a young attorney — former gubernatorial campaign aide and political activist — looking to serve in the state legislature. Knocking on doors in his suburban Portland district, Barton would be able to combat the issue but still have to prove to people that he was not that young.

Barton's race was one of the most contentious in Oregon in 2008 — and one of the most expensive in state history. He and his Republican opponent would trade barbs back and forth in order to win. In some ads, Barton would be attacked for resumé inflation based on how he stated what he did during a law clerkship in a prosecutor's office. He would attack his opponent — an incumbent — on her record. With so much of voting being subliminal, his opponent was looking to exploit Barton's youthful looks in the attack mail. "All of the attack mail showed a picture on a blog taken in 2004 where I look like I'm 15," Barton said.

Getting to Salem for his first legislative session in 2009, Barton would find the fact that he looks young brought up again but not in a serious way. He notes that he has been treated like a colleague by other House members and that his age has not been a disadvantage. Barton also has lucked out by entering the legislature at a time when young elected officials are a rising trend in Oregon. "I am teased several times a day about how young I am," Barton said of his time in Salem. "It's all good natured."

Jeffrey Graham knows a bit about an opponent bringing up age in the race. Graham was 26 when he was elected mayor of Camden, South Carolina, in 2008 and he had people asking him from the day he started his campaign how old he was. "I look much younger than 26," he said. But the real challenge he had to overcome was not constituents asking him in their doorways about how old he was. He was able to overcome the questions easily by talking about his vision for the city and how he wanted to bring new energy to city government. Graham was following a young elected official's playbook to an extent, promoting himself as the candidate of change. Graham's opponent was an incumbent mayor who was 34. She focused her campaign not on being the candidate of change, like Graham but by stressing her experience. Experience becoming code for Graham's age, by raising things Graham would not have been doing because he was in college or starting his career at the time.

Walker Hines was elected at the age of 23 to the Louisiana House of Representatives in 2007. Even before he was halfway through his four-year term, Hines was doing battle on multiple fronts in Baton Rouge. Hines' big issue has been ethics reform and restricting the influence of lobbyists in the state. Louisiana is a famously corrupt state, with stories of governors going to jail and a reputation that eclipses New Jersey and Illinois for corruption at many times. Coming into office a few short years after Hurricane Katrina devastated New Orleans, with stories of corrupt levee boards and mismanagement, Hines believed it was the right time to address ethics in government.

At the same time, Hines has had a second battle in the legislature. When he's not trying to get stronger ethics laws passed, he has to handle the fact that many of his colleagues believe he is there representing a district of young professionals instead of a district of diverse ages. That impacted how they involved him in some discussions early on. "For better or worse they put me in a box if it is not a bill that impacts young people," he said. "The worst part about being a young elected official is that your colleagues view you as being in a box." Hines would find the issue of age coming up during debate over his bill to limit the ability of a state legislator to have lunch with a lobbyist and have the lobbyist pay. Hines could be seen as attacking the longtime core values of Louisiana state government with this bill. "Some accused me of being young and immature and that it was great to have lunch with lobbyists," Hines said.

Young elected officials do face challenges based on their age and the reaction to their age. The question is how will they receive and react to those challenges. Many will have to face the question of how old they are, particularly if they look younger than they are. They will need to prove that they are not that young and that they are qualified to hold the office. They will need to work harder to overcome any perception that young people are immature and do not know what they are talking about. They will need to show that life experience is not the only way that someone can be deemed competent to discuss public policy issues and run a government. They will need to show that a variety of backgrounds can work in government. Many bring unique perspectives that are based on their age. They can espouse change and are not wedded to how things have always been done. They can look at things from perspectives not seen before. In an effect they let their age define them, but from a policy perspective not from an age perspective.

Working the extra mile though will continue to be the hallmark that young elected officials show in order to overcome any questions they get about their age. They will need to be policy wonks, ready, willing and able to dive into issues and learn everything they can. They need to study everything they can about the issue and avoid speaking in pithy soundbites and instead focus on conveying every detail. They will need to show that they are just as prepared as any of their colleagues.

Young elected officials will need to show a certain seriousness at times to show that while they are young they have the maturity to serve in the office they have been elected to. But this maturity should not be conceived as having to act overly serious at all times and give up any public nature of being in your 20s and 30s. They can have fun and continue to be someone in their 20s, but they need to show that they are serious about their jobs when they are doing their jobs. Some young elected officials talk about the change in their personal life and how they find themselves acting more seriously when they are in a public setting. They do not want to be seen as being young and immature when it comes time to face the voters the next time. Some young elected officials compensate so hard for any desire to act like a regular person their age that they sometimes make themselves look more serious at the end and could turn off the young professionals in the area.

Young elected officials can overcome perceptions about how they will act while in office or what they will support while they are in office. These are only perceptions, which can easily change as new elected officials take off and take on a life of their own. They could suddenly have the young elected taking a side that is the opposite of his generation, ignoring that some are following the needs and desire of their entire district and not just the young people.

Even with more young professionals opting for elective office, it would only be natural for the question of their age to come up either in casual conversation or as a part of a larger conversation. People will second guess many as they take office, often questioning whether a young person has the ability to serve in office at a young age. It will be up to the young elected officials to demonstrate that they can do anything and are willing to stand up for their districts during arguments for the issue that will help their district and show that they can deal with any issue that can come along. They need to avoid being shoeboxed into one issue area or issues effecting youth.

CHAPTER 4

The President in Waiting? The Ambitions of Young Elected Officials

The week before Labor Day 2008 had two iconic political images that are seared into the collective memory of the nation. That Thursday evening, an articulate, polished, energetic, intellectual man stepped into a makeshift amphitheatre in Denver to accept his party's nomination for President of the United States. That day, Barack Obama, then a senator from Illinois, helped move the nation forward, becoming not only the first African American to accept the presidential nomination of a major party, but also becoming the first person born in the 1960s to become the nominee of a major party.

The next morning, hours after the images of Obama and his young family waving to the crowds packed into the outdoor stadium in the Rocky Mountains, another piece of news had moved forward in the public imagination; news that would be confirmed hours later on a stage in Ohio. That day, a self-described hockey mom from Wasilla, Alaska — young, energetic, accompanied by her newborn son and young children — stepped onto the stage and accepted an invitation to run for vice president of the United States on a ticket headed by a man old enough to be her father. That day, Sarah Palin, then the governor of Alaska, helped set a new standard for women in politics. No longer was a major party female national candidate an older woman like Hillary Clinton or Geraldine Ferraro, whose children were grown. Instead, the country was looking at a woman chief executive with a newborn and only one child out of high school.

At the same time, another person stepped up on the national stage. Obama's running mate, Delaware senator Joseph Biden, was in his mid-60s when he accepted the vice presidential nomination of his party, but he had been around so long that it was hard to remember that he was a young elected official himself when he started out in his career. When he was elected to the Senate in 1972, Joe Biden wasn't even constitutionally eligible to become a senator. He was only 29 years old and while several examples exist in the nineteenth century of those under the constitutional age of 30 being sworn into the Senate — 29-year-old Henry Clay's swearing-in as a senator from Kentucky in 1806 being one of those — times had changed. In the 1800s, birth records were not as well kept, people may not have known the exact year they were born, communication was more difficult, Senate officials could not talk to Kentucky officials to find out Clay's exact age, so they let it be and seated him as a senator. But times were different; in fact Senator Rush Holt of West Virginia had to wait several months in 1935 until he turned 30 before he could take his seat. But in Biden's case, he turned 30 in December of 1972, while a senator-elect, and he was able to take his seat on the day his term had started. Of course this wasn't Biden's first foray into politics: he had already served two years as a county commissioner before being elected to the Senate.

Biden is not the only one of the three that started in politics and elective office at a young age. Actually in terms of the 2008 election, the vice presidential contenders were actually the early birds in the political arena. John McCain's pre-political career is well known and it's common knowledge that he pursued the military long before he relocated with his second wife to her native Arizona and chose politics as a second career. Obama also was a latecomer to the world of elective politics based on the work of Biden and Palin and many other young elected officials around the country. Based on the criteria I have used of young elected officials being those who are 35 years and under, Obama just makes the cut, having been 35 years old when he was first elected to the Illinois state senate in 1996. If you make the case that in his Senate district in Chicago, that the Democratic primary is the real election, Obama was 34 years old at the time of his election to the state senate. Biden and Palin were both in their 20s when they got their starts as a county commissioner and city councilwoman.

The group in 2008 were not alone: a look at those who have served as presidents and vice presidents since the end of World War II, along with those who have lost general election races for the presidency and vice presidency in the same time period, show that many started as young elected officials. Five[1] out of the 12 presidents who have served since that time were young elected officials at the beginning of their careers, along with 7[2] out of 13 vice presidents. Out of the 13[3] defeated general election presidential candidates, who have never served as president or vice president, 7[4] started their careers as young elected officials. Of the 20[5] defeated candidates for vice presidential candidates, who have never served as president or vice president, since World War II, 9[6] started as young elected officials.

Young elected officials are by their very nature ambitious individuals. Who else would want to put themselves through the circus like atmosphere that running for public office can be? They need to raise money, knock on doors, take positions on issues that they may have never thought of before, and keep giving the same elevator speech day after day, night after night, on doorsteps, on the phone, at fundraisers, and at nightly coffee gatherings. All the while dealing with a prying press and an opponent who could do or say anything to win the election. It is not a normal lifestyle and not one that the average person willingly signs up for. Having some sort of ambition is a precursor to seeking an elective office at any age, but when one is barely out of college, or in some cases high school and not even into your 30s, it is almost a requirement. "When you are young and in office the perception is that you're ambitious," Colorado state senate minority leader Josh Penry said.

But the ambition to start in elective politics at a young age is not just an ambition that ends at being elected to public office at a young age. It continues through since many of those who are elected at a young age are by very nature people who are looking to continue in politics for a long time, people whose very age put them in a position to help shape the direction of American politics for a number of years, in any number of offices. Young elected officials are by and large the next generation of American politicians. The intrigue and discussion of political dealings will continue to include young elected officials and what offices they plan on seeking.

Let's take Henry Clay as an historical example to start. Seated in the U.S. Senate at 28, he would not see his career end in that brief Senate term. He would move to the House of Representatives, serving as Speaker for a number of years. He would progress to being a presidential candidate and secretary of state, eventually rejoining the Senate. Clay's career would become one of the most enduring in the nineteenth century, one that would have an impact on the future of the Republic and the Senate as a whole.

Or in terms of the three from 2008: Did the voters who placed a young Sarah Palin on the city council foresee her ending up governor or running for vice president? Did the voters who elected Joe Biden to the county commission see the future longest-serving U.S. senator in Delaware history and one-day vice president in their midst? Or looking back further, the voters in Boston who voted in a young war hero named John Kennedy to Congress in 1946 did they see him one day ending up the president?

American history is taken up by many young elected officials who moved up in the political arena and continued with their ambition and desire to serve in higher office. Many continue to serve until this day.

Young Western New Yorkers Continue to Press Ambition

Let's take one region of the country to start. Western New York may not be the place one would first think of as a place to find ambitious young elected officials, but it has had more than its fair share. Dominated by the cities of Buffalo and Niagara Falls, Western New York is a region that is similar to many fading industrial bases along the Great Lakes. Factories have moved out of the region, leaving behind the employees but taking the jobs. Abandoned factories dot the landscape in many corners, with many young people leaving the region after college in search of a better job and better life in another region of the country.

Looking at the last 30 years of politics in Western New York, there are multiple examples of young elected officials in the landscape. In an interesting coincidence, the men who presided over the rise and fall of the Republican majority in the House of Representatives in the 1990s and early 2000s both got their starts as twentysomethings in the Western New York region. Bill Paxon was elected just out of college to the Erie County Legislature, moving onto the state assembly and then to Congress. In Congress he would take over the National Republican Campaign Committee (NRCC), helping usher in the 1994 Republican majority and marrying another young elected official, then congresswoman Susan Molinari of Staten Island. At the same time, in another part of Erie County, twentysomething Tom Reynolds got his start as a member of the Town Board in the Town of Concord. Holding a series of political staff posts, Reynolds would also see his career move to the county legislature and the state assembly — becoming minority leader in both bodies — before succeeding Paxon in Congress in 1998. He would show the same fundraising ability of Paxon and the same political skill. Reynolds would also head the NRCC, guiding it successfully in 2004, before presiding over the loss of the majority in 2006. Reynolds would end up retiring from Congress in 2008, a decade after taking office.

While both were not young elected officials when they were in their Washington heyday, both had gotten that start as twentysomethings toiling in the political vineyards of Erie County. Serving in town and county government, passing out literature at festivals in the summertime, helping more senior politicians. In short, doing everything possible to forge a career in the political arena in the long term and put themselves in a position to dominate GOP politics in Western New York and in Washington.

In the present day, there continue to be examples of young elected officials showcasing ambition in their careers in Western New York. Take Democrat Kyle Andrews and Republican Jack Quinn III as cases in point. Both have taken different paths into political office, but yet have similar goals going forward. Andrews was 21 when he was elected to the Niagara County Legislature in 2001, while a college student. Helped by a grandfather who had been town supervisor in their rural Niagara County town, Andrews did not have strong ties to the political history. He even pulled off a victory as a Democrat in a Republican district, holding his seat unopposed in four consecutive reelection bids. Quinn entered elective office in 2004 at the age of 26, winning an assembly seat just as his father, Jack Quinn, was retiring from Congress after a dozen years. Quinn was a recent law school graduate at the time, with a very short stint as an assistant district attorney in Erie County on his resume. His name was his greatest asset going forward. Beating back a former assemblyman in a district encompassing suburban and rural areas south of Buffalo, Quinn found himself in the assembly's almost permanent Republican minority, winning easy reelection in 2006 and 2008.

But at the same time while their paths into elective office are different, Quinn and Andrews are both highly ambitious politicians who have indicated a desire to move into higher office. Quinn didn't have to do anything to position himself for higher office — or at least have the speculation that he would be running for an office higher than state assemblyman. With Quinn's father being succeeded by Democrat Brian Higgins — himself a former young elected official — and the Quinn name being the political gold standard in Western New York, the young assemblyman was immediately considered the chief Republican rival to Higgins and the one most likely to challenge him in 2006.

Quinn does not deny that he has an interest in possibly one day taking his father's career path and serving in Congress. But he took a pass in 2006 and 2008, choosing not to make the race against Higgins but instead focusing on reelection to the assembly. In 2006, the year Higgins would have been the most vulnerable, Quinn declined citing the need to gain more experience in the assembly before making a race for Congress. As Higgins gains a more entrenched place in the Western New York political landscape, it is becoming clearer that while Quinn harbors ambitions for a seat in Congress, that seat will not come soon enough. When Higgins was listed as a potential replacement for Hillary Clinton in the Senate in 2009, many Western New York politicians — in both parties — told me that Quinn was the GOP frontrunner for the special election to fill Higgins' congressional seat in the event that he was tapped by Governor David Paterson to become a senator. The same people also mentioned that Quinn was not only his party's frontrunner for a special election to Congress, but also an overall frontrunner in the special election, which would be held over a short period of time.

This is not to say that Quinn does not have a desire to move up. In 2008, he briefly considered a race for the vacant district attorney's chair, before deciding against it on the basis of experience. But he notes that he continues to maintain an interest in becoming Erie County's chief prosecutor. In March 2010, Quinn announced he was not seeking a fourth term in his safe assembly seat and instead was seeking a state senate seat in a Democratic-leaning district. In doing so he took on a race thought by many to be key to reclaiming the Senate for the GOP. In fact, Quinn was heavily lobbied by state GOP leaders to jump into the Senate race, instead of running for reelection or seeking a county judgeship, which he publicly considered.

Quinn entered a Senate race considered winnable. With his famous name and overlap from his assembly district, he is the most serious Republican candidate. The seat is held by a 28-year Democratic incumbent, Bill Stachowski, who was already facing a primary challenge from a county legislator. The timing could add up to a perfect storm for Quinn and also make him a potential power player in Albany by helping to reclaim the Senate.

Moving up to Niagara County, Andrews was not finding himself on many frontrunner lists for higher office. At the same time though he was putting together what he would need should he choose to run for higher office in the future. He gathered the record and the relationships. Starting in the days where he unseated a longtime Republican incumbent in a heavily GOP district where he was listed as vulnerable in his first reelection, Andrews had formed a close relationship with Republican leaders along with maintaining his position within the Democratic Party. His boss in the private sector, where he was an attorney, was for a number of years Henry Wojtaszek, the head of the Niagara County GOP.

Andrews makes little secret of his desire to one day serve in Congress. Admitting it in various press reports and during a November 2006 panel discussion on young elected officials at the Columbia University Club of New York, he admits to having a desire to run for higher office one day, being the most blunt of the four young elected officials then sitting on the panel in the private club in Midtown Manhattan. While Andrews has a desire to run for Congress, he also has to deal with the fact that a seat is not coming open and in any event he would need to compete in a very competitive environment where frontrunners come out of all corners of the district. The redistricting of New York's congressional districts following the 2010 census, where the Empire State is likely to lose at least one seat, also weighs in the process. While desiring a seat in Congress, Andrews also has to deal with all of the circumstances impacting such a race.

At the same time, Andrews is not sitting back and keeping a seat warm in the county legislature. In November 2009, just after winning his fifth legislative term unopposed, he announced his candidacy for Niagara county treasurer, an office where the incumbent was retiring after almost four decades in the office. Andrews took a few risks in order to make the race, quitting his law firm job is one of them and also putting himself in a race for an office that could either be viewed as a political stepping stone or backwater office, just based on past treasurers in Niagara County and in other parts of Upstate New York. At the same that Andrews made the announcement that he would seek the treasurer's office in 2010, he was also in the final run-up to his impending New Year's Eve wedding.

Andrews found himself making it to higher office even before the November 2010 election. At the end of January, Niagara County's longtime treasurer, David Broderick, announced his resignation from office, leaving the job vacant through the end of the year. In March of 2010, Governor David Paterson announced he was appointing Andrews to serve as county treasurer for the rest of the term, making him, at 29, the youngest countywide official in the history of Niagara County. Taking office only hours after Paterson's appointment was filed with the state comptroller and county clerk, Andrews started implementing the centerpiece of his campaign platform, internal reforms to the treasurer's office. The reforms came from a state comptroller's report detailing mismanagement in the office during Broderick's tenure.

There is some precedent in Andrews trying to turn being a young elected official in a countywide office in Niagara County into a congressional seat. In fact, the last person to do that went just a bit further. Republican William Miller was 34 years old when he became the district attorney of Niagara County in

1948, a post he would hold for a handful of years before he was elected to Congress in 1950. Miller would spend 14 years in Congress during which he spent the Kennedy years as chairman of the Republican National Committee. Ending his tenure as the nation's top Republican, Miller would also take a chance at the highest office ever run for by a resident of Niagara County: vice president. The Lockport native would be the running mate of Barry Goldwater in the Democratic year of 1964.

In making reference to Andrews' boss in his private law practice, you are also making reference to a former young elected official in Western New York who has displayed an amount of ambition to move into higher office and to make politics his career. Henry Wojtaszek was elected the city attorney of North Tonawanda, New York, in 1997 when he was 33 years old. North Tonawanda is an industrial city with a suburban section on the Niagara River where the Erie Canal meets the river. The city was known as the terminus of the Erie Canal until 2007, when Governor Eliot Spitzer and the state legislature chose to move the end to the historic section in Buffalo, which had been the end until the canal was changed to end in North Tonawanda. North Tonawanda is one of the few cities that elects the city attorney. In charge of providing legal advice to city government and handling city litigation, it is not the sexiest of political offices. In fact it is almost tough to campaign for. How do you excite the public over who will be the city's chief lawyer?

Wojtaszek came to the office following service in the U.S. Navy Judge Advocate General Corps and as an attorney in private practice. He has also helmed the North Tonawanda Republican Party for a period. Being reelected to a two-year term in 1999 and to the city's first four-year term for city attorney in 2001, Wojtaszek was safe in the job. By the time of his election to a third term, Wojtaszek had also taken on the chairmanship of the county Republican Party, a post he took in 2000. Wojtaszek had put himself into a position of power. He would give up the chairmanship briefly in 2002, in order to run for Congress. Returning to the county chairmanship, he would end up resigning the city attorney's position and moving into a larger law firm while also focusing on the county chairman's job, a job where he orchestrated the retaking of the county government on the Republican Party's behalf. In 2008, when a congressional seat opened up and his local state senator was for a time the leading Republican nominee, I reported for a New York State political publication that Wojtaszek was the leading GOP contender for the Senate seat, speculation Wojtaszek did not deny at the time.

At the same time of concentrating on the fate of the Republican Party in Niagara County, Wojtaszek also moved statewide, taking a role in the state party, including that of first vice chairman of the New York Republican State Committee. Wojtaszek would then announce his candidacy for the chairmanship of the state Republican Party in 2009. The race would come up short; the state chairman's post would go to Ed Cox, the husband of President Nixon's daughter Tricia. Wojtaszek stepped down as the party chairman in his county at the end of 2009, but remains politically active and a power behind the scenes. While ambitious he has stepped back a bit, moving into the background as Cox dominates politics statewide. But Wojtaszek remains at the forefront of the political process helping to maneuver endorsements behind the scenes on a variety of levels.

In an interesting twist, Western New York is not just home to politically ambitious former young elected officials like Wojtaszek: the homegrown cases are supplemented by those who come from outside the region to make their home in Buffalo and continue their political careers there. To many in Erie County, Kevin Hardwick is now known for two main things: being a professor of political science at Canisius College and hosting a political call-in show on a local radio station for several years in the 2000s. But he has been involved in politics as well, starting in his native Broome County and then moving to his adopted Erie County, where he was elected to the county legislature as a Republican in 2009.

Hardwick got involved in politics when he graduated from high school in the rural Town of Binghamton and started college at nearby Binghamton University. Hardwick's political career then expanded to service on the Town Board. Already a political veteran during his college years, moving into his second office, Hardwick would also take another career move while pursuing his Ph.D. in political science at Binghamton University. He would become an aide to longtime New York senate majority leader Warren Anderson, a Republican who dominated Binghamton politics for decades. Anderson retired from the Senate in 1988 and Hardwick relocated to Buffalo to begin his teaching career. Bitten by the political bug, Hardwick chose to not just focus his attention on the academic side of politics when he moved to Buffalo from Binghamton. He became involved in politics in the City of Tonawanda, including service on the city council for several years.

At the same time, Hardwick continued his involvement in the Erie County Republican Committee. This included being recruited to challenge longtime Legislator Chuck Swanick in 2001, a race Hardwick lost. Hardwick turned around to run again in 2003 when the unusual happened to him: Swanick made a deal with the Republican county executive and other county Republicans to return to the chairmanship of the legislature in exchange for becoming a Republican, a move considered unusual given the angst county Republicans had shown towards Swanick during his many years in the legislature. Now, Hardwick had a new challenge, he wanted to run again but the Republicans who backed him against Swanick in 2001 were now backing Swanick. Swanick would beat Hardwick in that race and Hardwick would return to a full time academic life at Canisius and start a weekly political radio show called *Hardline with Hardwick*. The show kept Hardwick politically viable interviewing newsmakers and pundits (for the record I've appeared twice as a guest on his show, analyzing New York State politics) and generally being out there before the public and the listening class of politicians.

In 2009, Hardwick wanted to pursue that same political bug. Swanick had long since retired from politics and Democrat Michele Ianello had taken the seat. The new Republican who had become county executive was looking to put more Republicans into the county legislature to help move his agenda forward and saw Hardwick as a way to recapture the seat in the Tonawandas. Running in a year when incumbents were not in vogue across New York State, Hardwick was able to move into the realm of being a county legislator and continue those ambitions first formed as a young elected official in the rolling hills of rural Broome County.

Ambition in the Prairie

Of course, politically ambitious young elected officials are not contained to Western New York. They are all over the country, scattered from coast to coast. In America's heartland, Democrat Jasper Schneider has proven himself to be a young man in a hurry. Born in 1979, Schneider is part of a North Dakota political dynasty. Growing up in Fargo, he was never far from politics, as his father had served as a state representative, minority leader of the state House of Representatives, and as the state's U.S. attorney during the administration of former president Bill Clinton. "It's a family thing," Schneider said. "I grew up in a political household. My father held the seat I have from 1983 to 1991."

Schneider would himself be elected to the state House of Representatives representing Fargo to a four-year term in 2006. Under North Dakota's legislative practices and state constitution, the legislature meets only in odd-number years, with occasional special sessions in the even-number years. Moving into Bismarck for the 90-day session in 2007, Schneider would quickly establish himself as a frontrunner to become a statewide officeholder, before his first term was up. Before he would have a chance to attend his second legislative session in Bismarck, he would take the chance statewide. It is something that was weighing on him when he first entered the legislature, given his family's pedigree in state politics and the thoughts that he was a young man in a hurry. "It is a delicate thing being a hard worker and being an advocate for what you believe in," Schneider said of his first days in Bismarck when he didn't want to be seen as a hard charger in the halls of the Capitol. "I had to be as humble as possible and wanted to learn from the other members."

North Dakota is a state that elects one of the most statewide offices, contrasted with East Coast states where power is centered in a strong governor, with New Jersey having only one other state constitutional officer elected statewide — the lieutenant governor and then it's a new office elected on a ticket with the governor — or Vermont where traditional offices like the secretary of state, attorney general, and auditor are elected statewide, but the governor retains control of many of the regulatory agencies. In the Upper Plains, much like the South, there is a general need to move away from the strong executive and disburse power across multiple offices elected directly by the people.

In North Dakota, the voters elect the governor and lieutenant governor on a ticket. The secretary of state, treasurer, attorney general, and auditor are elected statewide as they are in many states. The voters also elect the agriculture commissioner, insurance commissioner, tax commissioner, superintendent of public instruction and public service commission, offices that are common for election in the South and parts of the Midwest and West. Voters have the power to shape the regulatory functions of state government more than in other states. Voters in New Jersey rarely focus on the role that the governor will play in appointing a new banking and insurance commissioner or public utilities board president when they go to the polls. With New Jersey's auto insurance rates eclipsed by property taxes as the top issue on any voter's mind, the head regulator of insurance is not an issue. New York voters probably didn't even give a second thought to who Eliot Spitzer would name as insurance superintendent or taxation and finance commissioner when he was elected governor in 2006. The officials simply exist, do their jobs and stay out of the limelight. In a state like New York, the insurance superintendent is only in the news if the department fines an insurance company or in the case of Governor George Pataki's last insurance superintendent, an ethics scandal breaks out.

But in North Dakota, these offices are in the limelight. Maybe not daily, who concentrates on the day-to-day focuses of these offices. In many states, election to these offices is almost for life. Get elected secretary of state once and that's it – you're in until you give it up, die or some kind of scandal happens. But in North Dakota these offices also serve as important stepping stones to higher office. In the sparsely populated rural state, there are only three federal officeholders, two senators and one congressman, all of whom got their elective starts as state constitutional officers. Senators Byron Dorgen and Kent Conrad are both former state tax commissioners and Congressman Earl Pomeroy is a former insurance commissioner. One North Dakota politician reminded me that these offices may not seem big deals outside North Dakota but inside the state they are considered the stepping-stone jobs, particularly those of insurance commissioner and tax commissioner.

In October 2007, the state's insurance commissioner resigned, with Governor John Hoeven naming former county prosecutor Adam Hamm to the post. Hamm, 36 when he took the job, would only hold it until the end of 2008, facing voters for a full four-year term in the 2008 election. Seeing the job open up and seeing what has happened to past holders of the state's regulatory commissionerships, Schneider saw an opening, even though he had only one session behind him and most of his state legislative term to go. "I had a very successful first session," he said. "I was successful in getting things I was passionate about passed and I worked well with the other parties. When the opportunity came up I felt I was a better candidate than the commissioner." Looking back on his first legislative session, Schneider notes that he had success in bringing workers compensation reform and children's health insurance reform up and to the discussion and achieving some changes to the laws. Building on that success, he focused on the issues during his 2008 statewide run. During his first term he was able to work on legislation that opened up health insurance to 5,000 more children in North Dakota.

North Dakota is an interesting state politically. Of the ten state executive offices that are elected, Republicans hold eight, with only the agriculture commissioner and superintendent of public instruction being Democrats. In the case of the education boss, the job is officially non-partisan. The three federal representatives though, are all Democrats. Schneider was up against a Republican trend in state politics when he ran. At the same time he also had to deal with a tough political environment for a Democrat in North Dakota. Hoeven was up for reelection, wildly popular and looking like a shoe-in, which he was. And while the country was going for Obama for president, North Dakota remained solidly in the McCain camp, barely giving the Illinois Democrat a second glance in his historic bid for the White House. "What's interesting about North Dakota politics is that with the national success for Democrats it was not good for us in North Dakota," Schneider said.

While North Dakota is small in population with only a few large population centers in Fargo, Grand Forks, Bismarck and Minot, and some of the cheapest television, radio, and newspaper advertising rates in the country it is still not immune to the realities of modern political campaigns. Because the state still is a small state where personal voter contact matters more than in, let's say, California, Schneider had to travel the state attending county fairs and other events. He had to get his message across in literature and advertisements and hire campaign staff to work with him.

Schneider had another battle going on in the statewide run: he was a Democrat. By running for an office like insurance commissioner where Republicans have historically done better in recent years in North Dakota than for the federal offices, Schneider was placed in what would be a tough race. But it had another impact, fundraising was a lot tougher, since the Democratic Party had a few scattered home ports in the state and the trends showed that a Democrat was not the frontrunner for an office like insurance commissioner. To combat all of this, Schneider could only do one thing. "I announced a year before the election," he said, in a move that some from more populated states would question, given the differences between North Dakota and California.

Campaigning statewide, Schneider would encounter the age issue on several occasions with people asking if someone in his 20s could serve as the chief regulator of the insurance industry in North Dakota. Compounding issues is the fact that Schneider looks younger than he is, almost having people think that a high school or college student is running to be their insurance commissioner. Schneider notes that while the issue came up in the race, it was not the top issue or the issue he was asked about the most.

Because the governor's race, congressional race and other statewide races were not that competitive, Schneider found that the race for insurance commissioner was at the forefront of the political debate in 2008, something that would come as a surprise to people in many other states. "Our race was the one to watch," Schneider said of his contest with Hamm. "We were both relative newcomers to the state political scene." At the end of the day, Schneider ended up losing the election. But given all that he was up against as a Democrat seeking to become state insurance commissioner in North Dakota, Hamm only edged him out by a half a percentage point.

While he lost the race for insurance commissioner, Schneider said he has no regrets about running statewide. He said that he was able to return to the state House of Representatives for the 2009 legislative session in a position that was remarkably different from the situation he approached when he entered in 2007. "It puts me into a better position now than before," Schneider said of his statewide run before he turned 30. "I am a better legislator and have a better network." Schneider does not remain coy about his desire to run for higher office again, even though he has temporarily left elective politics. Following Obama's election, Schneider started seeking a state-based appointive post in the administration. His name came up for the U.S. attorney's slot, but he was instead made head of the state's office of the Rural Development Administration in the U.S. Department of Agriculture. In fact, it's a perfect office for a politically ambitious young elected official to hold in a largely rural state. In the job, Schneider can continue to travel the state, maintaining his contacts and learning about rural issues. He also can hand out checks in ceremonies statewide and help develop rural development projects across the state. In this job, Schneider can continue to keep his name recognition high.

When asked about higher office in an interview before he was appointed to the rural development director post, Schneider said that he wants to make the run. "I do. I enjoyed my race," he said. "If I knew I would have lost I still would have run. I love this state. The best part of the race was meeting thousands of people I would not have met otherwise. I don't want to run to run though." Schneider said he wants to run for an office that he thinks he has a mission for and one that fits with his background. He notes that the insurance commissioner job melded well with his background and notes that state attorney general would also work, in addition to a seat in the federal delegation. He ruled out races for state auditor, secretary of state, or tax commissioner, noting that he does not see any of them as a good fit. He summed up the impact he has seen on his career by making the insurance commissioner race, something that many young elected officials see when they make the race for higher office. "Being younger and running a good statewide race, people say run again soon," he said.

State representative Corey Mock, a Democrat from Grand Forks, is seeking to copy Schneider's 2008 race, with one exception: he wants to see it through to a win. In February 2010, Mock announced a bid to be North Dakota's secretary of state. A 25-year-old native of Minot, Mock was elected to the state House in 2008, representing the state's forty-second district, where he and his colleagues all were under the age of 30 when elected. Representing the University of North Dakota, Mock has made his name on higher education issues, including tuition and fees. At the same time, Mock has indulged his interest in redistricting and electoral administration during his tenure in the House and his legislative agenda.

In the secretary of state's race, Mock is facing an 18-year Republican incumbent, Al Jaeger. Mock is using his age as a benefit in the race, seeking to play up his ability with technology and the need to infuse technology in the office. He talks about what he sees as the difficulty in navigating the secretary of state's website and the fact that Jaeger has not issued a press release in two years. He brings up the need to put voter registration information online in order to allow new residents to easily access the information. He speaks with the savvy of a young elected seeking to think outside the box in a low profile administrative office charged with running elections, registering corporations, and regulating boxing and martial arts.

At the same time, Mock realizes that he cannot look at young voters like he did in his legislative race. His district is a national phenomenon, with three young legislators, and a large base of college student voters. It's a district where being a former fraternity president is a plus. On a statewide level, Mock needs to cater to a variety of voters and show them the benefits of bringing youth and new thinking into the office. He talks about mobilizing colleges, but also of reaching out to older voters in many parts of the state and talking with them about his plans for the office and how he wants to upgrade the work of the office.

A Mock win will be national news, as he would become the youngest statewide elected official in the country. He would also be in line of succession to the North Dakota's governorship, putting him in the unusual position of possibly succeeding to an office that he is constitutionally too young to run for.

While Schneider and Mock hail from the urban part of North Dakota, they are hardly alone in being young North Dakotans with an eye on higher office, at the statewide level. Ben Vig was elected to the North Dakota House of Representatives on the same day as Schneider in 2006, representing a large rural district in the state. After Mock's 2008 election, the two became seatmates and close friends, with Vig being one of Mock's first supporters in the secretary of state's race. A farmer by profession, Vig speaks with passion about the state's rural history and agriculture economy. He notes that he wants to work on agriculture issues in the state legislature and in his public service career.

Vig does not deny his desire to run for a statewide office one day. "Well yes," he said when asked. "North Dakota elects 17 statewide officials. Three to DC and 14 to the Capitol tower."

While not sure when he will make the race for a higher office, noting he has a lot he still wants to accomplish in the legislature — and a reelection race to run in 2010 — he keeps it in mind. He notes that the young political base that the North Dakota Democrats have at the farm team level could serve as a jumping off point for a future collection of statewide candidates.

In considering options for a statewide race, Vig keeps a similar mindset to Schneider noting that he wants to continue to focus on a job that will allow him to help rural parts of his home state. The most obvious office would be that of agriculture commissioner, where he would be in charge of the state's agriculture regulation and promotion, a job that seems tailor-made for the young farmer. At the same time, he notes he has another option: one of the three seats on the Public Service Commission, where he could become a regulator of the utilities industry, which he said would allow him to contribute to the rural parts of the state. While narrowing any thought he has about higher office to the agriculture commissioner or public service offices, Vig notes that he doesn't want to completely close any doors on his political career, especially when he's still in his 20s and his political career is in its infancy. "Those are two options," Vig said of races for agriculture commissioner or public service commissioner. "We will see what the future holds. In politics, people should never say never."

The North Dakota trio is pretty open about a desire to run for a higher office, in the cases of Schneider it's hard for him to deny, he's already made the race for higher office. The desire to make public a run for higher office is one that many politicians hem and haw on. They want to seem committed to their current constituents while at the same time they want to position themselves to run for higher office in order to gain institutional support, financial support and help edge out the competition before they get off the ground, ambition and young elected officials are a double-edged sword.

Making His Ambition Clear

One young elected official who does not keep his desire to run for higher office to himself is Republican Anthony Sytko, a councilman in Garwood, New Jersey. Garwood seems like an unlikely place to find a candidate for higher office. It's a small town, just over 4,000 people. It's a blue-collar community sandwiched in between two better known and more prosperous suburbs. It's also a town that has not yielded many political success stories. The only Republicans to run countywide from Garwood in recent years have been unsuccessful, including one woman who lost four consecutive runs for county freeholder.

Sytko was first elected to the Borough Council in 2007 at the age of 25, on his third try for office. He also served a brief term on the borough's Board of Education. From the beginning you knew he had his eye on a higher office. In fact, he does not hide the fact that he sees himself as a future governor of New Jersey. "I like the executive branch," Sytko said of a desire to end up as governor. "I don't mind being in a legislative branch, but I prefer being in the executive branch. I have no aspirations for federal office."

Sytko showed desires similar to Schneider in his first term on the council. He announced for higher office in 2009, just as his first year in office came to a close. His council term runs for three years. But the office he announced for was tough — likely even tougher than Schneider had it as a Democrat running for insurance commissioner in North Dakota — he wanted to be a county freeholder.

Union County, New Jersey, has nine freeholders elected at-large to three-year terms. The freeholders are similar to county commissioners in other states. Serving in a county legislative function, the freeholder board has been all Democratic since the 1997 election. With the freeholders being elected at-large and several large urban areas and Democratic bastions dominating the county electorate, Democratic freeholder candidates are given the edge.

Sytko decided to remain undaunted, throwing himself into a race that many Republicans declared unwinnable. The race had become so tough for Republicans, the party often had times filling all three nominations, either putting in placeholders or in the case of 2009, not even running three candidates. Republicans also suffer from anemic freeholder candidate fundraising and lack of desire on the part of the base to campaign hard for freeholder candidates. Over a decade of constant defeats for countywide offices can do that to even the most dedicated political party volunteer. Sytko ran on a platform to change the way county government was run. It was an aggressive campaign; in fact one incumbent Democrat would characterize him as angry during her comments about the one and only debate.

But at the end of the day, Sytko joined the same pile as the other Republican freeholder candidates who have run in Union County since 1997. Actually when the results came, he finished fifth, behind the other Republican candidate, Nicole Cole, an attorney making her first run for elective office. While Sytko found himself defeated in the freeholder race, he notes that he is not deterred in his desire to run for governor one day and to move up the political ladder and make politics a career.

A Faded Star Rescued by a New Governor

Sytko can always look to another part of the Garden State in terms of a young elected official who saw some of his dreams dashed for higher office but then rescued in the appointive realm. Republican Bret Schundler was a conservative wunderkind after his election to the mayoralty of Jersey City in a 1992 special election in his early 30s. With Jersey City being a bastion of Democratic politics and a strong Democratic machine, for a Republican, let alone a conservative Republican, to win the mayor's office was stunning. Schundler was helped by the circumstances of the race, an open field of 19 candidates in a non-partisan winner-take-all ballot. Coming after a career politician mayor was indicted, Schundler as the businessman-turned-candidate was seen as a different path in Jersey City.

Coming into office, Schundler was viewed as a placeholder, someone who would be ousted in the regular election in the spring of 1993. Quickly pushing new development along the city's Hudson River waterfront and rearranging the city's finances, Schundler moved into the mayor's office on a long-term basis and quickly was being talked about nationally as the future of the conservative Republican movement. He won easily in 1993 and 1997 and continued to push conservative philosophies, including charter schools.

Following 1997, Schundler took the path of running for governor, hoping to position himself on statewide stage after eight years of governing the state's second-largest city. Schundler quickly found opposition among the state's Republican establishment, which is moderate to the core and had rallied behind acting governor Donald DiFrancesco for the 2001 nomination. Following a series of articles attacking DiFrancesco's ethics, the governor dropped out of the race and the establishment rallied around former congressman Bob Franks. Schundler ended up pulling off an upset, defeating Franks in the primary only to lose easily to Woodbridge mayor Jim McGreevey in November. Schundler even lost Jersey City to McGreevey, showing that while he was a popular mayor running on a non-partisan ballot, he was not that popular when his name appeared on a partisan ballot.

Schundler ran again in 2005, gaining some support in the GOP establishment statewide, but not enough. The establishment this time rallied to businessman Doug Forrester, the moderate choice in the field of seven. Buoyed by his statewide name recognition, Schundler narrowly lost to Forrester in the primary. He then retreated back to Jersey City, doing some consulting work, teaching, becoming chief operating officer of a Christian liberal arts college in the basement of Manhattan's Empire State Building. Schundler toyed with a bid for the Jersey City mayor's office in 2009, but ultimately declined.

Suddenly in January 2010, Schundler's dream of a statewide post came back, in the form of an offer from the current leader of the state Republican establishment who had spent so many years trying to block the former Jersey City mayor's ascendancy to the top of the state's political heap. Chris Christie, the state's new governor, named Schundler as his education commissioner, asking him to tackle issues like charter schools and taking on the state teacher's union, issues that Schundler has been discussing for over a decade.

What remains to be seen is if Schundler's career as education commissioner will be a temporary comeback in the public arena, a capstone to his public career and a way to honor the two-time candidate for governor and former big city mayor. Or will it be something more? Will it be his comeback into statewide politics? A chance to push a conservative agenda at the center of the ring again, a chance to push his ideas on charter schools and education reform and a chance to travel the state generating headlines in local print and online publications from Westfield to West Deptford. A chance to try to have a second chance (or, in Schundler's case, third chance) to make a first impression with statewide voters. A chance to become relevant again on a statewide basis positioning himself for another run for governor or a run for the U.S. Senate one day. It is an interesting discussion and something that Garden State politicos will be having for a while. It is also an interesting discussion nationally since Schundler is still young, not even 50, and someone who would be angling to regain the national limelight he had in the days when his tenure in city hall was in its infancy.

Riding a Reform Wave to Higher Office

Schundler's toying of a mayoral run in 2009 could have set him up on a collision course with Councilman Steve Fulop, a former marine and political reformer first elected to the Jersey City Council in 2005 at the age of 28. Fulop was considered a frontrunner for mayor from the day he entered the council. With a loyal army of followers in the city's reform community, an interest in pushing legislation to reform the government in a city long considered corrupt by outsiders, a zeal for fundraising and a knack for getting publicity, Fulop was long considered a potential candidate against Mayor Jerry Healy in 2009. A Schundler candidacy could have been mutually assured destruction for both Fulop and the former mayor, since they both appealed to many of the same voters in the city's booming downtown.

Fulop ultimately decided not to make the 2009 race, citing the economic downturn and the impact on his day job on Wall Street. Easily reelected in 2009, as was Healy, Fulop would see his fortunes jump considerably in July 2009 when the arrests of 44 public officials statewide, including several with ties to Healy, made reformers in Jersey City in vogue. Following public rallies on the steps of city hall calling for resignations of arrested Jersey City officials, Fulop continued to cement his status as a reformer. Headed into 2013, Fulop has become a frontrunner for mayor, which he has said is an office he has an interest in seeking.

Fulop's ambitions are also being pushed and fueled by considerable speculation. His name circulated as a potential congressional candidate in 2008 and as New Jersey prepared to swear in a new governor in January 2010, his name circulated on another list. He was listed as one of ten people to watch during the Christie era by a state newspaper. The article noted that he is likely to run for mayor and has positioned himself as a reformer, similar to the values pressed by Chris Christie during his gubernatorial campaign.

Notes

1   John F. Kennedy, Lyndon B. Johnson, Richard M. Nixon, Bill Clinton, and Barack Obama.
2   Richard M. Nixon, Lyndon B. Johnson, Hubert Humphrey, Walter Mondale, Dan Quayle, Al Gore, and Joe Biden.
3   This number includes the following third-party candidates: Henry Wallace, Strom Thurmond, George Wallace, John Anderson, and H. Ross Perot. They were included for being third-party candidates who attracted a strong national following their presidential campaigns. Both Thurmond and George Wallace received electoral votes during their races.
    Richard M. Nixon and Hubert Humphrey were not included in this list because they had served as president and vice president.
4   Thomas Dewey, Strom Thurmond, George Wallace, George McGovern, John Anderson, Michael Dukakis, and Bob Dole.

5 Thomas Eagleton is counted in this list for his brief 1972 race for vice president. Eagleton was nominated by the Democratic National Convention but dropped out before the general election, being replaced by Sargent Shriver.

This list includes the following third party candidates: Glen H. Taylor, Fielding Wright, Curtis LeMay, Patrick Lucey, and James Stockdale. They were the running mates of Henry Wallace, Strom Thurmond, George Wallace, John Anderson and H. Ross Perot, respectively.

Bob Dole is counted on both lists for his 1976 race for vice president and his 1996 race for president.

6 Fielding Wright, Estes Kefauver, Henry Cabot Lodge, William Miller, Edmund Muskie, Thomas Eagleton, Bob Dole, Patrick Lucey, Lloyd Bentsen, Jack Kemp, and Sarah Palin.

CHAPTER 5

The Challenges Faced by Young Elected Officials Running for Office Today

At the time of writing, 2010 is shaping up to be a year where those who started as young elected officials or are still young elected officials will be making their moves to higher public office. It makes sense in many ways. The 2008 election shows that the public is looking for the next generation to step forward and run for office. The 2008 election and the inauguration of President Obama shows that the public is receptive to younger candidates in higher offices.

The results of 2008, and even 2009, show that the American public is looking for a change. They are looking for new leaders and to promote new and younger leaders to higher office. Following the crises that dominated the country in the 1990s and 2000s, they are looking for a new generation to step forward to govern. It is not uncommon, it is just part of the grand scheme of how the country's political development occurs. It occurred following World War II and in the late 1960s and early 1970s when distrust over the Vietnam War and Watergate pushed through younger officials and again in the early 1990s when the end of the 1980s boom brought in a new perspective in public life.

Andrew Romanoff was 34 when he was elected to the Colorado House of Representatives as a Democrat in 2000. A self-described policy wonk, who also pursued a law degree while serving in the legislature, Romanoff has been working to position himself for a higher office.

Romanoff did not spend his eight years in the legislature — Colorado has term limits — regulated to the backbenches, he wanted to move forward. He moved into what could be deemed a thankless job, serving as the House minority leader, running a Democratic caucus that seemed to be an almost permanent and entrenched minority. Romanoff decided not to sit back and continue to run the minority, but looked at the trends of Colorado where Democrats have been gaining ground, he saw a prime opportunity to take control of the House in 2004. He was able to lead the Democratic Party to the majority, becoming the first Democratic Speaker in 30 years.

Moving into the speakership, Romanoff was instantly thought of as a frontrunner for the vacant governorship in 2006, a race he ultimately declined to make, even though he had support against Bill Ritter, the then district attorney of Denver County, in the primary. "I was not convinced that I would be a better governor than Bill Ritter," Romanoff said diplomatically. "I really enjoyed the job I had. I did not have a great burning desire to seek the next shiny object that was there." Romanoff's thoughts on the 2006 governor's race almost sound like the opposite of politicians. They are thought to want to run for a higher office and to show ambition and to reach for a shiny object because it's there. Romanoff's work as Speaker has also been receiving praise with *Governing* magazine picking him as the state official of the year 2008.

Wrapping up his House career in 2008, Romanoff did start looking to what he would do next. Coincidentally he had two opportunities thrown at him. The Colorado secretary of state's office was vacant after the secretary was elected to Congress and a U.S. Senate seat was vacant after President Obama nominated Ken Salazar to be the new interior secretary. Both seats would be filled by Ritter until elections could be held in 2010. Romanoff's name came up for both and he looked at both, with his eye on the Senate seat, not the chance to be secretary of state.

While he had pressed his case for the Senate and why he was someone who could hold the seat in the 2010 election, a January 2009 entry to the U.S. Senate was not in the cards for Romanoff. Ritter instead picked Michael Bennet, the little-known head of the Denver schools system, as the new senator. "I have a great deal of disappointment especially over the Senate seat," Romanoff said in a 2009 interview, noting that he found Ritter's search process for a senator to be a mystery. Romanoff's Senate desires have not cooled off. He announced in late 2009 that he was going to challenge Bennet in the 2010 Democratic primary. He wanted to let the voters decide who will be the next senator from Colorado for a six-year term. It is a race where Romanoff suddenly had the entire state Democratic establishment jumping for him to not make the race and the Obama White House pressing him to drop out. He was the first Democrat to announce a primary challenge to an appointed senator in the 2010 election, something the White House has been looking to avoid.

Romanoff does not hide any of his ambition, noting that he wants to continue to remain involved public life, no matter what the Obama administration says. He has been active on the campaign trail during 2009 and 2010 pushing Bennet in the election and looking to bring his legislative career to Washington. "If I can figure out a way to make a difference and make a contribution," Romanoff said in describing what would drive him to run for a higher office during an interview in 2009 before he announced his Senate candidacy.

Romanoff is not the only young elected official in Colorado who thought 2010 was their year to end up in statewide office. Josh Penry was thinking the same thing. Penry and Romanoff have several things in common. They are both young and from Colorado and both have been elected to the state House of Representatives. Romanoff stayed in the House, while Penry moved into the state senate, an early sign of his ambition and desire to move to the upper chamber of the legislature, while Romanoff concentrated his career in the House. Both would move up to the leadership of the state legislature. While Romanoff would become minority leader and Speaker, Penry would become minority leader of the Senate. Penry did start off younger than Romanoff, winning a House seat in 2004 at the age of 28, after serving as a congressional aide.

In 2009, Penry started exploring a race for Colorado governor, looking to make a move into the chief executive's office after six years as a legislator. At the same time, he was not the only Republican looking to take on embattled Democratic governor Bill Ritter. Penry's campaign turned out to be a non-starter in the end. He dropped out of the race several months after launching his bid for the governor's mansion, after Republicans started rallying around others in the race. In the end, Ritter would end up joining him, announcing in January of 2010 that he would not be seeking a second term in the state's governorship.

During an interview in early 2009, long before he announced his bid to become governor, Penry noted that he would not just run for any office, that he was looking for an office that would allow him to have an impact. As the quote earlier in this chapter shows, Penry knows that his age in entering elective office shows to people that yes he is ambitious and shows that he has an interest in moving up in public office. But at the same time he does not want to be perceived like many young elected officials are, that of someone who will run for any office that comes along just because it is a step up the political ladder. "When I decide to do this, I want to have the maximum policy impact," Penry said months before he made a brief and aborted campaign for the job that has the biggest public policy impact in the state of Colorado.

At the same time, Penry dropped hints that he has other desires than the governorship of his state. He spoke fondly of his time as a congressional aide, talking about the impact he was able to have during that time and the issues he worked on during his stint in Washington. At the same time he talked about how he decided to run for a seat in the capitol in Denver because of how it could lead to a seat in Washington one day. "In Colorado most people in Congress started in the Legislature," he said in early 2009. "Many tried to jump past the Legislature and ran for Congress and they didn't succeed. It's the way it's done." Words that show that Penry has his sights set on a higher office in the future. Words that show that Penry may look to replicate what many former congressional aides have done in the past and go to Congress themselves.

The duo from Colorado, and Kyle Andrews, are hardly the only young elected officials seeking a higher office in 2010. Moving to Oregon, state representative Brent Barton is proving to be a young man in a hurry. Elected to the state House of Representatives in 2008 representing the Portland suburbs, Barton is not seeking a second term in the politically competitive House seat he has held for a single term. Instead, with the retirement of a sitting state senator in a district that encompasses his House district, Barton has chosen to run for the Senate instead.

Moving to Wisconsin, two young elected officials are looking at 2010 as their year to make a move. Sean Duffy is not known nationally for his political career, in fact it is a blip on the radar screen for his national fans. Instead he is known for his time on the MTV reality show, *The Real World*. Starring in the show's Boston season in the 1990s, Duffy was on the show when it remained true to its original premise of being a documentary of a group of twentysomethings living and working together in an urban environment. Sure there were typical twentysomething scenes and parties, etc., but the show had turned into the party atmosphere with fights, steamy hot-tub scenes, and drunken debauchery. Duffy was still there when a conservative Republican lumberjack enthusiast could still do reality television.

Duffy is also known for his marriage to Rachel Campos, another Real World alum, and by far the more famous of the couple. Campos starred on the show's iconic San Francisco season. Campos, a social conservative ended up in conflict early in the season with Pedro Zamora, the AIDS educator who was living in the house with AIDS in an effort to promote awareness of the disease. While Campos later became friendly with Zamora, the story arc remained central to the San Francisco season. Campos would later do other television projects including twice being a finalist to be a co-host of *The View*, losing out to Lisa Ling and Elisabeth Hasselbeck. Actually, his wife not being tapped to sit around a table with Barbara Walters and Joy Behar debating politics and dieting may not have moved her career forward, but it has helped Duffy's career. If his wife had been picked for *The View*, the couple and their children would have needed to relocate from northern Wisconsin to New York, and Duffy would likely be toiling in a Manhattan law firm in the typical anonymous lifestyle of those married to the famous in New York.

Duffy instead has moved into elective office. He is now district attorney of Ashland County, Wisconsin, a northern rural county. He was first appointed to the post by Governor Scott McCallum in 2002 and has been reelected several times in his own right. If his wife had been tapped for *The View*, Duffy said in an interview, he would have resigned from the district attorney's office in order to relocate to New York and support his wife's career. It's an office which has spurred political ambition. His predecessor is now the state attorney general. Duffy himself made an effort for promotion, unsuccessfully seeking appointment as the U.S. attorney for the northern district of Wisconsin following President George W. Bush's reelection in 2004.

Duffy remained content in the district attorney's office until 2009 when he announced plans to challenge longtime Democratic congressman Dave Obey. Obey is not just an institution in northern Wisconsin, where he has served in the U.S. House of Representatives for decades, he is also a baron on Capitol Hill. Obey is the chairman of the House Appropriations Committee, the chief writer of all federal spending bills, a position where he can easily distribute federal funds across the land and across his district. Obey has served on the Appropriations Committee for decades, briefly serving as chairman in the last days of the 40-year Democratic majority in the House of Representatives, which ended in 1994 and then assuming the committee's ranking minority member slot for a dozen years. He reclaimed the chairmanship in 2007. Safe to say, Obey has been safe for years. But in the backlash to the Democratic control of federal government and the anti-incumbent wave riding the country at the end of the first year of the Obama administration, Duffy, who is safely at the right end of the political spectrum, decided it was his time to move past the district attorney's office and into a congressional race.

Brett Davis has a different political story than Duffy. Davis is from a more urban part of Wisconsin, he made his political name working with Tommy Thompson, the state's long-serving governor, who is a political icon in the Dairy State. A former legislative aide, Davis moved to the governor's office when the legislator he was working for mentioned the governor was looking for someone to work on his tax staff. When Thompson moved to Washington in 2001 to accept President George W. Bush's invitation to serve as secretary of Health and Human Services, Davis went with him. Settling in to the Department of Health and Human Services as an aide to Thompson, Davis would later move back to Wisconsin to seek office.

Thompson, though, did not inspire Davis to enter the political arena. Learning about President John F. Kennedy in elementary school was the trick that interested Davis and also told him that he could get involved in the political arena as a young professional. Kennedy was 29 when he was elected to Congress in 1946 and became the nation's youngest elected president in 1960 at the age of 43. Following the interest taking shape, his basketball coach helped get him an internship in Madison and that led to work on a political campaign in Oshkosh and then he was able to get a staff position in Madison in the legislature, a progression which led to his work for Thompson in the governor's office and the Health and Human Services Department. At the same time members of the legislature started explaining to Davis what he needed to do if he had a desire to join the legislature himself one day.

Having previously served as a legislative aide in the Wisconsin legislature, the 29-year-old Davis would himself join the legislature in 2004 with his election as a state assemblyman. Reelected twice, Davis too looks at 2010 as his chance to make a move to higher office, declaring his candidacy for lieutenant governor. The state's gubernatorial politics are in flux. The Democratic governor and lieutenant governor are not running again, the Republicans have a competitive primary for both offices. Davis is looking to make a race for the number two spot in order to move into a higher office at the end of the day.

During a 2006 interview for this book, Davis said he was interested in higher office but noted that he was searching for the right office, a common theme of many politicians regardless of age. Davis noted that a Republican faces an uphill climb in Wisconsin and that no matter what office he should choose it will be a challenge. In Wisconsin, Davis will be on his own in the lieutenant governor primary but then will have to run on a ticket with the nominee for governor. "There are some people who run for office to run for office," Davis said in 2006. "I would want to know I had a chance to hold the office."

Davis' interest in the number-two office in state government is shared by Democrat Jessica Sferrazza, who has announced for lieutenant governor in Nevada. A three-term member of the city council in Reno, Sferrazza has worked on issues relating to youth in her city. The lieutenant governor's office could put her in an interesting position in Nevada, as one of the official duties is chairing the state's tourism commission, possibly putting a young elected official at the center of the state's most important industry.

Romanoff and Penry are not the only young elected officials who are looking at the top statewide races in 2010. The end of 2009 and beginning of 2010 has been anything but normal in South Carolina. Following a series of unusual gubernatorial sex scandals in the first decade of the twenty-first century — with New Jersey's Jim McGreevey resigning after announcing he was gay and New York's Eliot Spitzer being involved with a high-priced prostitute — the circumstances surrounding South Carolina governor Mark Sanford were downright bizarre.

As Sanford was engulfed in the scandal and held press conferences to apologize to most of the country, and people focused on whether Jenny Sanford would get a divorce sooner rather than later, Republican Andre Bauer, the state's young lieutenant governor, found himself in the middle of the chaos. Elected twice independently from Sanford, Bauer had an uneasy relationship with the governor and the First Lady. In fact Jenny Sanford had endorsed his opponent in his 2006 reelection bid. Bauer was a logical candidate for 2010 — most lieutenant governors are — but the Sanfords hoped to block the rising star who had moved from state representative to state senator to lieutenant governor very quickly. At the same time, Bauer, who readily admits a desire to be governor, announced a plan that he believed would help the state, even if it was confusing the political chattering classes. Bauer said that if Sanford was impeached, he would assume the governorship but he did not plan on seeking a full term in 2010, a decision which surprised many. How could a rising star who has been thought to be obsessing over the governorship for years even consider not running once he gets the job?

In the end of the day, Sanford was not impeached and he did not place Bauer in the position of having to become a short-term lame duck and almost-placeholder governor. Not succeeding, Bauer decided to announce his candidacy for governor, mentioning his differences with Sanford and that he was a new face. Bauer started gaining in the polls for the governor's race, but at the same time having to battle the handpicked candidate of Mark and Jenny Sanford.

Over in Kentucky, a Senate seat opened up following the retirement of Senator Jim Bunning in the 2010 election. Bunning, a Republican, had been considered the Senate's most endangered incumbent as many Bluegrass State Republicans even sought to run away from the incumbent. The first choice on the minds of Kentucky Republicans to fill the Senate seat is Trey Grayson, the secretary of state. With term limits close to forcing Grayson out of the secretary of state's office in 2011, he was beginning to look at a move. He acknowledged during an interview in early 2009 that he was looking at a possible run for state attorney general or for the Senate seat. Grayson also made clear that he was not trying to run Bunning out the Senate. Bunning's decision to not seek reelection helped open up the door for Grayson making it easier for him to run for the Senate rather than attorney general. Grayson is considered the Republican most likely to keep the seat in his party. Kentucky is the opposite of North Dakota, with Republicans winning the Senate and House seats in Washington and Democrats dominating state government including the governorship and the state constitutional officers.[1]

Ohio is also looking to be an epicenter of current and former young elected officials making statewide races in 2010. Republican state representative Josh Mandel, 31, is the party's nominee for state treasurer, while Republican state representative Seth Morgan, also 31, unsuccessfully sought his party's nomination for state auditor, following the incumbent auditor's decision to run for lieutenant governor. The Democrats have picked Hamilton county commissioner David Pepper to run for auditor. Pepper was first elected to office in 2001 at the age of 29 as a councilman in Cincinnati. Mandel is on track to face State Treasurer Kevin Boyce, a Democrat who was appointed to fill a vacancy in 2008. Boyce was 29 when he became a city councilman in Columbus in 2000. Republicans have nominated state senator Jon Husted, a former Speaker of the state House of Representatives, for secretary of state in the election. Husted was first elected to be a state representative when he was 34. In an interesting twist, a win by Husted would give a young elected a seat on the board that redistricts congressional districts in the state. The race for secretary of state is considered competitive because of the seats the officeholders hold on a board that could redraw districts which would have a large impact on the future of the U.S. House of Representatives in one of the most competitive states in the country.

Mock may be the youngest major party nominee for a statewide office nationally in 2010 but he is not alone. In Illinois, 27-year-old Jason Plummer is the Republican nominee for lieutenant governor. An executive in a family-owned lumber company and former county party chairman in rural Illinois, Plummer beat several better known candidates to take the second spot on the ticket behind state senator Bill Brady. Plummer's primary victory is not a total surprise, given the fact that Illinois' lieutenant governor is charged by statute with rural affairs duties, giving the office a greater importance to voters from the rural part of the state. While past lieutenant governors have hailed from Chicago, rural voters give an edge to candidates from the rural part of the state in the election. Plummer went from the primary to team with Brady on a general election ticket.

Two young political scions are making congressional races in 2010. In Arizona, 33-year-old Republican Ben Quayle has announced his candidacy for Congress for an open seat. Quayle is seeking to become his family's second young elected official, following his father, former vice president Dan Quayle, who was elected to Congress in 1976 at the age of 29. On the east end of New York's

Long Island, 31-year-old Republican Christopher Cox, the grandson of President Nixon, has announced his candidacy for Congress, seeking to unseat Democratic incumbent Tim Bishop. Nixon, who was elected to a California congressional seat in 1946 at the age of 33, was himself a young elected official.

While several young elected officials have decided to make a race of it in 2010 and turn it into a year that could see several current and just former young electeds make it into statewide office, there are those who have decided not make the race. Democrat Mike Gerber was 32 years old when he was elected to the Pennsylvania House of Representatives in 2004 representing the Montgomery County suburbs of Philadelphia. He is someone who is considered a rising Democratic star in the commonwealth. He and another young elected from Montgomery County, Josh Shapiro, have been tapped to run the House Democrats campaign arm, an assignment that usually helps a rising star move up the ranks, especially with the access to fundraisers needed to run a statewide race in a state as large and diverse as Pennsylvania. Gerber does not deny having an eye on running for a higher office one day. "I do enjoy being in a position to have a positive impact on people's lives and I would enjoy being in a position to have a greater impact on people's lives," he said.

But he notes he has a young family and it would be tough on them as he seeks to make the race. Gerber would have to balance the campaign with his current responsibilities in Harrisburg and his law practice and his family life. With term limits opening up the state's governorship and lieutenant governorship in 2010, Gerber started giving thought to making a race for lieutenant governor. With signs pointing to the Democratic nominee from governor hailing from the Pittsburgh area and tradition of splitting the ticket between both halves of the state and many believing that the Philadelphia should have one of the two top spots in state government, a Gerber for lieutenant governor campaign made sense on the face of it. But the need to spend two years running statewide, attending pancake breakfasts in small towns like Dickson City and visiting festivals in Johnstown, proved to be something Gerber did not want to do while having a young family. He chose to pass on the lieutenant governor's race.

Gerber said he gets asked about 2012 and the possibility of making a statewide race that year. In the presidential election year, Pennsylvania voters will need to pick an attorney general, auditor general, and state treasurer. Would the ambitious Gerber want to make a race that year? He said he is likely to not make the race that year for the same reasons he declined a lieutenant governor race in 2010. While ruling out statewide offices, he has also ruled out a bid for Congress for the same reasons. "I have no desire to go to DC because I have a young family," Gerber said.

A discussion about Gerber would not be complete without a discussion of Shapiro. The two represent the same suburban Philadelphia County in the state House of Representatives, both are considered up-and-comers in Harrisburg and the state Democratic Party. With the two being allies it is likely they will come to a deal to avoid any face-off in the future.

Shapiro was mentioned as a potential candidate in 2010 for the U.S. Senate seat held by Arlen Specter. Specter, a longtime moderate Republican senator, was considered vulnerable if the right challenger came along. Some thought was given to the young state legislator and Shapiro considered the race. But a lightening bolt struck and suddenly transformed the Senate race and Pennsylvania politics — Specter bolted his longtime home in the GOP and became a Democrat. While some Democrats started discussing races against Specter, Shapiro decided to not make the statewide race.

In an interview in early 2009, Shapiro played coy about making a race for higher office. Taking a stance that many young elected officials take, where they don't want to specifically acknowledge any interest in higher office but also want to show interest in higher office, Shapiro wanted to straddle both lines. "I love what I do," Shapiro said. "I love serving my constituents and in the future if there is an opportunity to serve more of Pennsylvania I would consider it."

Ambition Tempered by Personal Circumstances

Personal life impacted the higher office Pam Iorio of Tampa, Florida, chose to run for when she was term-limited off of the Hillsborough County Commission in 1992. Iorio was elected to the county commission eight years before becoming one of the youngest county officials in the Sunshine State. The county commission job is a full-time one in Hillsborough County, with commissioners meeting to make policy decisions for the county and oversee the county departments and also serving as members and chairs of various boards for authorities governing everything from land use to mass transit to the airport to stadiums. During her time as a county commissioner, Iorio would become the commission's chairwoman, thus being the highest elected official in the county, along with chairing the Metropolitan Planning Organization, which handles land use for the Tampa Bay region and chairing the Hartline Board, which is the main mass transit agency for the region.

In 1992, Iorio had two young children and what some viewed as a limitless political future. With her term expiring on the county commission, advisors were encouraging her to look at a move to Tallahassee and run for state representative or state senator. Others were encouraging her to make a run for Congress. But home issues were impacting what Iorio wanted herself for her next move in public life. "I was not ready to run for a post where I would not be home," she said in an interview. Instead, Iorio looked at an office that at first sight would not be considered by many up-and-coming elected officials. She wanted to be the county's supervisor of elections. The largely administrative post involves running all elections in Hillborough County from collecting petitions, designing ballots, counting votes, and registering voters along with any related tasks relating to the administering of elections in the county. Barring a confusing design of a ballot and the results of a president election thrown up in the air, a low profile job is one that is not controversial.

Iorio also saw other perks to serving as the county's chief elections official. "I could get administrative experience and be home," she said. "I would have never focused on supervisor of elections without kids." Moving into the office, Iorio found the job fitting what she was looking for in an elective office. Her hours were predictable, with few speeches and evening commitments that dominated her time as a county commissioner or were part of the normal life for a state legislator. Yes there were some times of the year, namely election nights that were late nights, but she has no regrets because of the fact that it allowed her to remain in public life while at the same time being home with children when she wanted to.

And the job also gave her a brush with history. As the 2000 election got underway, Iorio became president of the county election supervisors association in Florida, helping advocate for the election supervisors statewide and providing assistance to other supervisors around the state. A role that did not give her any chance to help design ballots though.

Sitting in her office at around 11 a.m. on the morning of the election, an aide said that she was receiving calls from state Democrats asking about Palm Beach County and the design of the ballot, saying there are problems. "That was my first inkling," she said. Iorio decided to call Theresa LaPore, then the elections supervisor in Palm Beach County, to find out what was going on in her county and see if there was anything she could do. When she called LaPore's office she was told that she was busy. Still curious about what was going on in Palm Beach, Iorio called another county supervisor. "I called another supervisor and he said Theresa was having problems," Iorio said, with little knowledge that LaPore's problems would spawn multiple recounts, a Supreme Court case and the eyes of a nation focusing on Palm Beach and Tallahassee waiting to see who would be the next president.

In the aftermath of the 2000 election, Iorio was thrust into the statewide debate over elections reform helping to design new procedures for the administration of elections and new voting machines. She ended up helping do away with voting machines that created the infamous hanging chads that helped create the chaos that left the country wondering who was the president for weeks. Iorio also decided to take her administrative experience and start looking for a new post when 2003 rolled in. With her children older, she decided that she could spend more time away from home and did not have to be tied to the elections office. She chose to run for mayor in Tampa, capturing the seat and winning reelection in 2007.

Garcetti, Miller, and Padilla: A Study in Legislative Leadership for the Ambitious

Penry and Romanoff showcase one trend in seeking higher office as a young elected official, moving into a leadership role in the legislative chamber that they are in. Los Angeles is the nation's second-largest city, with a city council governing the legislative side of the city. Two consecutive presidents of the city council were young elected officials when they started. In some cities, the position of city council president is independently elected by the voters with the council president serving in a hybrid legislative and executive position, but in others the council chooses its own president. Los Angeles is the latter, with the council members being elected in districts and then coming together to elect a president from among the membership. One of the duties of the council president is to serve as the acting mayor in the absence of the mayor from the city and to succeed should the mayor leave office. Thus, the second-highest ranking official in the nation's second-largest city is only elected by a small subset of the entire city population; a recipe that actually makes it easier for young elected officials to move into the job.

Alex Padilla was 26 years old when he was elected to the Los Angeles City Council in 1999, and 28 when he was elected council president in 2001. Term limits proved to be his best friend in terms of getting the presidency. Many of the council members were going to be out of office in 2001 because of term limits and the president's job would be opening up. He started going out to solicit support. "Timing was helpful," Padilla said of his election to the council presidency. At the same time, Padilla worked to gain the help of the other young member of the city council, Eric Garcetti. With Garcetti working as his campaign manager and making calls on his behalf and being the first to endorse Padilla, he was able to secure the post. As with many elections to legislative leadership positions, Padilla notes that relationships mattered. He said he went about forming relationships with the other members of the council early on and was able to translate those relationships into a victory for the council president's office. With the term limits coming up he focused on those who would be returning, getting a jump on the competition in order to take the president's gavel. At the same time he realized he had to gain as much institutional memory as possible.

Padilla's story is remarkably similar to that of Gifford Miller, a young city councilman in New York City who became that body's Speaker after term limits forced all but a handful of council members out of office following the 2001 election. Miller was first elected in 1996 during a special election and reelected in 1997 for a full term. Representing Manhattan's Upper East Side, Miller was the youngest council member at his election and looked younger.

2001 was set to be a year of change in New York, similar to Los Angeles. It would be the first year that term limits swept the city, requiring most of the 51-member city council, all three citywide office holders and four out of five borough presidents to leave office. Miller was not impacted by term limits that year, being able to run for another term on the council, an election he won easily. In a twist of fate, even though Miller looked barely old enough to be out of college, he would be the most senior member of the council in terms of seniority, and he started plotting his bid for Speaker.

While Padilla was able to build relationships and start working an inside game to get elected, Miller didn't have that luxury, he had to run an inside and outside campaign for the speakership, with the council being larger than in Los Angeles, with members representing the city's diverse neighborhoods. The Speaker of the council is different and similar to the Los Angeles council president. Both set the agenda, both are the body's spokesman, both set the tone, but the New York Speaker is not the presiding officer, a role set aside for the city's elected public advocate, who holds little power compared to the Speaker. The Speaker also does not have the charter power to serve as acting mayor or succeed the mayor. New York's allows the mayor to designate one of the appointed deputy mayors to serve as acting mayor in his absence and in the event of a vacancy, the public advocate is acting mayor until a special election is held a short time later.

Miller had to figure out how to go after the council Speaker's office; he decided to help candidates citywide. With the help of one of his young advisors, Jessica Lappin, Miller set up Council 2001, a political action committee dedicated to identify and support council candidates in districts around the city. Council 2001 did not just identify and send financial support to the council candidates, it helped out in other ways.

In 2001, I was covering the race of Democrat Eric Gioia for a city council seat in western Queens and as part of that I went to a candidates' forum at a senior center in the Sunnyside neighborhood. As you entered the senior center, gathered on the street were a dozen volunteers handing out Gioia literature, but they were not clad in Gioia shirts, they were wearing Council 2001 shirts. A Gioia aide confirmed to me that the Miller group provided the assistance to Gioia and was providing volunteers in other districts citywide. Not surprisingly, after Gioia won a council seat, he became one of Miller's closest allies on the city council and his wife, political consultant Lisa Hernandez Gioia, would become Miller's chief fundraiser.

Miller would not just raise funds and provide volunteers for his candidates through Council 2001. Many of the candidates shared the same political consultant as Miller's group and Lappin often consulted the campaign staffers for Council 2001-backed candidates during the primary races that decide most elections in heavily Democratic New York. At the same time, Miller traveled the city neighborhood by neighborhood, knocking on doors with and for the council candidates he was backing. He was winning friends on the council, but also making other contacts that would be helpful in a future citywide campaign.

Miller did capture the council speakership in January 2002 when the new council took office. At the end of the day, the outside game he played worked well, it provided a sizable base of loyal council members who helped him win the inside game. To understand New York City politics is to remember the city is a remarkable patchwork of neighborhoods that are diverse demographically, socioeconomically, ethnically and from a political basis. It is a city where anyone looking at any citywide office — and the council speakership is a citywide office to a degree — needs to understand the needs of a blue collar worker in Bensonhurst, a liberal professor on the Upper West Side, the immigrant in Morrisania, the young family in Long Island City and the suburban family on the south shore of Staten Island. They also need to understand the degree of power the five county Democratic bosses have in the city where the Democratic Party means everything. Some counties are more boss-oriented, like Queens and Kings (Brooklyn), while New York County (Manhattan) is fractured because of the long reformist history of the neighborhoods below Ninety-sixth Street and the Bronx is regularly fractured in Democratic politics. Miller understood this and used his coalition. His coalition helped place pressure on the county party chairs in order to leverage support for Miller. But at the end of the day Miller also made some deals. Queens got two of the most powerful committee chairmanships in land use and finance, Bronx got the majority leader's post, key allies in Manhattan got health and government operations, Brooklyn landed less since they were not as enthusiastic and Staten Island got some.

The paths that Padilla and Miller took while leading their respective city councils differ as well. Padilla has a claim to fame from his tenure, which started in the early summer of 2001. Under the city's law that the council president is acting mayor when the mayor leaves the city, Padilla assumed that title one time when then Mayor James Hahn traveled to Washington on business. At the time Hahn chose to make the trip, September 11 occurred, making Padilla the acting mayor of the nation's second-largest city during a time of national attack. Miller was also impacted by this, seeing the city's Democratic primary delayed and then taking on the Speaker's office as the city was trying to rebuild from the attacks.

Padilla would focus on various projects for his district and citywide issues during his time as council president. He tells a story about how former Mayor Richard Riordon was surprised when he asked Padilla what he wanted in the budget — when he was a first year councilman — and Padilla asked for new sidewalks. Miller's time as Speaker was focused on one key goal — running for mayor in 2005 against Republican Mike Bloomberg. 2005 would see Miller forced out by term limits, while Padilla faced the same fate in 2007. The course both took differed.

Padilla could have run for mayor in the non-partisan mayor's race in 2005 but the race was already set to be a rematch between Hahn and former assembly Speaker Antonio Villaraigousa. Padilla likely had a chance but a tougher one against two politicians who had been running five years for the mayor's office in two elections. Padilla instead set his sights on a seat in the California Senate in 2006, looking to take his legislative career to Sacramento. He notes that while during his time as a councilman he was able to focus on the basic infrastructure needs of his district and his neighborhood and help deliver things from the central city government to the large disparate needs of the nation's second largest city, he could focus on big picture items as a state senator. California's Senate is different from the other 49 state senates in one important way. California is huge, the largest state by population with several major cities dominating politics. It is a country by all accounts. The amount of members of Congress serving the state goes up every census, but the state constitution sets the amount of senators at 40, meaning that every senator in California runs to represent more people and more territory than any member of Congress nationally. Only statewide officials in many states have larger constituencies than California senators. "When it comes to education, police and job training programs, I would have more influence as a state legislator," Padilla said of his desire to focus on a seat in Sacramento than a citywide office in Los Angeles. "The time had come to serve in a different capacity."

At the same time, Miller had to make a decision on what to do. As the council Speaker, he was the second most powerful person in city government. Under the city's form of government, he dominated the city council, to the extent he could. New York's City Council has never been known to not contain its share of gadflies and outspoken members who are willing to hold a press conference at the drop of a hat. With term limits originally scheduled to push all the new council members out in 2009, many were suddenly campaigning for higher office before they knew where the bathroom was in city hall. But at the same time, Miller was only elected by a small slice of Manhattan — the Upper East Side and Roosevelt Island — and his colleagues on the city council. Not something that translates easily into a citywide race in the nation's largest city.

Miller was not the only politician who thought he should be Bloomberg's opponent in 2005. Former Bronx Borough president Fernando Ferrer, the runner-up in the 2001 primary, Congressman Anthony Weiner, and term-limited Manhattan Borough president C. Virginia Fields all had the same thoughts. But Miller was considered a frontrunner given his fundraising ability, citywide contacts, citywide platform, and knack for publicity. But it wasn't meant to be. Not to say Miller didn't run a strong campaign. Miller may be an Upper East Sider, a neighborhood where people rarely venture to the outer boroughs. Upper East Siders like their niche and it's rare to find them below Manhattan's Fourteenth Street for anything other than work purposes in the financial district, let alone venture to Brooklyn or Queens. Miller was the opposite talking about his favorite restaurants in these communities. While many could dismiss Miller's love of pizza in Brooklyn as a campaign stunt, talking to Miller reveals a certain passion for New York's collection of neighborhoods that only a native New Yorker can appreciate.

Miller also tried to promote a legislative agenda that encompassed the entire city, hoping to make a dent in Weiner's role as the champion of outer borough interests. Miller fought hard for Staten Island, something you'd rarely see an Upper East Side or any Manhattanite do. Miller appeared on the suburban island regularly, learning the issues and trying to get the votes of the city's smallest borough. With Weiner championing outer borough interests and reminding people that he was in fact from Brooklyn and Queens, Miller was trying to make an inroad. At one point, Miller was able to pass legislation to expand Staten Island Ferry service between the island and Manhattan during the late-night hours.

In the end it didn't work out the way Miller had planned. When the results came in on that September day in 2005, Miller finished fourth in the primary — fourth out of the four major candidates. He was barely ahead of a fifth candidate who was so little known and forgotten about. It was an embarrassing defeat for a man who had spent four years as the second most powerful man in city government, commanding a large staff and a wing in city hall, negotiating the city budget with the mayor, giving his own state of the city address, moving about town with a retinue of aides and police bodyguards in his own city-issue SUV. He even finished behind his predecessor, Peter Vallone, when Vallone tried to move from Speaker to mayor in 2001. Vallone, who had also made a failed run for governor as the Democratic nominee in 1998, finished third in that election, beating out the city comptroller.

People had said Miller should not have made the mayor's race; that it was too early, that Ferrer and Weiner could not be beat. That Bloomberg was a shoe-in. The Monday-morning quarterbacks that populate politics and political punditry said Miller should have run for the vacant borough president's office, where his command of the Upper East Side and name recognition combined with the winner-take-all rules and Miller's fundraising prowess would allow him to become the borough's top elected official easily. While more a ceremonial and advocacy office than one of power and limited to Manhattan, it would have given Miller a platform. But, at the end of the day, Miller was drawn to the power of the mayor's office and wanting to move to an office that was equivalent to the one that he had held for four years. While borough president would be a move up the ladder for any backbench member of the city council, for a council Speaker it would be sideways at most, some would say a demotion, while mayor was the only office where he could go up. While Padilla went to the state legislature, that route was blocked for Miller. First, the legislators representing his neighborhood were entrenched; second, under New York's form of government the state legislature would have been a demotion for a council Speaker. In fact, many state legislators from New York City end up seeking the chance to run for the city council, citing many factors including shortening the commute, the higher pay scale of the council, and the increased power of the council for a backbench member, compared to the largely leader driven politics of the assembly and the Senate.

During an interview in 2006, Miller still looked clearly shell-shocked from his defeat in the mayor's race. It had been less than a year and he found it easier to talk about a shooting in the council chamber where his bodyguards needed to push him behind a bulletproof podium than to talk about the mayor's race. But at the same time he defended his decision to run for mayor and he defended his campaign, saying that he ran the best campaign he could and that he believed that mayor was the best race for him in the 2005 election cycle.

While running for mayor in 2005 caused his career to end, term limits did help give rise to another young elected official in city government. Jessica Lappin, his longtime aide, the former head of Council 2001, his district chief of staff won the election to replace him. Moving into the council, Lappin would also find herself as potential candidate for citywide office, due in large part to the term limits that continue to dominate discussions on the chessboard of New York City politics. In 2009, Lappin briefly considered a race for public advocate before deciding to run for a second term on the city council. Her name continues to be mentioned for higher office, either public advocate or Manhattan borough president in 2013, when there is a strong chance she'll be term-limited out of the council. At the same time though, Lappin was able to use her background to help gain a good spot in her first term, becoming chairwoman of the landmarks subcommittee, becoming a go-to person for any landmarks designation. With real estate being the driving force of the New York economy and a main part of the city's political process, Lappin's spot on the land use committee and landmarks chairmanship give her a spot in the influence of power in the council, helping to shape the future of how the nation's largest city looks.

Returning to Los Angeles, with Padilla moving to Sacramento and the state senate, the city council needed to elect a new president. Enter Padilla's old ally and friend, Eric Garcetti. Garcetti, first elected in 2001 when he was 30, comes with a name well known, not only to those in the City of Angels, but also to many Americans in the 1990s. Garcetti is the son of former Los Angeles County district attorney Gil Garcetti, who headed the prosecutor's office during the murder trial of O.J. Simpson. The elder Garcetti gained international fame during that time, helping guide the strategy of the prosecution in the Trial of the Century. The elder Garcetti would later be defeated in a future reelection bid for the county district attorney spot.

At the time of his son's run for city council Gil Garcetti was well known, but it is different, as Eric Garcetti likes to point out. His father ran countywide in one of America's largest counties. Los Angeles County is bigger geographically than Rhode Island, with a bigger population than most big cities and some states. Running a countywide race there is very different than the statewide race Jasper Schneider ran in North Dakota. The elder Garcetti did more television campaigning rather than retail campaigning. On the other hand, when Eric Garcetti ran in a district encompassing some of the young professional hubs of Los Angeles, he was able to rely on door-to-door campaigning, including having his father knock on doors. In addition, Eric Garcetti ran in a very liberal district — not the type that would embrace a former law-and-order career prosecutor.

When Padilla moved to the state senate, Garcetti considered it a normal course of action to seek the council presidency. He had worked closely with Padilla on his campaign for the president's post and then during Padilla's presidency, and he believed he could make the race. Again relaying on the path that he helped shape out for Padilla, Garcetti used the personal relationships he gained on the council to help move into the city's number-two spot.

Los Angeles did something that New York has done and changed the term limits law from two terms to three terms. With the expanded time in office and a third council term ahead of him starting in 2009, one cannot help but ask Garcetti if he has a desire to run for a higher office in a future race. Garcetti is articulate, energetic, liberal, and a believer in new ideas. He takes pride in many of the community service projects he has accomplished as a city councilman, including reducing graffiti by 70 percent. But he also talks about his time in the navy and intelligence, giving him national security credentials that could translate into a future congressional race or U.S. Senate race. Given the dominance of the Los Angeles media market and financial sector for fundraising, it would not be too out of the question for someone to try to make a jump from the city council to one of the down ballot state constitutional officer jobs. In short, Garcetti has only options ahead of him politically. The real question is what does he want to do and also what can he do. Many young elected officials are limited by the offices available when they want to run or by what they choose to do, Miller being just one of them.

Garcetti has no problem admitting that he is interested in making a race for higher office, openly expressing interest in the 2013 mayor's race when Antonio Villaraigosa will be term-limited out of office. It's the same thought process of Miller: successful service as council president and make the move into the mayor's chair. Of course there are differences, namely that Garcetti has a larger starting base, given Los Angeles' smaller city council, so he already has a larger base of voters that know him than Miller did when he launched his bid for mayor. In addition, Garcetti will have a longer time as council president than Miller did when he ran. And Miller was preparing to run against a one-term incumbent, while Garcetti is looking at an open seat race. But Garcetti is leaving some options open. "I am interested in running for mayor in four years but I am not sure if I want to do it," Garcetti said in an early 2009 interview. "I would be open to a run for Congress."

At the same time, while admitting to a desire to serve in a higher office and make a run for something else on the ladder, he does not want to plan out his political career. He knows a life in politics is unpredictable and many plans go astray for any number of reasons. Unlike Sytko he doesn't have a grand plan for his career, or if he does he's keeping it as secret as Sytko has made his public. "I don't want to be planning my life two political moves ahead," he said. "I don't want to commit to governor or president."

An Ambitious Young Elected Ends Up Vice President

As was said earlier in this chapter, there is no shortage of young elected officials in American history choosing to make races for higher office and growing in the political career. Many United States senators and governors started their political careers under the age of 35. Many presidents and vice presidents started their careers at a young age. Many started as the youngest and stayed to be one of the oldest. When Ted Kennedy was elected to the U.S. Senate in 1962, he was the bare minimum age of 30. When he died in 2009, he had the second most seniority of any sitting senator in the country, leaving behind a 46-year legacy in the Senate.

Dan Quayle is one of the most recognizable people in the country. A former vice president, Quayle is the first baby boomer to run on a major party ticket when he ran with the first President Bush in 1988. Now many Americans remember Quayle for his indirect contributions to the nation's comics during his four years in national office. Before Palin had inspired Tina Fey and every late night show, Quayle held the honor, just without the near perfect look-alike on *Saturday Night Live*. What is not remembered about the former vice president, though, is the ambition he showed as a young elected official in Indiana. An ambition that put him into place to one day become the vice president of the United States.

Quayle grew up in a journalism family, splitting his time between Indiana and Arizona and then moving into appointive posts in state government before going back to work in the family business in Huntington. Bitten by the political bug, Quayle gave thought to a run for the state legislature, before choosing to take on a 16-year Democratic incumbent for a seat in Congress during the 1976 election. Winning the House seat, Quayle would be reelected in 1978 but started thinking about what his political future held and did he want to stay a part of what seemed the permanent minority that the Republicans had in the House of Representatives at the time. "In the minority in the House you don't have much clout," Quayle said in an interview, noting that it would be tough for him to get anything done and he was looking to accomplish more.

Quayle cited the House rules for everything including which legislation moved forward and the deciding on which amendments could be considered on the floor. Debate was limited and time split, leaving members at times with only seconds to voice an opinion on the biggest issues facing the nation. Quayle started to look longingly across the Capitol towards the Senate. Senate rules give individuals more power, the ability to move legislation, unlimited debate and the power of the hold where one senator can block legislation and nominations.

One thing stood in Quayle's way in terms of dreaming about the Senate — three-term Democrat Birch Bayh. An Indiana institution, Bayh was a former young elected official himself, being in law school when he served in the state legislature and as the state House Speaker. A former presidential candidate, Bayh was considered unbeatable by many and they told Quayle he'd be throwing his career away if he ran. Showing the ability that many young elected officials have to take a huge risk and a chance that they may not take at an older age, Quayle jumped for it in 1980. "They said you are making a mistake," Quayle said in an interview. "I said Bayh was vulnerable and had close elections."

With the decision of Bayh to accept Quayle's challenge to seven debates and the landslide Republican victory of Ronald Reagan and Quayle's campaigning around the state, he was able to unseat Bayh and bring his career to the next level. In fact that race had helped put Quayle on the path to the vice presidency. If he had lost to Bayh, he would have retreated to the private sector and have become a former congressman, one of many around and unlikely to break out of the pack again. He would likely not have another run for the Senate, with new politicians gaining ground over time and elbowing him out.

Quayle's ambitions are pretty clear now in retrospect. While he may not have looked at the vice presidency when he first came to Washington in 1977 as a young congressman, Quayle had ambitions to move beyond the House of Representatives. He showed this when he took the chance to challenge Bayh in 1980 when people said it should not have been done. Quayle is an example of not only a young elected official showing his ambition but also a young elected official thinking outside of the box in order to achieve those ambitions.

Quayle would continue to show those ambitions by pursuing the vice presidential nomination when Bush came calling and then going for the job, becoming the first baby boomer to hold national office. While Quayle did not achieve his goal of the presidency, he was able to become the vice president, the nation's second-highest post, one heartbeat away from the Oval Office, in the room when key decisions on foreign and domestic policy are made, showing that, yes, a young elected official can be ambitious and see those ambitions fulfilled in a short period of time and on a grand scale, and showing that a young elected official can take some huge risks and see them rewarded as they move forward.

Senator Lives Childhood Dream

Bob Menendez started his political career as a high school student in Union City, New Jersey. The northern Hudson County town has evolved into a home of Cuban refugees and the centerpiece of the Cuban American community in New Jersey. The issues raised by Menendez, now a U.S. senator and the first Hispanic elected statewide in New Jersey history, are those you would expect a high school student to address and those you would not expect a high school student to address. But they underlie that in fact Menendez was a young man in a hurry who had ambitions to pull himself into a position of political power one day.

Entering his senior year in high school, Menendez was told by his teachers that he was eligible to enter the school's honors program. Looking to go to college, Menendez jumped at the chance to be a part of the program, until he found out about a catch: in order to participate in the program, and improve his chances of getting into a good college, Menendez would have to pay $200 for books and other school supplies, a sum he and his family could not afford. Without the $200 payment, Menendez would not be able to participate in the program, which surprised him, as he was in a public school. "I could not understand for the life of me that I could be burned," he said of the experience.

Menendez raised a ruckus regarding the fact that he was eligible for the honors program, but could not participate because of the $200 fee. To quiet him down, school officials agreed to waive the fee for him and he participated in the honors program, but that was not the end of the issue for him. He saw that other friends of his could not participate and many other students were in the same boat. He was outraged by the unfairness of the system and the $200 fee that was harming the educational careers of so many of his fellow classmates. While he was happy that his ruckus had allowed him into the program, he still wanted to change the system for the rest of the students in Union City.

Studying the matter, Menendez found that the city's Board of Education was to blame. For years, the school board had been appointed by the city's mayor and was responsive only to him. He found that the board did not keep student interests in mind and did not provide what he found to be a decent and quality education for students. With an appointed school board, change would not be forthcoming as only the mayor made the appointments and school board appointments would not command the attention of the electorate when voting out the mayor. In any case, William Musto, Union City's longtime mayor, was so entrenched that he could easily be reelected.

Menendez instead looked for an opportunity to change the way the school board functioned, an unlikely topic for a high school senior to be considering. Working with his friends, he circulated petitions and obtained a public referendum to change to an elected school board. The change would be major for Union City; not only would an elected board put residents in the driver's seat as to who sat on the board, but also the annual school budget would be approved by the electorate and not by the Board of School Estimate, chaired by the mayor and consisting of four mayoral allies from the school board and town commission. "I spent a long hot summer with my friends who felt the same" Menendez said of the movement to change the school board.

Union City residents changed the method for choosing a school board and the change would come into effect over a three-year period, as seats would come up for election as the terms of the appointed members expired. Having changed the town's school governance structure at the age of 19, Menendez did what he felt was natural, he sought a seat on the new Board of Education at the age of 20, in the first-ever election for a school board in Union City history.

Getting elected to the Board of Education, Menendez found himself in the middle of Union City's political world. Hudson County does not have a reputation as one of the most ethical places in New Jersey, as detailed in other parts of this book. Menendez would become an ally of the city's longtime mayor and state senator, William Musto. The relationship would evolve as Menendez moved off his volunteer position on the Board of Education to take a fulltime salaried post as secretary to the board.

During this time Musto was under federal criminal investigation for ethical issues surrounding construction in Union City and there was involvement from the school system. As one of the school system's chief administrators, Menendez found himself mentioned in the middle with many of the records. He cooperated with federal law enforcement officials and put himself in a position where he ended up receiving death threats from those tied to Musto. At the same time, Menendez decided that he wanted to make a move in the political structure of Union City in an effort to bring change to the city's government.

Union City is governed under the commission form of government, which began in the United States in Galveston, Texas, in 1900. Under this form of government, five commissioners are elected at large every four years to run city affairs. The commission chooses one commissioner to serve a four-year term as mayor. Each commissioner takes on executive responsibility as director of a department during their term. In addition to overseeing a department, the mayor is the head of the city government, presiding at commission meetings, setting the city's agenda and serving as the public face of the city. The mayor is typically the leader of the winning ticket in the city elections. While commissioners are all elected separately in the one election, teams run in each election and it is not uncommon for one ticket to sweep all five seats on the commission. Meeting together, the commission exercises all legislative functions for the municipal government. Like most municipalities in Hudson County, Union City elections are nonpartisan. While nonpartisan in nature, almost all candidates are Democrats and have some degree of alignment with the Hudson County Democratic Organization (HCDO). As mayor, Musto was one of the leaders of the HCDO, which is typically run by the county's mayors.

Entering into the 1982 mayor's race, the young Menendez faced a tough race, since Musto was well liked by residents because of the public services he had provided and the outreach he had done in the burgeoning Cuban community. But, as the first Cuban with a chance to become Mayor of Union City, indeed the first Hispanic in line to become a mayor in New Jersey history, Menendez had large support in the Cuban community. Although he was only 28, Menendez played up his decade of experience in city politics and had pressed for reform in several roles within government. He said his age rarely came up as an issue, because of the experience he was bringing to the table. "I had built a reputation as a reformer on the school board, as CFO and as a lawyer," Menendez said. "The Hispanic community had grown as a voting population and I was recognized as a leader in that community."

With Musto being convicted on federal corruption charges during the election campaign, Menendez' election should have been secured. With the mayor being sentenced to several years in federal prison the day before the election, and being required to vacate the mayor's office and his Senate seat, Menendez should have been the frontrunner going into the race. But the powers of longtime incumbency and a loyal political machine worked to Musto's advantage in the spring 1982 election, and the day after being sentenced to federal prison, Musto was reelected Mayor of Union City.

Being defeated in the mayor's race, by an opponent who had been sentenced to a federal prison term the day before the election, marked the lowest point in Menendez' political career. He began to question whether or not he should remain in public service, or whether his political career would end with his school board service. "I was so disillusioned that I said to myself that if people thought so little of me that I would get out of public service," he said. "I would use the law as a vehicle for social change." While Menendez moved on with his law career and focused on building a practice, Union City government and politics continued. Musto tried to retain the mayor's office but was forced out by state officials. He installed a loyal ally on the Board of Commissioners as the new mayor and a special election was set for Musto's seat as a commissioner. Musto's wife sought the commissioner's seat in the special election and won a place as a city commissioner.

With a city government controlled by Musto loyalists, a purge of Menendez supporters was started. The Musto forces started to identify city employees who had joined the Menendez-led reform movement. Many of those fired by Musto's allies were in civil service positions and had certain protections granted by state law. They started coming to Menendez, first to retain an attorney to fight the city to get their jobs back and secondly to encourage him to reenter the political arena and continue the reform movement he had launched.

Encouraged by those who had been purged by Musto's allies, Menendez reentered the political arena, helping them get their jobs back and advocating for reform within Union City. He began laying the groundwork for a second mayoral run in 1986, recruiting city commission running mates and outlining his proposals for reforming the way the city did business. Entering the 1986 race, the then 32-year-old Menendez would again be battling Musto, this time via the surrogates Musto was running the city government through. Hardened by his unsuccessful 1982 mayoral campaign and encouraged by the systematic expulsion of his backers from civil services positions by the Musto forces, Menendez pressed his message forward to win the mayor's seat. In doing so, not only did he become Union City's first Hispanic mayor, he became the first Hispanic mayor in New Jersey history.

Under the traditions that govern the Hudson County Democratic Organization, Menendez suddenly found himself in a position of extreme power. The mayors are the backbone of the HCDO, controlling many of the decisions made by the organization, including but not limited to endorsements in the county but also endorsements for governor, senator and even president in a Democratic primary. With the sheer amount of votes in a primary that come out of Hudson County and the importance of carrying the party organization's backing in a primary in New Jersey, this is a powerful role. Suddenly the 32-year-old Menendez was not the outsider seeking to change the political system, he was on the inside and a powerhouse in his own right in Hudson County. But he is not through yet.

For over a century New Jersey had an unusual tradition of letting elected officials serve in more than one elective office at once. Dual officeholders were commonplace across the state: mayors who were freeholders or state legislators. town councilmen who doubled as assemblymen, freeholders in the legislature.

On occasion you would find some individuals holding three elective offices at once, holding down roles as a city councilman, county freeholder, and state assemblyman at the same time. The tradition is almost at an end. In 2007, Governor Jon Corzine persuaded the state legislature to get rid of the dual-office-holding tradition, but he had to accept one caveat from a state legislature where dual officeholders held influential posts in the legislative process. Those holding two elective offices on a certain date in early 2008 were allowed to continue in both jobs, being grandfathered into the tradition.

Menendez was someone who was part of the tradition. In 1985, the unthinkable happened. Well, the unthinkable for Hudson County. Republicans won two state assembly seats representing northern Hudson County. The victories occurred on the coattails of the reelection of Republican governor Tom Kean, who won with the biggest landslide in state history and carried all but three towns statewide, including all of Hudson County. Democrats started looking for ways to reclaim the seats in 1987 in a race that they believed were easy to retake. After seeing the impact that state government could have on local government, Menendez was eager to head to Trenton in order to work on state issues. He joined the Democratic ticket as a candidate for the assembly, easily winning the seat and beginning his tenure as both an assemblyman and mayor of Union City.

Menendez' political career was not harmed by his early policies of reevaluating properties or laying off public safety employees. He was reelected as mayor in 1990 and was able to rehire the cops and firemen he had laid off shortly after his reelection. In 1991, his career in Trenton continued as he left the assembly and moved to the state senate. In doing so, he became New Jersey's first Hispanic state senator. This was not the Senate though that Menendez was aspiring to. Menendez has something in common with Sytko, something that Garcetti would cringe at. Menendez has had a political goal in mind since high school, one that he had set his mind on and hoped to make the move in the future: Menendez wanted to be a U.S. Senator and in 1992 he made a move that would put him on track to the Senate 13 years later, he ran successfully for a seat in the House of Representatives.

While the move to Congress helped put Menendez in a good political position to achieve his goal, he notes there were other reasons he made the race. He notes that he learned a lot about the interplay of federal and local government during his tenure as mayor and he could accomplish more in the federal government, helping to deliver more money for underfunded programs than he could do at the local level. In Congress, Menendez started moving up the ladder, rising to chair the Democratic Conference in the House, the number-three post while in the minority. He was on track to become Speaker of the House one day. But his desire for the Senate continued on his mind. After Corzine stepped down from his Senate seat in 2006 to start his four-year tenure as governor, he had to appoint his successor in the Senate. After a search that dominated the state's political chatter for weeks, Corzine installed Menendez in the Senate for a one-year term. Of course, to keep the seat, Menendez would have to compete against another former young elected official who had made a name as a reformer, Republican state senator Tom Kean Jr. of Westfield.

Former Governor's Son Settles in Young Elected Capital

Kean had moved up quickly, primarily on his father's name. The name gave him instant entry into state politics and instant access to some of the state's leading powerbrokers. He sought a seat in Congress in 2000, relocating to New Jersey from Massachusetts where he was in grad school and moving into a town which maybe not coincidentally was home to a leading political strategist who had run his father's 1985 reelection campaign. Losing the congressional primary, Kean quickly rebounded being elected to the assembly in 2001, over other local politicos who had been waiting years for one of the legislative seats to open up. A year later when the district's Senate seat opened up, Kean easily took it. Now Kean, at the age of 38, wanted to be a U.S. Senator.

The race was not an easy one for Kean. He had to emerge from his father's shadow and try to make an independent name for himself. He had worked on reform issues in the state legislature and decided to take the next level to the Senate race. Using Menendez' ties to Hudson County, Kean focused almost exclusively at times on ethics issues in the county. Kean's campaign mantra became "Bob Menendez was under federal criminal investigation," a line heard over and over again. In a state at a time when the U.S. attorney's office was indicting people on political corruption charges at a record clip, it would have been safe to assume that if something was found, an indictment would have been made. As of 2010, Bob Menendez has not been charged in any federal criminal investigation or officially implicated in any ongoing corruption probe.

Kean would lose the Senate race, becoming sort of like Miller, left wondering what happened in an election he thought he could win. Being blessed with the most famous name in state politics, it was assumed he could easily win a statewide campaign when the time came. With many national and international interests, Kean would fit in more at the federal level and with federal issues, than he did in Trenton dealing with state issues. Undaunted, Kean returned to Trenton and easily dispatched a former Long Hill Township mayor who challenged him for reelection in 2007. While Democrats typically don't contest Kean's district seriously, given the strong Republican advantage, they took a chance in 2007, according to the local political grapevine, mainly because of Kean's aggressive stance in the 2006 race against Menendez.

Still in Trenton, Kean took a similar path that Romanoff and Penry took in Colorado when the 2008 session began: he became minority leader of the Senate. Unlike the duo from Denver though, the minority leader's post was not vacant when Kean expressed interest. Republican Leonard Lance of Hunterdon County was safe in the seat. Following a political path well worn by many legislative leaders across the country, be it Romanoff and Penry or Padilla and

Miller, Kean began working on relationships with existing and new senators. He was helped when 2007 brought in a new influx in the Senate Republican caucus, a younger one and one that would allow for a new stance in leadership. Many had complained that Lance was not aggressive enough, a charge that could hardly be leveled against Kean following the 2006 race, where at times negative commercials from Kean dominated the airwaves. In the end, Kean rounded up the votes and was able to find a soft landing spot for Lance as the Republicans' chief member of the budget committee, allowing the state budget expert to put his talent to use.

Interestingly, right after Kean won the minority leader's post, he faced a dilemma. Republican congressman Mike Ferguson, a thirtysomething Republican who had beat Kean in the 2000 congressional primary, announced his retirement. Suddenly Kean had to decide about whether he wanted to continue his time as minority leader, which had barely started, or whether he wanted to pursue his dream of federal office, in a race where he would have cleared the Republican field in an instant and entered a highly competitive race against a Democratic assemblywoman who had almost defeated Ferguson two years before. Of course, Kean had another dilemma: another defeat for higher office would have basically ended his political career. Of course he'd remain a state senator and minority leader, but a third loss for federal office would have left him marooned in Trenton and not in contention for higher office down the line. At the end of the day, Kean decided to honor his commitment to the Senate Republican caucus and not run for Congress. He also announced his endorsement of Lance who would win the primary and the 2008 election.

Kean may have been up to something, though, in his decision to move to Westfield. There is a small tradition of young elected officials heading into elective office in the town and also looking to be ambitious. Kean is in the leadership of the state senate and his legislative district counterpart, Assemblyman Jon Bramnick, is similar to Kean. In his early 30s when he was elected to the Plainfield City Council, Bramnick would later leave the council to focus on his law practice and his family life. But he also relocated out of the urban Plainfield, which has a high crime rate, and into bucolic suburban Westfield, where he would establish himself as a local Republican powerhouse. This includes heading the town's Republican Party and getting elected to the assembly to succeed Kean. In the assembly, Bramnick has followed the path of many and moved to the number-two slot in the leadership.

Kean's Senate predecessor is Republican Rich Bagger, who was a law student when he was elected to the Town Council in the 1980s. He was elected mayor at 29 in 1990 and then to the state assembly a year later; a political movement that continued and led many think of him as a rising star on a statewide level. In 2000, Bagger surprised many by taking a pass on the open congressional seat, a move that allowed Kean to run and establish himself as a young elected official in the state. In 2001, Bagger moved to the state senate continuing to establish himself in Trenton. But Bagger would pull the plug on his elective career in 2003 when, after just a year as a senator, he accepted a promotion in the government affairs department at pharmaceutical giant Pfizer and decided to focus full-time on his business career. Kean would succeed Bagger, thus giving Bagger the claim to fame of helping to launch the younger Kean's fast rise in state politics. In late 2009 it was announced that Bagger would leave Pfizer and, instead, return his focus to state government by becoming chief of staff to the new governor, Chris Christie, the second most powerful job in state government.

Bagger's second successor as mayor was also young and in a hurry. Democrat Tom Jardim made Westfield history in 1996 when he became the first Democrat in a century to win the mayoralty. Westfield has long been viewed as a rock-ribbed Republican bastion, a town viewed statewide as one of the most Republican in the Garden State. Becoming mayor, Jardim was suddenly a state star, with people wondering where would the youthful mayor go next. Reelected in 1998, people were beginning to wonder was it a fluke based on a series of political conditions beyond his control or was Jardim on to something. To be on the safe side, Republicans were able to get legislation passed at the state level changing the mayor's office from two-year terms to four-year terms and moved to odd-number years when the governor was up. The fear was Bill Clinton's 1996 reelection had helped move Jardim into the mayor's office. Interestingly, while Westfield has continuously gone Republican locally for years, since 1992, Democrats have won the presidency in town.

Jardim followed local tradition and stepped down in 2000 after two terms in office and Republicans reclaimed the office. But he would continue to be heard. The next year he became one of the few Democrats to seriously contest the local assembly district, running against Kean for one of the two seats in the district. Unsuccessful, Jardim made one more comeback, challenging appointed Republican mayor Andy Skibitsky for Westfield's first four-year mayoral term. Be it the new election cycle, the lack of a controversial opponent like he had in his previous two runs or Skibitsky's habit of showing up to every event in town, Jardim lost the mayor's race that year and has moved to the backbench of politics.

And in one more quick Westfield note, in 2001, Democrats captured control of the Town Council for the first time in history. One of the seats that helped sway that control was 28-year-old Kevin Walsh, who won one of the town's third ward seats. Walsh would only serve one year of the two-year term. He decided to switch his ambitions away from politics and on to his legal career, accepting a position as an assistant United States attorney.

In addition to all of these young electeds in recent years in Westfield, Schundler, the former Jersey City mayor and new state education commissioner, is a Westfield native.

State to City: Moving On Up by Moving Down

The concept of politically ambitious young elected officials is for them to move from one level of government to the next level. In some cases, you will see someone move from the state to the city or county to the city because the job is higher or there is some sort of desire for them to work at that level.

In the case of Oregon Democrat Earl Blumenauer, his career for a while kept showing him running for a lower office before he made it to Congress. Blumenauer was a longtime liberal activist in Portland in the early 1970s, when a group of young Democrats sought to transform local politics and change over how the state is run. In 1972, he became one of the group to run for office, being elected to the state House of Representatives at the age of 23. The election followed work of his in college to lower the state's voting age and other liberal issues during the time of societal change in the late 1960s and early 1970s.

Settling into Salem, Blumenauer quickly found himself moving up in the biannual legislative sessions Oregon used. Within two sessions of joining the state House of Representatives, he was chairman of the revenue committee and gaining more clout in the legislature. But at the same time he was beginning to look for the next step. Where would a politically ambitious politician from Portland go? And with the legislature being part time, would he go for a full-time post. "The legislature was a great proving ground," he said. "It was not a full-time job, I was able to earn a law degree and work fulltime at Portland State University. It was a great launching pad."

With many around the country seeing the state legislature as a great place to move to, it is surprising to hear someone say it is a launching pad. You may hear it in a place like New York or California or the Chicago area where city politics is more dominant or in California's case, where lifetime term-limit bans take effect. In 1979, Blumenauer thought he found the office he should make the next race for — Multnomah County commissioner. "The county was an opportunity for full-time service," he said.

In 1987, Blumenauer decided to promote/demote himself yet again. He wanted to run for an office that was lower on the protocol chart but actually more powerful and a place where he could make changes that he could not in county government. He had decided to run for the Portland City Council. "In our community the city council is an opportunity to do more," Blumenauer said. "The city has a rich mix of services."

Portland is one of the largest cities in the country to be governed by the city commission form of government. All of the council members are full time and have a mix of a legislative role and an executive role. The mayor assigns each councilmember a portfolio of city agencies to work with, where they will provide executive leadership, set policy and push legislation on the council. Collectively the entire council will set policy, adopt a budget and push other legislation. It is a mixed bag of a job. Blumenauer likes to note that during his tenure as a city councilman, he managed a $250-million budget and almost

1,600 employees directly in the departments he oversaw. His portfolio always included the city's transportation agency — not a surprise for an advocate of transportation alternatives, including bicycle and pedestrian-friendly cities — along with areas including city planning, the environment, purchasing, emergency management, cable television, and personnel management. "It is the best local government job in America," he said.

Blumenauer tried to become mayor in 1992, losing out to Vera Katz, a longtime ally from the early 1970s when a group of Portland Democrats went out to change the world. In 1996, Blumenauer would make a political move that would show upward mobility in a traditional and power sense, he was elected to Congress. While he gave up his control of a multi-million-dollar budget in Portland city government, he's moved into a role where he can push issues dear to him on a national stage and help set other policies. Clearly Blumenauer has become a young elected official who has pursued a somewhat different career path and different definition of career advancement, but also one that kept working out for him.

Term Limits Send Legislator to County Government

The concept of the impact of term limits which drove Miller, Padilla, and Garcetti and the move from state to county government and that drove Blumenauer comes together in Andy Meisner in Oakland County, Michigan. Elected to the state House of Representatives in 2002 at the age of 29, Meisner found term limits coming up and stated to look at other options in the public and private sectors. Looking at his options, he saw the most appealing in county government, taking a path that Andrews is now looking at in Niagara County, New York. Meisner chose to run for county treasurer and won. But thanks to a quirk in Michigan law, Meisner was elected in November 2008, but would not take office until July 2009, giving him an extra large transition to prepare for the treasurer's office.

Going into the county treasurer's office, Meisner announced plans to create a land bank to help the county's real estate issues in the last years of the first decade of the twenty-first century. Michigan was a hard-hit state in terms of foreclosures and Meisner saw the treasurer's office as not just keeping the county's books and signing checks and making sure the county is making money on their investments, but as a way to work on housing related issues in a time of crisis. With Oakland County being one of the wealthiest in Michigan, but still facing dropping property values and increasing foreclosures, Meisner was looking for a way for individuals to not see foreclosures as the economy continues to climb out of the peril of the past few years. "It is an important bully pulpit in the most perilous financial time of our lifetime," Meisner said of the county treasurer's office.

Being a young elected official who has found himself in a higher office after just six years in elective politics, Meisner finds himself being asked about making a move into higher office all the time. While in some places, an office like county treasurer could be considered a political backwater, in Michigan it has served as a launching pad for others. Candice Miller used her two years as county treasurer in Macomb County to become secretary of state for eight years and then a congresswoman and potential candidate for governor. With the question being asked, Meisner laughs it off but also shows that he has gotten used to answering the question. "I do not rule it out," Meisner said of a bid for higher office. "But I just got elected to a challenging job. The fellow is who is investing $1 billion of taxpayer money in challenging financial times. It will take everything I've got to do this job."

More to Life than Politics

There is always the occasion of a young elected official saying that they are not sure about running for a higher office. Granted many politicians say that, it's almost a force of habit for them to downplay their ambitions while at the same time also planning out a campaign for higher office. But in some cases, based on age and everything else, it would not be surprising for a young elected official to hold off on making a definitive decision because of the ever-changing circumstances of their lives.

Shane Brinton was elected to the Board of Education in Arcata, California, in 2005 at the age of 18. Just out of high school, Brinton decided to make the jump into elective office. The son of a longtime community activist, Brinton grew up going to rallies, sit-ins, organizing meetings and the other rituals of a life in community activism. After a few years on the school board, Brinton decided to take the next step in public life: running for the Arcata City Council. Winning the race in 2008 at the age of 21, Brinton also is in a position of one day becoming the city's mayor since the council elects the mayor from amongst its membership to one-year terms. This form of government, common in many California communities, leads to a rotation of the mayor's office giving many council members the chance to say they were the community's mayor.

While Brinton is a leading liberal politico in the Eureka area, in an area where liberal enclaves dominate the political landscape, he is not sure if he wants to make a race for higher office or at least in the short term. He has experience in the higher office arena, having run campaigns for candidate for the county Board of Supervisors and he has an idea of what is needed to make the race and to serve in higher office.

Brinton readily admits his age plays a factor in why he is not sure if he wants to run for higher office at this point in time. During an interview in February of 2009, Brinton noted that he still needs to attend college and that he wants to be able to have a career outside of the political sector. While he is passionate about issues and notes he wants to continue to discuss and debate issues and be an activist, he is not sure if the political sector is how he wants to go about this and continue to be a part of the public policy debate. "The idea is appealing to me, but it is not in my plans right now," Brinton said in the interview. "Being on the council is an example of where I can achieve my goals. It if feels like the right time, I'll do it."

Unlike other young elected officials who look to the city council in a small town as the first stepping stone on a career to let's say the governor's mansion, Brinton does not view it that way. He stressed that he does not want to just progress from office to office on his way to making politics a career. He does not want his life to be viewed of him being a politician. But above all he wants to be happy with whatever job he has, whether it is a political job or something in the public advocacy field, which comes across as his passion. "A lot of people go to school and have a career and I don't look at life that way," Brinton said. "I do what is right at a given time."

At the same time, Brinton does not firmly close the door on a future run for higher office, like any good politician. With term limits constantly turning over the California legislature, a seat in Sacramento could one day be on the horizon or a seat on the county board of supervisors could become available. But at the same time, Brinton stresses that he is not running to run for office, he is running in order to pursue the issues that are dear to his heart. A councilman who as a high school student organized anti-war groups during the opening days of the Iraq War, Brinton takes issues to heart. Any politician who has to stress "I am not a Communist," during an interview because the label was thrown at him because of his strong anti-war stance, which led to his student group to become affiliated with the Communist Party, it is safe to say he is committed to his liberal beliefs. "If organizing and activity takes me to office in the future, I won't shy away from it," Brinton said.

Brinton's decision to say that he is not sure if he wants to one day hold a higher office is not unusual amongst young elected officials. Derrick Seaver was 18 when he was elected to the Ohio House of Representatives in 2000, an incredibly young age to hold a seat in the state legislature of any state. Most young electeds at Seaver's age end up serving on city councils and boards of education and possibly as a mayor, the state legislature is down-right shocking.

Seaver's career had more ups and downs than many politicians at an older age. Elected as a Democrat in rural Ohio, Seaver suddenly became part of his county's Democratic elite because of his service as a state representative. Seaver would end up the chairman of his county party, moving into a leadership role on a dual front that many politicians twice his age never achieve. But at the same time, Seaver found himself growing more conservative. In the years following the September 11 terrorist attacks and the War on Terror growing and President George W. Bush talking about the dangers poised by Iraq, Seaver started to find himself thinking more about national security and agreeing with the Bush administration

As the 2004 presidential election came closer, Seaver found himself in the position of being a county chairman of the Democratic Party who was happier with President Bush than with John Kerry. Seaver chose to step down from the county chairmanship, become a Republican, and endorse Bush for reelection; a stunning choice on many levels. While party switchers are not a new thing in politics, they come in all shapes and forms at all levels of government. I once covered a woman who went from Democrat to Republican to Independent in six years, and lest we forget Ronald Reagan and Hillary Rodham Clinton did not start off in the parties they would become most associated with. But to have a county chairman, the leader of the party in a certain area in the biggest swing state of the 2004 election switch parties in order to endorse the Republican is stunning.

As the 2006 election approached, Seaver found himself in the position of running for one more term in the House of Representatives, before Ohio's term-limits law kicked in and he would find himself unable to seek another term in the House. Many politicians in similar situations will run again unless there is another office they can run for first before they find themselves involuntarily dismissed from office. Seaver did not do that. At the end of the day a series of personal issues and a desire to attend college weighed on the 24-year-old and he chose to move forward with his life at the end of his third term and he did not run for a fourth term in office, voluntarily ending the career of the nation's youngest state legislator following a wild ride in office, one that could have led him to higher offices.

Assembly Ambitions

In some cases, young elected officials want to focus their careers in a certain direction and on building institutional power and possibly not on gaining support at a higher office. Andy Hevesi was elected to the New York State Assembly representing the Forest Hills section of Queens in his late 20s filling a vacancy in the spring of 2005. The son of the then state comptroller, Alan Hevesi, he had seen his father hold the assembly seat for a number of years, concentrating his career on trying to become assembly Speaker, a dream the older Hevesi would not see. The older Hevesi would instead spend two terms as New York City comptroller before losing a bid for mayor and then being elected state comptroller twice. Alan Hevesi would not serve his second term as comptroller, due to an ethics scandal that emerged in the closing days of the 2006 campaign involving the use of official cars assigned to the comptroller's office. He would resign in the closing days of his first term and decline to take office for a second term. His son remains in the assembly.

In an interview conducted in the summer of 2006, just a year after Andy Hevesi was elected to the assembly and before the allegations that ended his father's political career were revealed by the older Hevesi's little-known opponent, Andy Hevesi indicated a desire to keep his career in the same pattern his father had intended to do for so many years. Andy Hevesi had been the chief of staff to an assemblyman from the Bronx early in his career, along with working in the Queens County district attorney's office and as an aide to the city's public advocate. He noted that during his time working as an assembly staffer and now as a young assemblyman, he was studying the political game in Albany and getting to know what he needed to do to get legislation passed and to deliver for his district.

In talking about this, Hevesi focused on how he wanted to continue in Albany and the assembly and gain the clout that comes with seniority. The New York State Assembly is a body built on seniority. While many legislative chambers are built on the seniority system, with 150 members from across the state and a tradition of a strong Speaker, it is just as important in Albany. More senior members can obtain committee chairmanships and access to the closed door discussions where much of Albany's business is conducted. Seniority also equaled more resources for your district in the form of member item money — aka "pork" — that is given to legislators to distribute to organizations around their district on an annual basis. No competitive bidding needed for the money, it was all up to the individual senators and assembly members scattered across the Empire State.

The idea of gaining clout and power in the assembly is what Hevesi said appealed to him in the opening days of his career, rather than positioning himself for a higher office. For someone who had seen his father as a longtime assemblyman and then as a citywide and statewide officeholder, it is interesting that he wanted to follow the first career path and not the second one that his father took. But then again it isn't that surprising in retrospect given the sheer amount of negative press attention his father received in the closing days of his political career. "I hope to stay in the assembly for a long time," Hevesi said in 2006 when asked about future political ambitions. "It is like many other businesses. I am a better elected official today than when I first took office. There is always something to learn and always something interesting. It is a lot of effort but it is worth it. I hope to be an elected official for a long time to come."

Hevesi is not the only ambitious young elected New York assemblyman to look to make the assembly his career. Heading back to the Western New York theme from the beginning of this chapter, it is fitting to mention Democratic assemblyman Sam Hoyt on using the assembly as a platform for future ambition. Hoyt succeeded his father in 1992 following his father's sudden death on the assembly floor. In his early 30s, a former aide to a U.S. senator and possessing a famous name in Buffalo politics, Hoyt was considered someone who would serve for several years in Albany and then move to another level. Hoyt has long been known as follower of the Chuck Schumer approach to politics — announcing just about anything in a press release or press conference. It worked; Hoyt quickly built a public profile in a region with multiple assembly members.

Hoyt seriously considered a race for lieutenant governor in 1998 on a ticket with Lieutenant Governor Betsy McCaughey Ross. McCaughey Ross had been elected to the state's number-two post as a Republican on a ticket with Governor George Pataki before having a contentious falling-out with him, she became a Democrat and announced a bid for governor. Hoyt was one of the first to endorse McCaughey Ross and talked with her about the lieutenant governorship. In the end he declined the race, which was likely a good thing, McCaughey Ross lost the gubernatorial nomination and while the lieutenant governor nominee is chosen separately in the primary, 1998 was not a Democratic year statewide. The eventual Democratic nominee, New York City Council Speaker Peter Vallone, lost to Pataki in a landslide with his running mate, Brighton Town Supervisor Sandra Frankel. Losing as a lieutenant governor candidate didn't even help Frankel in a future bid as she was relegated to obscurity even before votes had been cast in her statewide bid. A Hoyt for lieutenant governor campaign could have ended badly with the ambitious assemblyman relegated to obscurity before his career took off.

It was a standard joke for years that Hoyt wanted to be Buffalo's mayor one day and as the mayor's office opened up in 2005, many thought he'd face off against state senator Byron Brown for the seat. Following a tough assembly reelection in 2004, funded partially by Brown allies, Hoyt suddenly declined a bid for the mayor's office. There were many theories on why Hoyt declined this race, but Hoyt remains emphatic that a desire to spend more time with his family and not to allow the media intrusion that a mayoral campaign and serving as the chief executive of New York's second-largest city would bring into his family life were his chief concerns.

Hoyt would instead refocus his attentions more on Albany, building a closer relationship with the assembly Speaker and with new governor Eliot Spitzer, becoming a political leader in Erie County. Hoyt would also help get allies elected to the city council and county legislature as time moved on. In Albany, he took on the local government committee chairmanship, becoming a would-be architect of any attempt to reform New York's arcane system of local government, an effort that lost political clout when Spitzer resigned. Hoyt also battled back a tough 2008 reelection when a past affair he had with a graduate student intern became an issue in the continuation of his political career.

Young Elected Officials Will Continue to be Ambitious

As you can see in the stories told in this chapter, many young elected officials are ambitious and will continue to be ambitious. While many will continue to deny or underlay their ambitions like a Shapiro, there will be others like Andrews who will be upfront about their ambitions. Shapiro will continue to be the norm.

But at the same time, the lifestyle of a young elected official will complicate the issue of their ambitions. While the impact of being a young elected official on the personal life of the person involved is fully discussed in Chapter 7, it is important here to discuss the impact that personal lives have on the career potential of a young elected official.

The concept of a person trying to balance career and family is not new. It is a story that has existed for many years and will never go away. People will look at work/life balance in all that they do. Many will look for ways to spend more time with children and spouses and trying to advance in their jobs, while others will put career advancement ahead of all else. As can be seen in this chapter, there are multiple examples of young elected officials trying to balance their family with their career ambitions.

The unique nature of politics as a career and the demands placed on the life of an elected official play a big role in trying to combine the job with their personal life. Elected officials have to work during the day in their elective job, attending meetings and conferences and events and doing desk work. If a legislator they will also have to attend meetings that could stretch into the nighttime hours. But they will also have the political end of their job to do, something that is further complicated with the concept of the never ending campaign. They will need to raise money, attend events and make contacts with those who could be of political benefit in order to win the next election. Their constituents will also demand their presence at events in the community in order to see their elected official. These events will also give the elected official a good feel for the pulse of the community and what the ever changing issues impacting the community are.

At the same time many young elected officials serve in local and state government. Those serving at this level of government will likely be serving in a part-time capacity. Thus, they are continuing in a full-time job in another career. By doing this they are holding down two full-time jobs in all likelihood. In some cases they will have staffs to assist them, in some cases it may be one person to help them. But in other cases there are no large staffs and the elected official is on their own. While the voters are willing to cut them a certain slack that they have a full-time day job and cannot attend certain events or be available at certain hours, they need to make it up at the times that they can be available. That means nights and weekends. To be a local elected official, at a young age or any age in America today, means sacrificing your nights and weekends in order to attend community events and meetings and be able to stay in office.

All of these issues will weigh heavily on young elected officials as they try to decide which office to run for and if they want to move up on the rungs of the political ladder. Many will end up having the family concerns that are weighing on Gerber or weighed on Iorio. The idea of taking a pass on running for higher office because of the impact of a statewide campaign or the commuting between your home district and Washington could have on a young family. Or choosing to run for an office that would not have been the first one you would have jumped for because it worked better as a parent, is a role that they have done and many young elected officials will continue to go.

One of the oldest lines in American politics is when the retiring or resigning politician gives up high office because they "want to spend more time with my family." Most of the time this usually translates to "I know I am going to lose the next election" or "I am likely to be indicted soon so maybe the jury will remember that at the end of the day I am a huge family man." Unfortunately the line developed that reputation because that is what it has been mainly used for. Plus the public perception that no ambitious politician would ever give up power in order to do such a thing as spend time with their family. In some circles ambitious politicians are supposed to use their families as campaign props and spend occasional events with them, with the BlackBerry ever present.

But in the case of many young elected officials, from the ones that I have talked to in the process of writing this book, I have found it to be true that many of them are interested in their families and will use family concerns to dictate future career ambitions. Many will think like Gerber in what is in the best interest of their families. Many of them will look and think that the chances of waiting to move up the political ladder in order to better accommodate their family is better than jumping for the first office to come along. As I said before, this is a surprising statement to many in the political arena. I remember a conversation I had a few years ago with a political staffer who questioned why any elected official would place their family before their career except for the public consumption of the phrase. But at the same time it comes clearly across that young elected officials are concerned with their families and want to make sure the interests of their families are balanced with the interests of their careers.

There are also the young electeds like Seaver and Brinton who want to be young while at the same time looking at any career in politics. They will decide to move away from politics for a while, get a college degree or focus on their personal life for a while. It is a large demand that is being asked for from young elected officials that they be on display at all times and focus their entire lives at times on their careers, when many of them are still trying to be the same person that their friends are. It is to be expected that some of them may take the chance of giving up their careers or leaving office for a few years in order to reclaim some semblance of a normal life. What may work for a 20-year-old will not work for some even a few years older. It also could be nothing more than a need to move for work or take a new job that will help with career enhancement. Look at Westfield's Kevin Walsh — he spent most of 2001 knocking on doors and working to defeat a longtime incumbent to turn around after a year and resign in order to take a new job as a federal prosecutor, which required him to step down as a councilman. He would be able to advance his legal career but at the same time would need to give up his elected office.

With many younger people looking for careers that interest them and stimulate them, along with being fun, it is not surprising that many of the young elected officials are apt to look at certain career opportunities in order to find the offices that they believe best fit their image. This runs in contrast to the common perception of a politician who will run for just about any office that comes along because of a desire to hold the power and prestige that comes with the office and not because they want a job that interests them or possibly want the job that will have the best possible impact.

Hevesi is a good example of this. Life in the New York Assembly for a backbench member can be tough. There are 150 members of the assembly and it is a body that is driven almost exclusively by the whims of the Speaker. Yes, the Speaker will be influenced by his caucus because of the need to keep caucus support to stay in office, but, at the end of the day, the Speaker has the most impact. The Speaker can give a member the chance to shine, a better office space, more staff, access to the taxpayer-funded publicity machine, campaign money and good committee assignments. Please the Speaker and you're on the powerful Ways and Means Committee; upset the Speaker and you're representing an urban district and debating dairy policy as a member of the agriculture committee. And this is life in the majority, for a minority party member like Quinn, life in Albany is a lot different with the elevator operator wielding more power than the average backbench assembly Republican. To work into a position of power and prestige in the assembly normally takes time. With seats in the New York State Legislature turning over less than the Soviet Politburo did, time won't even open up these seats. Gaining power and influence in the assembly is a wait-and-see game.

But Hevesi remains undeterred and indicated that he wants to make a career in the assembly and move up in office because of this. He does not want to explore higher offices like his father did, but rather focus his efforts on growing in Albany and the assembly. Saying he is willing to take on the long waiting game that is rising in the assembly ranks shows that Hevesi is ambitious but also tempers that ambition with a desire to stay where he is, where he can continue to gain power by sticking around for decades. This thought process could be interpreted that Hevesi has no shot at running for higher office and has decided to take the desire for a longtime assembly career instead, but it can also be interpreted that he has found what he is looking for and has decided to pursue his career in the assembly chamber in Albany.

But for everyone in this end there are young elected officials like Schneider, Shapiro, and Grayson who will be looking for the next step up the ladder and will be looking to balance it with their personal life, but also look for what is the best move to make politically. They will also look to balance the needs of the future in doing this. In another chapter I have written about young elected officials thinking outside the box and taking risks and it is clear that this can also be addressed in this chapter about ambition. They will be looking to take these risks and use this as a way to help further whatever ambition they have. Looking at Schneider he took a risk in running for insurance commissioner that, yes, he could win a statewide office in his 20s or do well enough in a losing campaign that he could set up a statewide network and name recognition for a future statewide run. Or he could lose badly enough that he would be considered a failure and not able to run statewide again. Schneider is also taking the risk of moving into a federal appointed post that could help him move about the state easily but take him out of the elective office that could be a springboard to another elective office. But he could also have put himself in a position that could allow him to travel the state and garner headlines in communities from

Fargo to Minot, which show him distributing federal funds across the land. It is a risk that could either help or hurt his political ambitions and it is one that he is taking and one that can be attributed to his age. In the end, most signs point to Schneider being able to succeed based on the risks that he is taking in his career. His political ambitions will likely succeed because of this career path.

The ambitions of politicians will exist as long as there are politicians, and those who were elected at a young age will continue to push these ambitions because they are by nature ambitious people. No one willing to jump into the almost bizarre lifestyle of an elected official cannot not be ambitious at some point. The need to be ambitious is almost a prerequisite to run for office in the first place, to do it at a young age is a guarantee. And these ambitions do not usually get extinguished early on. While in some cases they are pretty much on display from day one, in other cases they will smolder beneath the surface until it bubbles up as a young elected official looks at the next path in their career. With term limits continuing to gain steam in many corners of the country, they will help dictate the career paths of a young elected official. Some may choose to retire and head into the private sector or a lobbying job because of them, becoming in some regard the Jeffersonian ideal of a citizen legislator. In other cases they will choose to run for another office in order to continue their careers at another level. Or in some cases they will see an opportunity for advancement in a legislative chamber because of a turnover in the jobs because of the forced retirements of others.

Ambitions will be a part of the story of young elected officials going forward, but it should be kept in mind that it is not the only part of the story and that it is possible for a young elected official to actually check their ambitions at the door because of the particular circumstances that come with their age and their position in life.

Note

1   Trey Grayson lost the Republican primary to Rand Paul to succeed Jim Bunning in the U.S. Senate.

CHAPTER 6

"I got asked constantly what my husband thought": The Challenges Faced by Young Women in Elective Office

Massachusetts has two great competitive activities: sports and politics. Both are taken seriously, endlessly debated and at times becoming a blood sport. In the run-up to the 2000 election for president, there was a lot of talk in the commonwealth about the impact the presidential race would have. There was speculation that if Al Gore won he would tap Senator John Kerry to be his secretary of state. If George W. Bush won, the Republican governor Paul Cellucci would join his administration.

It was with this speculation in mind that Cellucci invited his lieutenant governor, Jane Swift, to a private lunch at his Statehouse office to discuss a variety of possibilities and how the speculation would affect her. Swift was 35 years old at the time and had been in elective politics for a decade. Following a stint in her early 20s as a legislative aide on Beacon Hill, she entered the state senate in 1990 representing western Massachusetts. She gave up her Senate seat in 1996 to unsuccessfully challenge a Democratic congressman. While she lost her race for Congress, the moderate Republican Swift was recognized as a political dynamo, raising over a million dollars for the race and running a strong campaign.

Following her loss for Congress, Swift would move into executive positions within state government with then governor William Weld naming her to head small airport development for the Massachusetts Port Authority and then Cellucci tapping her for his cabinet as consumer affairs secretary. Heading into his 1998 bid for a full term as governor, Cellucci would ask Swift to be his running mate for lieutenant governor.

Swift's campaign for the second-highest job in Massachusetts government came at the same time that she and her husband were trying to start a family. She was upfront with Cellucci about her personal life and situation and he was supportive of her. Swift would campaign while pregnant and gave birth just days before her election to the lieutenant governorship. Her early days as lieutenant governor were marked by her age and the fact that she was combining mother-hood with the job. Her husband became a stay-at-home husband and, rather than move the family from their western Massachusetts home to Boston, Swift would commute two hours in each direction and sleep occasional nights at her brother's apartment in Boston.

In some ways it was a double standard. Many male politicians of the same age with young kids and a stay-at-home wife would not be the focus and subject of news stories about their ability to combine work and family. But in the masculine world of Massachusetts government the young woman in the number-two job was something to talk about. Massachusetts has never elected a woman to a statewide office above lieutenant governor. At the same time as Swift's lieutenant governorship, the state would also see Democratic treasurer Shannon O'Brien give birth to a child and take a maternity leave from her post as the state's chief financial officer.

Moving back to the lunch Cellucci and Swift had the day before the historic 2000 presidential election, the governor told Swift how the election would likely affect her life. He told her that if Kerry was tapped to head the State Department in a Gore administration, he would be appointing her to fill the state U.S. Senate seat, becoming the first woman to represent the state in the Senate. He also told her that if Bush won, he would be seeking a place in his administration, which would mean he would vacate the governorship and Swift would move up to become the first woman governor of Massachusetts. Swift reacted by sharing an announcement of her own with the governor. "I had to tell him after he gave me this opportunity that I was pregnant and was having twins," she said. "The look on his face was priceless."

Laughing as she recalled the story of how she ended up on the road to the governorship, she said the story did not end there. Attending Bush's inaugura-tion in January 2001, Swift was told by Cellucci that he would be nominated for the ambassadorship to Canada in the coming weeks and would likely be leaving Beacon Hill by the spring, paving the way for Swift to not only become Massachusetts' first woman governor but the nation's first pregnant governor. Cellucci would step down in April and Swift would be the first governor in Massachusetts history to be addressed as "Her Excellency." Under state law she was technically acting governor, retaining the duties of lieutenant governor too, which meant she presided over meetings of the governor's council in addi-tion to running the state.

Her governorship got off to the interesting start of her being close to giv-ing birth. She would spend the last seven days of her pregnancy on bed rest, governing Massachusetts from a hospital bed. Swift didn't take a maternity leave in the formal sense, preferring to take a modified maternity leave, which would involve her continuing to work from her western Massachusetts home while also focusing on her newborn twin daughters. Modern technology, and a dedicated staff in her Boston office, allowed her to take the working maternity leave. She could use computers, e-mail, and fax machines to keep in touch with top aides and continue to fulfill constitutional duties as the acting governor. If Swift had chosen to temporarily step aside, the governorship would have temporarily passed to Democrat William Galvin, the secretary of state and next in line of succession since the lieutenant governorship was still technically held by Swift.

Not only is Swift the youngest woman to hold a state governorship in U.S. history, being just a year over the maximum age I set for a young elected official for the purposes of this book, she was the first to be pregnant and give birth while in office. She gained national and international publicity for being a governor who gave birth; only a handful of members of the U.S. House of Representatives had given birth while in office, and no senators had. Massachusetts had a very unique situation during Swift's four years as a constitutional officer of the commonwealth, with O'Brien also giving birth. When Swift retired from the governorship in 2002, O'Brien was the unsuccessful Democratic nominee to replace her.

It would take seven years until the country had another governor give birth while in office: Sarah Palin of Alaska. Several differences do exist between the two governorships. Swift's pregnancy was well known for months, while Palin kept hers a secret until the end. Palin reported back to work days after giving birth to her youngest son, Trig, while Swift chose to have a maternity leave and Palin would end up moving up to make a run for higher office, in her run for vice president several months later. Swift would leave the governorship in January 2003. In addition, Palin is the first elected governor to give birth while in office.

Swift being the first governor while in office does highlight the differences in having a young woman in elective office. Many of the women governors prior to Swift were older, either childless or had raised their children already. Some had teenage children while serving in office. It was rare that a woman with young children had taken on a political office such as the governorship. When Swift gave birth in 2001, three women in Congress had given birth, all of them young and all of them newsworthy. Almost 20 years elapsed between the first, Yvonne Burke of California, and the second, Enid Greene of Utah, giving birth while serving in Congress. It was more common to see at the local level than at the federal or statewide levels. A lot of this came to a belief that for a woman to be able to serve in elective office, she would need to be childless or have grown children. The first woman to run on a national ticket, Geraldine Ferraro, had grown children by the time she made her run for the vice presidency in 1984. Of course in the ensuing 24 years, as women in executive roles in the private sector became more common, the number of women senators went well above the two that had dominated the chamber for decades and Swift had paved the way for pregnancy in the executive chamber, the landscape changed. Palin was a sitting governor with young children and a candidate for vice president. Palin was also younger than Ferraro was when they made their national candidacies.

Young elected officials who are women do not see a need to behave any differently when they are in office and do not see a need to pursue different policies, for the most part. Some have acknowledged that they have to be tough and work hard, because they are first overcoming the questions about their age and in some cases the question on whether a young woman could take on some of the challenges.

It should be noted that young elected officials who are women do not shrink from the challenges that they face in their duties in office. Swift is a case in point, and not for her pregnancy or her having governed from a hospital bed. On September 11, 2001, the two planes that slammed into the World Trade Center and started the terrorist attacks took off from Boston's Logan Airport. Pretty quickly, people were questioning security at Logan and the hiring and management practices of the Massachusetts Port Authority. Swift found herself taking on one role during the attacks that day, commanding Massachusetts' response in the state war room and then another in the weeks after, working to determine what had gone wrong at Logan and helping to determine a plan to remedy what had occurred there and prevent any other large scale security breaches in the future. "It was a little surreal," Swift said of what was going through her mind on September 11 as she was sitting in the state's war room. "It was a time when the privilege you have been given to serve comes with the real responsibilities. To make the best decisions, some of the most important decisions you made are the ones where you have the least information."

Swift is not the only young woman to take on some of the toughest challenges in elective office. Democrat Elizabeth Holtzman was 31 years old when she was elected to Congress representing Brooklyn, New York, in 1972, becoming the youngest woman ever elected to the House of Representatives — a record that stands as of early 2010. Getting to Congress, the former aide to New York mayor John Lindsay had to dislodge a Brooklyn institution, Democratic congressman Manny Celler, who had served for 50 years and chaired the judiciary committee.

Entering Congress, Holtzman would assume a seat on the judiciary panel. It was a time when the committee was beginning to wrestle with one of its biggest issues in history: the impeachment of Richard Nixon. New to Congress and elective office, Holtzman would suddenly find herself questioning witnesses, listening to testimony, studying evidence, and being immersed in the biggest constitutional questions in American history and trying to decide if the Watergate conspiracy warranted Nixon's impeachment and potential removal from office. Of course the final votes on this issue were cut short with Nixon's resignation, but the tough issues facing Holtzman and her committee colleagues continued under the Ford administration.

When President Ford took office one of his actions in his first month in office was to pardon Nixon, ending any future prosecution of the former president for any role he had in the Watergate affair. This set off an immediate debate over whether the new president made a deal with Nixon when he was appointed to the vice presidency or before Nixon's resignation to pardon Nixon in order to become president. Ford agreed to unprecedented testimony before the House judiciary committee regarding the pardon. Holtzman found herself sitting in judgment of a second president in her first term in Congress.

During Ford's testimony, he was not directly asked about a deal exchanging a pardon for the presidency as the questioning moved down the seniority ladder of the committee. When the time came for Holtzman to question the president, she immediately stepped up and asked him the question that was on everyone's lips: was there a deal? Ford immediately stepped up to deny any deal, but the question was out there and Ford had to answer the question being debated across the country. While her more senior colleagues sat back and praised Ford on being the first president to testify before Congress and asked him questions regarding other aspects of the pardon, the youngest congresswoman in the nation's history showed the impact young elected officials can have on the debate and on public policy by asking the toughest question that could be asked of Ford.

Holtzman would not shy away from tough positions during the rest of her career in public life, continuing to showcase the personal will and fortitude that she showcased as the youngest woman in Congress. During the remainder of her eight years in the House, she would serve on the first-ever budget committee and chaired the immigration subcommittee. She left the House in 1980 to run unsuccessfully for the U.S. Senate. Beating some of the biggest names in New York politics in the Democratic primary, including Lindsay and former Miss America Bess Myerson, Holtzman was considered a frontrunner in the three-way race against Republican Al D'Amato and Republican senator Jacob Javits, who was running as the nominee of the Liberal Party. The active campaign of Javits on the Liberal line and the 1980 Republican landslide contributed to Holtzman's narrow defeat.

She bounced back a year following her defeat for the Senate, being elected to the first of two terms as Brooklyn's district attorney, becoming the first woman elected to be a district attorney in New York City. Following her days as a prosecutor, where she helped create a sex crimes unit and combat domestic violence, she would become the city's first female comptroller. Given all of these firsts in tough jobs, Holtzman though does find it amazing that women in politics have only gone so far, including not dethroning her as the youngest woman to win a congressional seat in the nation.

New York remains one of the most socially progressive cities in the country, a city where women in elective office remains at a high, with women in the city council, the state legislature, and the congressional delegation, including in one U.S. Senate seat. But the depth of the pool of young women is small — something Jessica Lappin noticed when she launched her bid for the city council representing Manhattan's Upper East Side in 2005 at the age of 30.

Lappin launched her bid for the council after years working for her predecessor, former council Speaker Gifford Miller. She worked on Miller's staff, headed his political action committee, served under him in the Speaker's office and was his district chief of staff. With Miller forced out by term limits, Lappin decided it was time to step up to the plate herself and make a race for office. At the time, Lappin was newly married and childless. One of the first things she did was to attend a campaign seminar for women candidates, where she discovered something: she was in a small minority of young women in the room. Most were either older or, if they were young, they were unmarried and childless. "I think that it is a few who run for office, serve and have a family," she said. "That is not something I am afraid of. If you look at the women in the council, most are younger." Following Lappin's election, one of her first votes was to elect a 39-year-old woman, Christine Quinn, as the new Speaker of the council, succeeding Miller. Quinn and her partner do not have children.

Heading out on to the campaign trail, Lappin was surprised by some of the questions she would get while shaking hands at subway stops and meeting voters at street fairs. Questions that she was unprepared for in a neighborhood represented by women in the state senate and in Congress, along with Senator Hillary Rodham Clinton, who had won the area. "It was always interesting to hear the questions," she said. "I got asked constantly what my husband thought. I doubt a male candidate would be asked that. I was asked if I had kids."

For the record, Lappin's husband, Andrew Wuertele, supported her decision to run for the council; in fact, he serves as her campaign treasurer. At one point she was even asked if Wuertele knew she was running for council. Yes, she'd mentioned it before the signs went up. She found it odd because of her experiences with Miller, who was not that much older than her. During her time with Miller, who had two young sons while he was a councilman and was running for mayor in the 2005 election, the issue had never come up. No one had asked Miller if his wife, Pamela, supported his decision to be a councilman or run for mayor. "If you are going on a job interview, your interviewer would never ask what your spouse thinks," Lappin said.

Lappin shows no signs of stepping down her career and has shown interest in running for higher office. Her son, Lucas, was born after the election and she has balanced being a councilwoman and a mother, as, she says, any working mother needs to do. In 2009 she showed some interest in running for the vacant public advocate's office, but declined. Her name also had circulated for Congress in the event that Representative Carolyn Maloney declines to run again. With term limits likely to push her out of office in 2013, Lappin is considered a rising star in Manhattan politics and a likely candidate for either public advocate or borough president in the next election.

Lappin is not the only young woman running for office who has encountered challenges during the campaign because she was a woman. Greenville, Mississippi, and the Upper East Side of Manhattan could not be further apart culturally, geographically, and politically. In fact many would not put the two together in any description of politics and government, except in this case. Heather Hudson was 27 years old when she made her first race in 2003 for the city council, followed by a successful bid four years later to be the city's mayor. Hudson has multiple distinctions in her political career. Not only is she the youngest person to hold the mayor's office in her city, she is also the first woman and the first African American to hold the office.

When Hudson embarked on her city council and mayoral races, she chose to run like any other candidate in city history, not giving any consideration to her gender when she was campaigning. One of the things that many politicians in Greenville do during the campaign is speak from the pulpit at churches in the city, something that Hudson found to be a challenge. "It was very different," Hudson said of her campaign. "I would go to certain churches and they would not allow a woman on the pulpit." Cut off from the pulpit part of the campaign, Hudson focused on grassroots campaigning, stressing her background and plans for the city. In running for the mayor's office, she focused her attention on discussing the community service work as a councilwoman, including pressing for infrastructure upgrades in the city and talking about how she would continue on these issues in the mayor's chair.

Guttenberg, New Jersey, is a small working-class community in northern Hudson County, just across the river from Manhattan. The most densely populated town in the country, Guttenberg has not had a long history of electing women to elective office or younger officials. In fact, Hudson County has not been a hotbed of women in elective office, with the first female mayor taking office temporarily through succession in 1992 and no women being elected mayor until 2009 in Hoboken. Jennifer Credidio stepped into this situation to serve her hometown in 2002.

Twenty-six years old, Credidio was already a political veteran by the time she was asked to become a replacement candidate for a seat on the Town Council. She had been an aide to a local assemblyman and had obtained a master's degree in public policy from Columbia University. A graduate of Seton Hall Law School, Credidio had started practicing land use and municipal bond law. She also became politically active in Gutternberg, serving as a Democratic Party committeewoman and becoming chairwoman of the planning board.

After being picked as a replacement candidate, she was on the fast track in the November election, since Democrats routinely win Guttenberg elections. Taking office, she was appointed to oversee recreation issues in town, a position she would hold for her entire four years as a councilwoman. Now serving alongside men old enough to be her father, and being a woman, Credidio needed to fight to get herself heard as a councilwoman and make sure that the needs of the town's recreation department were heard. "A lot of the time I had to be more aggressive than I would have been," she said of her time in office. "There was a certain amount of table thumping I had to do to get heard. I was not going to sit there with my mouth shut. I think the guys were good, especially the guys I had worked with before. I had to win over the other two councilpeople."

This was not the first example that Credidio had to deal with people underestimating her as a young woman in the political arena in the rough and tumble of Guttenberg. Another time was during her time as planning board chairwoman, when an attorney came before the board and proceeded to lecture her, calling her "little lady," and then she had to inform him that his entire argument was wrong. Credidio's career in elective office was brief, with her choosing to not run for a third term in 2006 and instead focus on her legal career. With the demands of a job that required her to attend municipal meetings of clients in other towns across the state, Credidio did not have the time to attend to town business in addition to her legal work. She also noted that getting out of elective office would give her a different lifestyle all together. "It's not a normal lifestyle," she said of her time as a young elected official.

If there is anything the 2008 election did for the country, it was to educate the country about the differences between Alaska and the rest of the country. No matter what you may think of Sarah Palin and her politics or anything else that may have come out during her bid for the vice presidency, the education in the culture of Alaska was a benefit for the country. The largest of the states in terms of land size, Alaska is still largely rural, especially the interior villages. Many places are accessible only by plane, with small airlines playing the role of taxicabs in the Lower 48. Juneau is the nation's only capital not accessible by car. Alaskans continue to vote down proposals to bring a highway to connect Juneau to the rest of the state or to move the capital to Anchorage. The capital can only be accessed by air or sea.

The state legislature meets a couple of months a year in Juneau. In other states this means different things. The smallness of Delaware allows for legislators to commute back and forth. In California or New York, state legislators are like members of Congress with regular commutes back and forth to the capital and the district. In state like North Dakota or Wisconsin, legislators come to the capital for the short sessions, and commute back on weekends. None of this is possible in Alaska with the location of Juneau, the need for air travel to many parts of the state and the winter weather. Consequently many state legislators spend the entire session living in Juneau, often moving their whole families to the capital city for the several-month session, uprooting children from schools and spouses from jobs in order to perform their duties in Juneau. It is something that hits both men and women in the Alaska legislature.

Mary Kapsner was elected to the Alaska House of Representatives representing a district consisting of several rural villages at the age of 25. Commuting back and forth to Juneau during the first decade of the twenty-first century, she would encounter issues similar with those she was serving alongside in Juneau. In the era of having to move her family back and forth, she did not need to also deal with the sexist response she received. "Most of my colleagues are retired and are men," she said. "A lot of them feel women should be home raising kids. It is a reality for most Americans and most Alaskans that you cannot make it on one income."

Kapsner noted that her husbands have been able to make the adjustment to her lifestyle of living in two different cities because of her job and the desire to move the family in accordance with the legislature's schedule. Her first husband was a commercial pilot and her second husband worked for the university system. She did say the lifestyle is toughest on her children though. "We've always traveled together," Kapsner said in an interview. "You have to pack every thing and children have a lot of stuff. I believe being a public servant is hard on families. It is interesting to see how my kids handle living in two places."

Heading back to Massachusetts and Jane Swift, Swift notes that her time as governor who was a mother was of benefit to how she approached issues and the decisions coming across her desk. "I have said that that I was a better mother because I was governor and a better governor because I was a mother," she said. In terms of policy, Swift, a self-proclaimed policy wonk noted that being a woman and a mother gave her insights in education and children's issues that she believes benefited her state. She notes that she was able to reform the state's testing system and work on issues relating to the foster care system and have certain insights as a young mother that she would not have normally had. This included developing more funding for foster parents and helping place foster children who were determined to be high risk.

At the end of the day, Swift's children helped her decide not to run for the governorship in her own right in 2002. Swift was hammered from almost the very day she took over as governor in 2001 and had to deal with periods of bad press from her days as lieutenant governor. She notes that she was unprepared for the sheer amount of negative publicity she received during her governorship. "I was completely unprepared for the focus and attention to my life," Swift said of her life from the moment Cellucci put her on the 1998 ticket. "To this day, some of the political challenges I dealt with later were from that and not being prepared for it."

In 2002, Swift was getting ready to face businessman Mitt Romney, the future presidential candidate who was preparing to self finance a campaign, Following a year of bad headlines, Republican Party leaders were coalescing around Romney, with the state GOP chairwoman stepping down from her post to become Romney's running mate. Looking at the political situation going forward, Swift found several issues. She saw the primary as tough, while she felt she'd beat whichever of the three Democrats won the nomination. With the state's finances in bad shape and other policy issues she wanted to address, Swift suddenly found herself faced with two all-consuming jobs: that of governor and that of gubernatorial candidate. She also found herself asking questions of herself. "When facing an opponent who had a bottomless base to self-finance, I knew I could not win a primary," Swift said. "I was not going to run a race giving it my all and not having a chance to win."

Bringing a range of backgrounds and experiences to the political spectrum is key for young elected officials wishing to have an impact on society. This includes having a broad mix, including young women, in office. With more and more colleges being at least half, if not more, female in the student body and women taking on more roles in the executive suite and in all aspects of society, this translates into the arena of elective office. The thing is there is still a double standard that exists today regarding young women running and serving in elective office. Lappin illustrates the debate with the questions she was asked during her campaign in Manhattan where she was being asked if her husband was supporting her campaign and if she had children. Miller, her predecessor, did not get questions on those issues. These are questions that people will continue to ask if a young woman can balance having a child or wanting to have a child with serving in elective office and can a woman take time off for maternity leave and then move back into office.

As the country moves forward it becomes less and less of an issue. Swift showed how a woman can successfully give birth to twins while still running a major state. Lappin is showing that she can help govern the nation's largest city and be a young mom. Kapsner found ways to balance the needs of her job in Juneau with the unique challenges of being a politician in Alaska. Women who are young elected officials have more guts and less to fear in certain areas at times. Having overcome certain challenges posed by others, they have shown that they are willing to overcome anything in order to accomplish what needs to be done. Holtzman's biggest challenge was toppling a Brooklyn institution in the 1972 primary, which paled in some comparison to sitting in judgment of President Nixon or questioning President Ford. She continued to show this desire to take on tough challenges by running for district attorney and city comptroller, two of the toughest offices in city government.

Looking ahead, women will continue to be an important part of the story of young elected officials and will continue to forge ahead. As more take on various legislative and executive roles in government and more people are accustomed to two-career couples, young women will get fewer questions than Lappin. While a woman like Holtzman is considered a trailblazer for her election in the early 1970s, young elected women like Lappin and Hudson continue to blaze that trail in order to allow more young women to run for office. One of these days it is likely Holtzman will be unseated from her perch as the youngest woman ever elected to Congress as more young women get involved in politics.

CHAPTER 7

From Dating to Parenting: The Impact of Politics on the Personal Lives of Young Elected Officials

Many young people first starting out in the workforce complain about the impact of work on their personal lives. Associates at large law firms, medical residents, analysts at the large investment banks, all have many things in common. The hours are long, the work is tough, the environment is a far change of pace from college life. Days measured in the double digits are not uncommon, spending more time at work than home is normal, stress on the job is a way of life.

The lifestyle of a young elected official is no different, yet also very different. Young elected officials end up putting in long hours for the job they hold. They have to attend numerous committee meetings, general meetings, briefing sessions, and put in hours reading background material and doing research. For many, they have little to no staff support, meaning much of the research a more senior elected official can farm out to a staffer has to be borne by the elected official. They have constituent obligations to attend to, planning and attending town hall meetings, going to events in their district and responding to constituent requests. They help track down benefits for a widow or fill a pothole. Again many of the tasks falling to them were based on the little to no staff support.

But again, being a young elected official is, in reality, two jobs: the first — that of being in elective office — is described above; the second is being a candidate. In today's permanent campaign cycle, where the reelection campaigns begin at 9 a.m. on the morning following the election, politicians are never not running for office. This job includes attending meetings of party committees in their district, raising money, attending political and community functions, maintaining close ties to key community groups and party leaders, attending strategy sessions and meeting with advisors to plan out the future. For those running for or looking to run for a higher office, there is research on future races that needs to be held, more strategy sessions to be conducted and the almost mandatory attendance at various community and political meetings and events in areas outside of the present district, but in parts of the new district. All in all, a pretty demanding job with unusual hours. Just because the elected official is available during the day does not mean that members of the community are available to meet during the day. Thus, many meetings and events occur at night.

At the same time, this is not the only job the young elected officials hold. Most hold elective offices that are part-time posts, meaning they have day jobs that keep them just as busy and have them working morning, noon, and night in order to accomplish their day job, their governmental role and their political role. They sacrifice time with friends, with family, with spouses, with dating, in order to take on the role of being a young elected official. And they sacrifice time at work, potentially hurting their day jobs at the same time.

But these are not the only personal sacrifices that young elected officials need to make in order to hold office. Many also have to change their behavior. To hold elective office is to be a public figure. To lead a public life is to have to operate knowing that a camera may be trained on you at all times. Are people watching? What will people think? In the age of the Internet, the 24-hour news cycle, anything can become news at a moment's notice. With citizen journalists and blogs it is easier and easier for a minor misstep to be blown out of proportion. With more and more traditional journalism moving online and the creation of hyperlocal newspapers online, there are more avenues to get potentially embarrassing information out in a journalistic format. Instead of seeing the speech written, a local official's speech can be recorded and posted online for all to see. The behavior of young elected officials ends up changing.

But this is all part of it.

Jane Swift was never not in politics in her early 20s. She was involved in political activities and as a state senate staffer. During this time she met and started dating another senate staffer and the two were on an equal footing for a time. Then Swift's boss retired and encouraged her to run for his seat. Her boyfriend was supportive of her political ambitions; he was in politics after all, how could he not support her ambition? That's what happens in politics — you are ambitious and know other ambitious people. And staffers aim to move up to be the politician themselves. How could this not be a good match?

It looked like a good match on Swift's end. Then things changed up a bit. In good news for Swift, she won the Senate seat, heading to Beacon Hill as a young female senator. It also upset the equal balance of her relationship. Suddenly she went from staffer to senator: she and her boyfriend were not on an equal footing. He ended it. Swift became convinced that her political career would end up having a major impact on her social life. Would anyone date her if she was a senator? "It is kind of tough to be a 25-year-old single woman in a visible position," she said. "Ironically I met my husband through my service in the Senate. I thought I was dooming my prospects when I ran and won."

Swift's husband was a dairy farmer in her largely rural western Massachusetts Senate district for which she was a senator. He came to her to discuss issues facing dairy farmers and the relationship blossomed into a friendship and then into more. At the end of the day, she would end up marrying and have children. She had her first child just before being elected lieutenant governor and then had twin girls just after taking office as acting governor of the commonwealth. Swift would also end up in the unique position of having her husband becoming a stay-at-home dad, sparing her some of the child care decisions of many mothers in executive positions.

Swift was 33 when she became lieutenant governor and 36 when she succeeded to the governorship. While her husband was able to stay at home, there were other demands on her personal life and her job of governing a state. Massachusetts is one of the few states that provide an official residence in the capital for the governor and no residence for the lieutenant governor. Swift chose to continue to live full-time with her family in western Massachusetts and commute daily to her office in Boston, staying overnight in the capital with her brother as needed. The commute was two hours one way, with Swift's home physically closer to the capitol in Albany, New York, versus the golden dome on Beacon Hill in Boston. Many criticized Swift for this decision and her time spent commuting among other issues.

Swift would end up in an incident as lieutenant governor where she used a state aircraft on Thanksgiving weekend to fly back to her home from Boston. Her daughter was sick at the time and traffic on the Massachusetts Turnpike was heavy, given the holiday weekend. Swift had the same thoughts of many working mothers, that she wanted to get home to her daughter, and to get home as quickly as possible. For Swift, though, many found it inappropriate that she utilized a state helicopter for a personal reason and then said it was because her daughter was sick. Some said she could have avoided this if her family lived closer to Boston. The decision would haunt Swift for her entire time in statewide office with many hammering at her until she took her lone walk[1] down the steps of the Beacon Hill Statehouse in January of 2003.

The biggest impact on the personal life of a young elected official is the time aspect. They have to balance the two disparate aspects of the elective office with their personal life. Jersey City councilman Steven Fulop said it has played havoc with not being in a relationship as he was for most of his first term in office. He noted that he had a lot of first dates, but the time became a factor. In some cases, it wasn't just Fulop's political work or even the combination of that with his private work in banking. He also for part of his first term pursued two masters' degrees — in public administration and business administration — at two different universities on a part-time basis at the same time.

Fulop's ward is a young one. Being just across the river from Manhattan and just south of Hoboken, there is not much in way of nightlife in his part of Jersey City. There is more than enough in the other two cities. But at the same time Fulop is concerned about his public image and the fact that he is in the public eye. It is not a decision that can be taken lightly. Jersey City mayor Jerry Healy, who is frequently at odds with Fulop over government reform issues and almost saw the young councilman as his chief rival during the 2009 mayor's race, has run into several issues due to his behavior while drunk. Healy has been photographed naked while sleeping on the steps of his home and was involved in a criminal case along the Jersey Shore. "I don't date in Jersey City. I don't go out in Jersey City. I try not to drink in Jersey City," he said.

Fulop's concerns that a casual drink or a date in Jersey City will suddenly end up on some Internet message board or in the *Jersey Journal* or in *PolitickerNJ*, are not just left to him. Many other young elected officials have the same concerns about their personal lives and worry that suddenly one misstep will end up in the public consumption. The rise of online media has contributed to this, with online newspapers being a place where anything can suddenly be posted, while community message boards and blogs are other places that an incriminating photo can end up. At the same time, many in politics have begun to use blogs and message boards to set the agenda, criticize opponents, spread information, and sometimes do more harm than good. Fulop himself has fallen victim to this, with community message boards in his downtown Jersey City district being populated by a small but very vocal group of residents who would love nothing more than to see him go. He's been accused of being the puppet of various people, not being competent, of being gay, and of being a flip-flopper. Unfortunately he is not alone in being a young elected official who is being attacked in the blogosphere.

Fulop's thoughts about drinking and going out in Jersey City are not just his. Dan Zwonitzer is a Republican state representative in Cheyenne, Wyoming. While they do not hail from similar areas, the two share a lot of thoughts when it comes to being in elective office and how it changes their lives. Zwonitzer was first elected in 2004 in his mid-20s and had his eyes on running for higher office one day. In 2008 he briefly pursued a seat in Congress before dropping out. But he keeps an eye out for what he can and cannot do. "I can't be as rowdy as I want at the bar," he said. "You have to be socially aware. I am more guarded on what I say. You keep in mind that if you say the wrong thing it could come back to haunt you and that's sad."

Unlike Fulop, who lives alone in a Jersey City condo, Zwonitzer started his legislative career sharing a house with friends in Cheyenne. Being in that position, he had to start worrying about other people and the impact they could have on his life. He started talking to his roommates and what they should avoid doing because of the impact it could have on his political career. One old roommate used to throw keg parties when Zwonitzer was not home.

Heather Hudson, the young mayor of Greenville, Mississippi, is active in a national network of progressive young political leaders in the country. In this organization she has the chance to talk with many of her colleagues nationally and hears many of the same concerns Fulop brought up. In fact, it is one of the most common she hears. She considers herself lucky to be married so she can avoid many of the concerns that other young elected officials have. "I have heard young elected officials say how hard it is to date," she said. "You want to go out and it is in the paper. It is the *US Weekly* and *People* magazine syndrome."

State representative Brent Barton of Oregon knows where Fulop is coming from on the dating front. First elected in 2008 at the age of 28, the two have many things in common. Both unseated long-term incumbents to get to their offices. Both had competitive races. Both are considered rising stars in their parties and regions. Both had formed alliances with leaders in their cities and states which helped them get a foot in the door for their first race. Both are ambitious and have made no secret of those ambitions. Of course they have a few things not in common. Fulop was the young upstart while Barton had family ties that helped him out. Fulop had almost no political experience when he first ran for office, while Barton had worked for his state's governor. But both are or were single when they first entered public office.

Barton is an associate with a large law firm based in Portland where he works outside of his stint in the legislature. Unlike Fulop, who has almost weekly meetings of the council and community meetings, Barton dedicates several months at the beginning of the year non stop to the legislature in Salem, followed by other work in his Clackamas County district the rest of the year. Outside of his time-consuming work as a lawyer and his work as a legislator, Barton is active in other political work that will likely one day help his political career. He recently announced a bid for a state senate seat in 2010, adding more to his workload.

Barton notes that being single and childless has been a blessing for his political and legal careers, given the sheer amount of time he has to dedicate to work on a daily basis. "I don't have kids and that's the only reason I can do this," he said. At the same time, Barton notes that his hectic schedule balancing both a legal career and a political career has a downside. A downside, which interestingly enough, helps fuel the amount of time he puts into the dueling careers. "I'm probably single because I work so hard," Barton said.

Not every dating issue facing a young elected official has to do with the amount of time he or she is putting into politics or the fact that they want to make sure there are no issues in their personal life that could explode one day in the press.

Anthony Sytko, the councilman in Garwood, New Jersey, has two dilemmas that are a bit different from anyone else. Sytko is not shy about his political ambition. In fact he knows what office he wants, he wants to be the Garden State's governor. Not only does he want to be governor he believes he is destined to be the governor. In fact at times it can be deciphered that his entire life is designed around a future campaign for the governor's mansion. He doesn't deny it. "Every decision I have made since I was 18 was about knowing the future," he said. "Would it come back to bite me?"

Sytko made the decision to become governor while a high school student in the late 1990s and he's continued to focus on this goal. While some elected officials are cautious in their public behavior or remain coy about exactly what they are doing and the intent of their actions, Sytko is anything but coy. In fact, knowing the age of digital cameras and social networking sites like Facebook, he keeps the issue out there at all times when he goes out in public, even if it's to enjoy a casual dinner with friends. "I am very cautious of my public image," he said. "I don't do anything that can be portrayed negatively."

Sytko's desire to be New Jersey's governor and belief that he is destined to one day occupy the state's highest office, does more than have him worried about a photo of him enjoying himself in a bar ending up on Facebook. It is also impacting his dating life. While Fulop and Barton are talking about not having as much time to date because of their busy schedules and Swift said it was harder to find a man who was willing to date and then marry a woman in the state senate who would one day become her state's governor. Sytko has a situation which is likely unique among young elected officials nationwide. "The biggest thing that I would say being young has an impact on is dating," Sytko said. "It is a combination of past politics and future politics. My wife will be the First Lady of New Jersey and I have to find a woman who can carry that mantle. I need to find a woman who can stand that I will be a public figure." Sytko said he views that his wife will be a first lady who is more in the mold of a Laura Bush, helping him in particular with the public aspect of his career. He said he keeps this in mind at all times. "I can usually tell right away," he said.

Wyoming's Zwonitzer can sympathize with Sytko. While the two have never met and have never been in each other's home towns, and Zwonitzer has not announced plans to one day be the governor of Wyoming, he shares a thought process. He notes that the women he dates he thinks about differently because of the responsibilities of his office. "I am more selective in who I date," he said. "I take them to receptions a lot."

While Barton, Fulop, and Sytko are busy dating and looking for a wife, regardless of what future title the woman could hold, state representative Don Calloway has a piece of advice that he wants to pass on to all of them and all other hopeful young elected officials dotting the American landscape from Portland, Maine, to Portland, Oregon. "Anyone thinking of running for office should know it is a huge strain on the marriage," he said.

While young elected officials like Fulop, Barton, and Swift said holding office had a negative impact on dating, and in Sytko's case holding office and aiming to be governor dominates every decision in his life, at least one young elected official said being in office actually helped his dating life. Josh Svaty represented rural Kansas in the state legislature. His district was small towns and farms. He represented the Kansas rural stereotype of wheat fields and the agriculture industry: the type of locale that residents of both coasts dismiss as flyover country. Svaty said he believes being in office helped him out from a romantic perspective. Svaty resigned from the legislature in mid-2009 to join the cabinet of Governor Mark Parkinson, as secretary of agriculture, noted that his hometown is a farming community. It is small. There is more wheat than people. It is the long beige rural strip that many on the coasts see of the state when they are flying between both sides of the country. Growing up in rural

Kansas he returned to his home but suddenly found himself in a less than ideal situation for a twentysomething bachelor. "It's difficult," Svaty said of single life in rural America. "One of the problems of moving to rural Kansas is that if you are single, you don't have a chance to meet people." While noting that he did not run for the state House of Representatives in order to help his dating life, he said it was a perk. Suddenly he wasn't spending all of his time in a rural part of the state. Svaty was now in Topeka on a regular basis. "I met my wife in Topeka," he said, noting that his wife worked for state government when they met. "It is different to spend four months away from the farm."

For those who are in serious relationships where they are not married there is still a strain in the relationship from the long time spent away from home and conducting political duties. Democrat Mac Schneider was elected to the North Dakota Senate in 2008 at the age of 29. In a serious relationship with his girlfriend in Grand Forks, he has moved with her from North Dakota to Washington, DC, where he attended law school and back again to allow him to practice law in their native state. Like many couples they have different schedules and at times they see conflicts in the time they can devote to themselves. During his first legislative session in 2009 he would find himself spending most of the week on the Senate floor in Bismarck and then coming back to Grand Forks on the weekends. Coming back to Grand Forks, his girlfriend would be gone. She's a track coach and would be out with the team for a Saturday meet, thus not coming home till late Saturday. Because of this, the couple would frequently only spend a day together during the entire legislative session. While their time together was limited while he was attending to his Senate duties in Bismarck, Schneider says he remains committed to the relationship and in moving it to the next level. "I am going to seal the deal one day," Schneider said in an interview in early 2009. "My mom will kill me if I don't do it soon." Schneider did seal the deal about a year after this interview. In February 2010, he and his longtime girlfriend, Crystal Cummis, became engaged, with a wedding planned for later the same year.

One thing that impacts young elected officials who end up in full-time elective offices — and even those in part-time offices — is that they are sacrificing the amount of money they pull in on an annual basis. Many are lawyers, working in jobs where they can pull in a six-figure salary, something many elected officials cannot bring in, especially at the state and local level. Other positions are equally more financially lucrative than government service and it becomes an issue. For those who serve in part-time office, the financial issues of balancing politics with a full-time career weigh heavily. Time spent attending to government meetings and political events is time that cannot be invested in their law firm or other business. Many companies will not tolerate this on a long-term basis, in particular law firms that view the time away as lost billable hours. Many young elected officials suddenly see their legal careers changing while they are in office. While the time in elective office provides free advertising and the chance to meet new people and potentially bring in clients, it can also have a drawback. The time away will be counted in when partnerships are awarded and other promotion decisions are made.

For Mike Gerber, a state representative in the Philadelphia suburbs, he made the sacrifice. Pennsylvania's state legislature can be a full-time job. With a generous salary and full staffs and offices in his Montgomery County district and in Harrisburg, Gerber has every incentive to be a full-time legislator. He isn't though. He maintains a part-time law practice with a firm in addition to his work in Harrisburg. A rising star in Pennsylvania politics whose name has been mentioned as a potential congressional or statewide candidate, he is, though, spending less time on law. With his Montgomery County — and fellow young elected — colleague Josh Shapiro, Gerber is helping the campaign committee for House Democrats, working to recruit, finance and elect Democratic state legislators across the commonwealth. Not a lot of time to devote to the practice of law.

But Gerber has found an upside. While the lifestyle of politics is time consuming it does not compare with his time in a large Philadelphia law firm. "It has a positive and negative impact," Gerber said. "From a positive impact I am happier which makes me a better Dad and husband. At a big law firm you are pressed with hours and to build a business." While Gerber says he is happier and his mental state is better by being a full-time legislator, there is a downside. "My income is half of what it would be if I was a full-time lawyer," he said.

Gerber notes that he sets aside time for his family on a regular basis and he protects it, not wanting other obligations to take away that time from him. With young children he said he knows the value of spending time with his kids and wants to make sure that his kids know who their father is. He wanted to make sure that people knew that he does not believe his career choices are impacting his kids or his family in a negative aspect. "I would not be doing it if I thought it as a detriment to my family," he said.

The concept of impact on a professional career has been approached by others as actually having an impact, particularly in the area of lawyers who are young elected officials. State senator Marc Keahey of Alabama said that his service as a part-time senator in Montgomery has taken a lot of time away from home and away from his family but it has also been a plus. A lawyer in private practice, Keahey said his service in the Senate has allowed him to meet a lot of people he normally would not have met otherwise and has allowed them to come to his legal practice. In addition, Keahey notes that he lives two hours from Montgomery, which allows him to divide himself between both worlds a lot easier than some legislators in other areas.

Gerber's Montgomery County colleague Shapiro agrees with him that his career is tough on his family life. With three young kids, there are nights where he gets home after his children are long asleep, after barely seeing them before he leaves for work in the morning. "That weighs on me," Shapiro said.

Calloway of Missouri was 29 when he was elected to his state's House of

Representatives in 2008 while having a newborn son. While his wife was dealing with middle of the night feedings and diapers and constantly changing clothes sizes, Calloway found himself in Jefferson City four days of the week in the first months of 2009, dealing with the state budget, working with a new governor, setting long-term policy, being a Democrat righting what he felt are the wrongs that former governor Matt Blunt set on the state. Calloway praises his wife for giving him the ability to serve in the state legislature and being able to handle the fact that he's in the capital for four days out of the week and not by her side being a father. He said he spends more time sacrificing moments with his son that he cannot get back. "My wife is a saint," he said. "It is a sacrifice that cannot be understated. It is heartbreaking to leave your child for four days a week. It is stressful on the marriage."

But at the same time, Calloway knows that he is being able to do things that others cannot do. He finds that while there is a sacrifice he is making and a strain on his marriage, he is also seeing things, meeting people and going to events that he would never have a chance to if he was not a member of the state House of Representatives. "I am somehow convinced that things in the future for my family are good," he said. "It gives you access to things in the community that you don't have otherwise.

Republican Brett Davis, a state assemblyman in Wisconsin, notes that the chance to be his own boss, a chance that the assembly affords, allows him some control on his schedule. While he cannot control the assembly calendar and he has little control over the various community events and political meetings he needs to attend in his district, he still has found time to focus on his children. "With a young family it can be a challenge," Davis said. "The nice thing about the job is there is flexibility. I can take time in the morning to spend with my son."

Davis is not alone in using the control over scheduling in helping to balance the demands of his job as an elected official with the demands of his personal life. Don Ness is the mayor of Duluth, Minnesota. First elected to the mayor's office in 2007 at the age of 33, Ness entered city government in 1999 when the 25-year-old was elected to the city council. As a mayor, Ness finds himself in demand to attend many events around the city, with people looking to him to discuss issues, meet new people and welcome businesses. The unique form of American government, where the duties of a head of state and the head of government are mixed in the executives at all levels of government come to play here. Ness has to handle the mix of ceremonial duties, which the public loves and demands more politicians attend to, with the governmental duties of running to the day to day affairs of city government, creating policy and handling the long term planning of the city.

Ness finds himself having to balance the ceremonial aspect of his job in order to balance the job with his personal life. The father of two young children, Ness finds himself with the constant tug of many working parents with demanding careers. He wants to spend more time with his children but also needs to spend more time with his constituents, who hold the fate of his career in their hands. Not going to an event in a certain neighborhood could hurt him; a neighborhood group will remember and possibly take it out on him come the next election. Skipping too many community events could seriously endanger Ness' political future, no matter how competent he performs the public administration duties of his job. It is something that has hurt many a politician, becoming labeled with the tag of being out of touch — something Ness wants to avoid while being a good dad. "I've made it a priority to find a balance,' Ness said of balancing the needs of his career with the needs of his family. I will be a much more effective mayor if I have that balance and have time to spend with my family and to refresh myself. To take on these massive challenges I have made it clear that I am not going to show up at every cocktail party and ribbon cutting because of the importance I place on that balance."

Ness said he talks to the community groups and business leaders about what he is trying to do. He explains that the reason he is not cutting at the ribbon ceremony opening a new business is because he wants to spend time with his family. That he will be going to a school event for his kids in place of attending a cocktail party benefitting a local charity. Ness said he has remained up-front with many people in the city so they know he is not trying to escape the duties of his office but is rather trying to balance them with his duties at home. He said that as he explains the need for this balance and his desire to spend time with his children he has won support in the community and understanding that he cannot be at every event.

Calloway's comments may have been said in 2009 when he was starting his career in elective office, but they are echoed by those who have been in elective office for years and have grown from the days that they were young elected officials. U.S. senator Bob Menendez of New Jersey has been in politics for over 30 years. Thinking back to the 1980s when he had two young children and a mix of political and legal jobs, he remembers the time commitment. At the time he was the mayor of Union City, a small community in northern Hudson County, just across the Hudson River from Manhattan, and a member of the state legislature.

Menendez' years in public life until his 1992 election to Congress, had a serious impact on his life. Even though he was both a mayor and a state senator, both jobs are officially part-time and paid at part-time salaries. He earned less than $10,000 as mayor and around $35,000 a year as a state legislator. With a wife and two small children, his political career was not bringing in enough money to cover his expenses. He had to work as an attorney full-time as well, in order to pay his bills. In addition to the time demands that holding three jobs put on him, the unusual hours he received phone calls as mayor changed his life. "I would get calls during the night at 3 a.m that the heat was out in a building," he said of constituents who wanted to talk to their mayor about whatever issue was happening at that moment. In addition the time demands meant that, while he tried to make every game or an event for his children, some public demands took precedence over family life. "You miss out on the little things along the way."

Calloway's thoughts in this regard are shared by Ben Vig, a young member of the North Dakota House of Representatives. He shares much in common with Svaty, in that they are both farmers and they both represent largely rural districts. Vig's district would be a shock to many urban politicians from New York or Los Angeles. While they can walk from one end of the district to the other in an hour or less, at the end of an hour in the car, Vig has barely made a dent in the large land mass of North Dakota that he represents.

He noted that serving in Bismarck, where he was first sent in 2006, has been a boon to his social life and professional life. Much like Svaty, he notes that has been able to make new friends and new contacts by heading to Bismarck for the session. Like Kander he is traveling on legislative business in the off season and headed around the state. For a young politician who has his eye on a statewide office one day — unlike Sytko he hasn't announced for North Dakota's governorship preferring a potential race for agriculture commissioner or state public service commission in the future — he is building a network, which can only pay off for a higher office down the line. "When I come to Bismarck I get to network with people from around the state," he said.

At the same time, he noted that his social life benefits from the fact that his rural district encompasses many communities and many of his friends in the legislature hail from around the state. One of his closest friends in the House is state representative Corey Mock, who lives in Grand Forks and grew up in Minot, a community in the state's extreme north where winter temperatures tend to run around negative 30 or more. "I have a lot of classmates who go to Fargo and Grand Forks for entertainment," Vig said, naming the state's largest city and main college town respectively. "Having campaigned I have seen a lot of neat places in North Dakota that are overlooked."

Being in elective office is also changing the family planning process for young elected officials. While Sytko is busy looking for a wife who could be his state's first lady and Barton is trying to find time to date, state representative Jason Kander of Missouri is married, has no children, and no announced plans to run for governor one day.

Kander's wife, Diana, knows politics. When he entered the political world, he did it with his wife. The duo started the group Heartland Democrats to help bring a new generation into politics in the Midwest. At the same time, Diana Kander knows how to cope with change and a certain amount of uncertainty in her marriage and personal life. Kander is a member of the Army Reserves, where he is gone from the home a couple of days a month on army duty. He's been deployed to Iraq for months, fighting a war and leaving his wife behind to tend to the home fires. Jason Kander's time at the beginning of 2009 in Jefferson City tending to the legislative session and then combining legislative duties with his law practice and army responsibilities is almost normal. At least she doesn't have to worry about her husband being shot at. "I am not in danger and I will come home from Jefferson City," he said.

Kander proves there is no such thing as a part-time state legislature. Yes, he spends only a few months at the beginning of the year in Jefferson City full-time during the session, getting home to Diana and their dogs in Kansas City on weekends. But during the off-season — if there is anything like an off-season in politics — he is busy meeting with community groups, conducting research into policy, drafting legislation, attending meetings, and traveling to Jefferson City. He's also preparing for his 2010 releection campaign and the 2010 legislative session. all the while being a lawyer and doing army stuff. It is not uncommon for him to play legislator and lawyer on the same day.

But at the same time, being a young elected official and a state legislator, while almost normal from his time in Iraq, is still changing his personal life. "It's not easy," Kander said of his life. "I miss my wife, she's in Kansas City, she makes it to Jefferson City a few days and it factors into our planning on when to have a family. That keeps changing." The impact of having a family weighs on single young elected officials. Many said they do not know how they would be able to do their jobs if they had children and the home responsibilities where they would be losing time from their children based on the amount of time they had to dedicate to their political careers. "With as much as the legislature pays, I could not do this with a kid," said Oregon's Barton.

Jeff Anderson is a city councilman in Duluth, Minnesota, a part-time position he combines with working in advertising for a radio station in northeastern Minnesota. He estimates that he spends 10–20 hours a week on city business, on top of the amount of time he invests in his full-time career. But while he gives that estimate he notes that is at the low end of the amount of time he can spend on city business each week. This includes council and committee meetings, meeting with community groups, attending events and reviewing reports and conducting research. He has found he has spent as much time on city business each week that he has spent on his professional career with the radio station on a given basis. Anderson agrees with Barton that his status being single helps him in his work as a city councilman. He also notes that his age gives him one unique advantage over other people in the political arena. "I feel that being a young guy who is single with a lot of time and energy to put into this helps," he said.

Andy Meisner was 29 when he was elected to the Michigan House of Representatives in 2002. By the time 2008 rolled around, Meisner had hit two things in his life. He moved to his second elective office as the treasurer of Oakland County and he was divorced. When someone ends up divorced in their mid 30s, they become a reflective person, someone who looks at what happened and why; someone who tries to figure out if anything could have been done to change things going forward or pinpoint an exact cause. While Meisner did not want to discuss the details of his divorce publicly he did make general comments about his time as a young elected official and the commute to

Lansing he made as a state representative. "It's fair to say that the lifestyle can be challenging for a family," he said. But at the same time, he started to look up and see the benefits of his move into county government. "I'm a pretty hard charging guy in any position I'm in, but I think this office will be better and taking out the three hours of daily driving time," Meisner said. "I am excited to be closer to home."

In some cases, the work of a young elected official leads to long separations and their lifestyle changing for several months. While Barton had to spend several months away from his law practice during the legislative session in Oregon, he could commute daily from Clackamas to Salem and back. In other states, legislators may spend two or three days a week away from home in the capital for a period of time. In North Dakota, they are gone from home every weekday for 90 days every two years, at a minimum.

For Corey Mock, who as a 23-year-old from Grand Forks was elected to his first four-year term in 2008, the time he spent in Bismarck for his first legislative session was a new change for him. Mock had no choice but to move to Bismarck for that period of time. North Dakota is too big for him to commute daily and the hours in the legislature too unpredictable. Plus the North Dakota winter, which occurs at the same time as the legislative session, makes it tough to drive halfway across the state on more than a weekly basis. But at the same time it is probably a plus that Mock and his colleagues are kept in Bismarck full-time during the week during their session.

With a citizen legislature — popular in many western states — and a tradition of keeping government to a minimum, North Dakota's representatives and senators only convene for 90 days every two years. Yes, there are study committees to review issues and prepare possible legislation in the interim periods. And there are occasional special sessions to tackle pressing issues or revenue related issues — uncommon for North Dakota even in the recession-wracked economy which has caused many states to teeter on the verge of bankruptcy in 2009. But, by and large, North Dakota legislators get the state's business done in that 90-day period. Time is vital then for the legislators and almost locking them in the capital city helps eliminate distractions and makes them focus on the business of the state.

Mock said this concept allows for two different things to develop. One is that he has made some close friends in the legislature, including several other younger legislators and several of the younger lobbyists, since he saw them all of the time during the 2009 legislative session. But at the same time he only sees the same people during his time in Bismarck. "You're social life while in Bismarck is the same with the same people everyday," Mock said. "You see them in the capital and when you go out at night. You are with the same legislators and the same lobbyists."

Consequently, when he went home on weekends to Grand Forks, meeting up with close friends and seeing his girlfriend, he wanted to try to disconnect as much as possible from the week in Bismarck. Spending his work and social life with the same people had led him to spend his weekdays focused almost exclusively on politics and state business. He could not escape the state legislature wherever he went. A political geographer by trade, who enjoys the minutia of legislative redistricting, he also has the issue of loving the political talk, which he found catching up with him at home in Grand Forks. "On weekends I have noticed I try to disconnect," he said. "I don't have the ability to disconnect from work for more than a few minutes."

Mock said his lifestyle in Bismarck also is different from any other life that his peers have. While it may be the same that someone in a Wall Street firm or a large law firm has while at work, the fact that his work and social life in the state capital combines together, he ends up finding himself with less time for typical pursuits for a 23-year-old. "I don't even go on Facebook that much," Mock said of his time in Bismarck. "My girlfriend acknowledges that we don't talk much during the session. I don't want to inundate her with politics."

It is interesting Mock made reference to Facebook and a modern method of communication as something he cannot do that much while he is in Bismarck. Other young elected officials made it a point to note that modern technology has made it easier for them to do their jobs in politics, their jobs in the private sector, and maintain some semblance of a personal life during the hectic moments of their lives. Like many young professionals from coast to coast, the modern methods of technology have continued to remain more and more important to keeping in touch and maintaining their lives.

Many, if not all, young elected officials remain glued to their BlackBerries at all times, including balancing Facebook and other social networking sites in addition to answering and sending e-mails. During an interview with New York assemblyman Jack Quinn III in June 2008, we were interrupted at one point with his BlackBerry going off, signaling new text messages. Checking the messages, Quinn was able to relay that his staff was informing him that Tim Russert had just passed away. This is not that unusual, as text messaging continues to be more and more of a method that young elected officials use to communicate with staff, colleagues, friends, and journalists in order to handle the work. As a journalist, I have seen cases where quick interviews can be conducted over text message, especially with younger politicians in place of a longer phone interview.

Alabama state representative Cam Ward who was first elected at the age of 31 in 2002, agrees with this assessment about modern technology and the young elected official. "The key is e-mail and technology," Ward said, comparing 2009 when the interview was conducted with the beginning of his legislative service. "Cell phones and BlackBerries have changed that. As long as you have a BlackBerry and a phone you can work anywhere in the world."

Modern technology helped Swift deal with her four hours of commuting time each day during her tenure as lieutenant governor and acting governor in Massachusetts. Driven by the state police, Swift was able to focus her attention on paperwork and making calls during her time in the car. She could send and respond to e-mails from the car and a fax machine was set up in the car for her to exchange documents with staffers in her Boston office while she traveled up and down the Massachusetts Turnpike. When Swift gave birth to twins in her first weeks as governor, modern technology allowed her to have a working maternity leave in her western Massachusetts home. She was able to exchange documents by e-mail, confer with staffers by phone, and in general perform the duties of her office, while she was located in her home on the other end of the state from Boston.

While Mock has found young colleagues to hang out with in Bismarck, the age factor is one personal life factor for Stephen Webber, a member of the Missouri House of Representatives. Elected in 2008, alongside Kander and Calloway and at the same time as Mock, Webber was 25 when voters decided to send him to Jefferson City. He notes that his time as a marine infantryman helped prepare him for a life in politics and spending four days a week for the first months of the year helping govern the State of Missouri. He said both lifestyles are nomadic, with a constantly changing schedules and no set way of life. In a way you can say that his background and life is like many young people in demanding jobs, be it state legislator, big law firm associate, medical resident, or editor of an online daily newspaper — the unusual is his norm.

But at the same time he noted that his lifestyle in Jefferson City is different from the work environments of many people his age. Those in Wall Street firms and in large law firms have jobs that are hectic and time consuming. Young investment bankers working on deal books and young law associates putting together briefs could find themselves practically living in their offices, a lot like state legislators working in Jefferson City during the session. But at the same time those on Wall Street and in law firms are mainly working alongside their peers. Many of the people working with them came in with them, are their age or within a few years, and while they work with those who are older, there are many of those who are around their age. For Webber it is a lot different.

While Webber has young colleagues in Jefferson City — Kander and Calloway are both in their 20s — he also finds himself in a new environment, different from his marine days. "The biggest thing on my personal life is that I am hanging out with people who are older," Webber said. "It's kind of strange. I don't think you grow up faster but it's a natural transition."

Webber notes he is happy that he is single and does not have children, for he spends a lot of time with Calloway and can attest to the issues that Calloway talked about. "I've seen how hard it is for Don Calloway who has a young baby and that's tough," Webber said. "I feel fortunate that I am not missing that. It's a lifestyle and you do give your heart and soul to it. You don't always hang out with friends but go to evening meetings."

It's interesting to hear many of the young elected officials debate the merits of whether or not having young children and being married impacts their time and ability to serve. In October of 2009, the issue of children and marriage came up in the race for a seat on the Town Council in Westfield, New Jersey.

The race for the council's fourth ward seat was the most competitive in town. A 41-year-old Democratic incumbent, Tom Bigosinski, was running against a 31-year-old Republican challenger, Keith Loughlin. Bigosinski is married and has two young sons, while Loughlin is unmarried; not an issue that was on anyone's radar screen until two weeks before the election.

Then during the one and only debate in the race — more of a forum than a debate — the issue of marriage and children became a campaign issue. Not over the time commitment or if Loughlin had more time than Bigosinski. It came up in the last minutes of the debate, during Bigosinski's closing statement, which I captured on video in my capacity as editor of *Westfield Patch.* "There are profound differences between the two of us," Bigosinski said during the closing statement. "Unlike Keith, I'm a husband, I'm a father, I'm a home owner and I'm a taxpayer and I have been for many years."

Bigosinski's comment became a story, the sort of news cycle that professional political operatives have heart attacks even thinking about. Being a local race, Bigosinski was spared being surrounded by a campaign staff that was being rushed to the local emergency room in the minutes after his closing statement. But for better or worse he made the statement, set a new debate, and caused at least some of the voters I talked to to vote for Loughlin in the election. Neither Bigosinksi nor Loughlin said they felt the issue had anything to do with age. Rather, Bigosinski said he was trying to show how he related to the residents of his ward. Loughlin hit back by bringing up being a lifelong resident of the town and his commitment to staying in Westfield. At the end of the day, Loughlin unseated Bigosinski.

Young elected officials will continue to change their personal lives to meet the demands of elective office. They will take time away from their jobs and their families and their love lives in order to serve in office. In some cases they are doing this because of a love of public service and in other cases they are doing it in order to put themselves in place for a race for higher office. In some cases they will not continue just making changes to their lives because of a fear of how a drink in public or a date or some kind of night of fun one weekend could end up on Facebook or on some sort of blog that day or one day in the future. The changed media environment has caused many to change their personal lives for this reason. It is almost a pattern of fear of what they can and cannot do. While President Kennedy did not have to worry about the press reporting on his parade of mistresses and President Roosevelt being in a wheelchair was kept from the public, the post Watergate media mindset has changed how politicians are reported. In addition, citizen journalists with blogs and those on message boards have changed the mindset of politicians. One blogger posts a photo and an entire media cycle can change.

In addition, the craziness of the world of politics just causes many changes to the lifestyles of young elected officials. From Fulop's many first dates to Kander's changing conception timeline to Mock's lack of Facebook use while in Bismarck to Calloway's guilt over leaving his newborn son behind while he is legislating in Jefferson City, many young elected officials will continue to make changes to their lifestyles and accommodate the life. These sacrifices will continue to shape the American political landscape and will shape the way young elected officials govern. Politicians like Calloway who have guilt about leaving their children will continue to exist. Those like Fulop or Barton who are trying to date will continue to exist. Those like Kander who are changing plans on when to have children will continue to exist and it will shape the landscape.

Swift did not change her career plans because being a state senator impacted her social life. She did marry and ended up giving birth to their first child just as she was elected Massachusetts' lieutenant governor and then gave birth to twins just weeks after becoming the commonwealth's acting governor. Swift holds a place in history as the first chief executive of a state government to give birth, beating Sarah Palin by seven years. But Swift could be an anomaly; many could end up changing their career plans because of the personal sacrifices that being a young elected officials asks of them. Many will look at what they are sacrificing and say that it is not worth it and decide that they want to have a more normal life and not the lifestyle. They want more personal time, more time to dedicate to a professional career or more of a balance in their life.

Seeing many of these young elected officials leave politics could have an impact on the future of the country and the political system. The many attributes — both positive and negative — that they bring to the discussion will be lost. The diversity they bring to the table will be lost. Politics and government will become the domain of those who have already raised their families, those who have already pursued careers and those who are farther from the education system. Fulop commented about how he had once thought of waiting until after he was married, established in his business career, and had children to pursue government service — a common theme of many on Wall Street. But if he had done this, many of the government reforms he pursued in Jersey City would not have been pushed and it is unknown if these are issues he would have pursued if elected to office at the age of 48 instead of 28.

The changes and impact of this would be great on the country and on many levels of government. It will have dramatic changes and cause issues. Work/life balance is not a new debate: it's been around for years. Companies have been making changes by allowing more work-from-home days, company gyms, day care, etc., in order to say that they appreciate their employees' personal lives. Politics unfortunately cannot be that way all the time. Many young elected officials can be like Svaty and meet their spouse in the state capital while others can be former congresswoman Susan Molinari and be able to bring their baby to work. But others will be like Gerber and Calloway and have guilt over not seeing their children, or like Mock where he has to balance being away from his normal life for days on end. Work/life balance is hard in politics, very hard. Especially for young elected officials who are looking to stay in office or move up the ladder.

While this continues, many will continue to reevaluate why they want to stay in office. While one of the biggest clichés in politics is the term "to spend more time with my family" when a politician leaves elective office, in the case of many young elected officials, especially those in part-time posts where they are balancing a second, full-time job, it is more of the truth than a comfortable line that can mask anything from a pending indictment to some sort of scandal to poll numbers so low that a loss is the most likely result of the next election. But in terms of young elected officials this will remain one of the more truthful reasons why they choose to leave office early.

Many young professionals in the twenty-first century talk about the need for work/life balance in any number of careers. While many are committed to being ambitious and spending the time needed to be ambitious in their careers, they also want to be involved with their families and pursue personal hobbies and other interests outside of work. Many companies these days talk about work/life balance in terms of what they offer to new employees and how they want to recruit people to their companies. In some cases, discussions of corporate work/life balance it is a smoke screen, where they discuss the work in order to help recruit top talent but the reality is a lot different. But in many cases it is the case where the professionals can have time to come and go as needed, indulge in personal interests and even work from home when needed, a perk that is popular with many with young children.

But young elected officials do not have this option on many occasions. Those in an executive post can do this, because the job is very much like any other professional job in an office. They can also control their own schedules and, like Ness, decide which events they are going to versus which events they are not going to. There is a lot of control that they can show on their work and how they approach the job.

For a legislator it is tougher, given the fact that legislatures meet in large groups and that quorums are needed on the floor and in committee rooms. Yes, a legislator can control their schedule in terms of which events they go to and which private meetings they take, there is less control given the need to be at the capitol for a meeting at a time set by others. In terms of those in part time legislatures there is a need for the time frame to be changed. The legislative session is condensed over a few months when total focus on the work of the government in the state capitol is needed. Time away from home will be a must for this period and the time in the capital will be intensely focused on the work of the government, where there will be little time for personal enjoyment or any private work. This makes it tougher to pursue other interests, either personal or professional.

This is where young elected officials have it different from other young professionals, excluding those in companies that have a strong policy on the amount of time they need to spend in their offices and the types of meetings they need to go to. The work of these meetings and demands on the time of those serving as young elected officials will continue and will send many to decide to spend their time outside of politics. They will continue to say that maybe it is time to move out of politics and decide to look for a new career path because of the demands on their time and the desire to refocus their time or their career.

At the end of the day, many young elected officials said that it is a choice for them to do this and make the change in their personal life that is needed for them to run for office and be in elective office. Andrew Romanoff, the late 30s former Speaker of the Colorado House of Representatives who announced in 2009 to challenge appointed U.S. senator Michael Bennet in the Democratic primary for the Senate seat, summed it up the best. Romanoff is a single policy wonk who pursued a law degree while serving in the House of Representatives at the same time. He has noted in many interviews in the Colorado press the amount of time he has put into his career and the impact on his personal life. "I have dedicated a lot of time to (my career)," he said before he announced his Senate candidacy. "I like this field and I enjoyed my job as a legislator. I had to take time from a personal life. That was a choice I made for better or worse."

Note

1   A Massachusetts tradition is that the outgoing governor walks down the steps of the Statehouse on the last day of office. Swift departed with tradition by inviting her husband and children to join her for the walk.

CHAPTER 8

Oregon's History of Young Elected Officials

Oregon has always been considered one of the most progressive states in the country. Home to voters who value progressive causes and who have been at the forefront of the environmental movement, the Beaver State is a state which is expected to think outside the box when it comes to politics. The political thinking of Oregon has allowed issues that would be unthinkable in the Midwest or the Deep South to see the light of day. Bicycling is a major issue, not as a recreational activity but as a part of the alternative transportation movement. Portland is a city dedicated to well-laid-out bike trails along with a light rail system to reduce dependency on car transportation. Going into other parts of the country it would be almost unheard of to try to promote alternative transportation, but Oregon's progressive history has always been a driving force behind these issues.

Oregon is the first state with mail-in voting as the sole way to conduct elections. The state's reputation for clean and fair politics has allowed this method to be utilized as the sole voting system; states such as New Jersey or Illinois, where political corruption is practically a branch of government, would never allow a total switch to mail-in voting because of the risk of tampered elections.

Based on this, it is not surprising that Oregon is a hotbed for young elected officials. In fact, it is a tradition that has gone on for a number of years, and in many cases organized movements helped bring the next generation into the political process. In the early 1970s, in the days following the Vietnam War protests and the optimism spurned by the presidential campaigns of Senators Robert Kennedy, Eugene McCarthy, and George McGovern, a group of young liberals in the Portland area started working together to discuss issues, work on campaigns, and get themselves elected. The group would grow into the Democracy Forum, dedicated to making decisions based on policies which would help the public good, not on what would help move the power elite forward.

Several of the group's members would start in elective office, serving as city council members and state legislators, becoming the next generation of

Oregon leaders. Barbara Roberts became the state's first female governor, Vera Katz the first female House Speaker and Portland mayor, and Earl Blumenauer a leading member of Congress. Of the three, only Blumenauer remains active in elective office today, but the impact of the Democracy Forum continues to be seen today. "They helped transform the political landscape of Oregon," said state representative Jefferson Smith, D-Portland.

Blumenauer notes that the Democracy Forum saw extraordinary success pretty quickly, as the culture of change that swept the country in the late 1960s and 1970s continued to move more people into elective office. "In four years we had a member of the Portland City Council, a county commissioner, and five legislators," he said. Placing a young elected official on the Portland City Council at the time was not just putting a young person in a legislative body making policy decisions for a major city in the Pacific Northwest. Portland has a city commission form of government, with each member of the city council being given responsibility for a portfolio of agencies in city government. Suddenly a young elected official was making day-to-day decisions impacting the daily lives of Portlanders. In the twenty-first century a new movement has started and allowed more Oregon youth to get involved in politics, and in some cases run for office. In fact it could be said that one non-profit civic engagement organization is the driving force behind the next generation of Oregon leaders and will provide the basis for a legacy that could drive the Beaver State for the next 30 years.

Jefferson Smith was born and raised in Oregon. His father had been a part of the Democracy Forum in the 1970s and he had witnessed firsthand the way a group of active young professionals could chance a political culture. Growing up, Smith, who had been born in 1975, had the principles of public service instilled in him by teachers and graduating from Harvard Law School in the mid 1990s, he settled into a judicial clerkship, a position which barred him from political activity. During this time he saw the Republican controlled Congress doing things that he felt went against the grain of what he had been exposed to growing up in Oregon, including repealing the estate tax. He followed his clerkship with a year in a white-shoe Manhattan law firm.

Coming back to Oregon, he started talking to a friend whose father had also been involved in the Democracy Forum, about how to get more young people engaged in Oregon's public life. The conversation started to center on recreating the Democracy Forum and trying to use a new group to help jump-start young professional involvement in politics.

Smith started seeing his work centered on one main theme, that of a lack of civic engagement. He saw his generation backing away from getting involved in civic life and public service and more focusing on making money and not making a difference. He noted how in the 1960s many Rhodes Scholars went into public service related careers, but in the twenty-first century many were going to work for large consulting firms with the promise of six figure starting salaries. He believed the lack of highly educated individuals ending up in public service was doing a disservice to both Oregon and the nation. Out of this belief, the Oregon Bus Project was born. "We got a bunch of folks together and said our generation is disengaged and our politics are not focused on the biggest challenges," Smith said. "We had to do something." The Oregon Bus Project centered on a basic premise. The group bought a bus and used it to transport young professionals around the state to assist in state legislative races. The group would assist candidates with knocking on doors and helping get the message out. Hitting 70,000 homes with 100 volunteers in the first year, Smith assumed the Bus Project would be a short-lived initiative. "We thought it would be a short thing and it ended up swallowing my life," he said.

The Bus Project continued working in each state legislative year to help candidates statewide. By 2004, the group had worked in ten races, helping nine successful candidates, a record that would be repeated in 2006. Many of the people who had gotten involved in the Bus Project had started to run for office themselves or find other ways to get involved in politics. Smith had started to see that he had recreated the Democracy Forum and was looking to transform another generation of Oregon politics. The Bus Project had also grown past the bus, including a variety of political boot camps for young professionals who were interested in working on campaigns and in grassroots public life. The groups started to expand to bring in college students to help and inspiring more people to get involved in public life. Smith was seeing himself presiding over a growing civic engagement organization, which had counterparts starting up in more states.

While Smith used the Democracy Forum as a template for setting up the Bus Project there are differences. Blumenauer is quick to praise Smith's work in setting up the Bus Project but notes that Smith has focused his organization primarily on campaigning and canvassing in order to get candidates elected. The Democracy Forum was focused more on policy and governance issues in its heyday than the Bus Project has been. The Democracy Forum was the incubator of ideas and then hoped to translate them into policy. The Bus Project is the incubator of candidates hoping they will be in a position to create the ideas. "We tapped into the progressive institutions in Oregon," Blumenauer said of the Democracy Forum. "It was less oriented to campaigning than the Bus Project. It ended up being successful in getting our people into office though."

By 2008, Smith had decided to bite the bullet himself and joined the growing crop of Bus Project veterans running for office. After declining offers to run, many of which were natural given his involvement in the Bus Project, Smith decided it was time, at the age of 35, to put his money where his mouth was and seek to represent a Portland-based district in the state House of Representatives. His name had first come up for speculation in the political world in 2005, when some thought he'd seek the governorship the following year, a rumor Smith continues to dismiss as "ridiculous." Smith jumped into the race, believing it was a good time to seek office. The incumbent state representative, House Speaker Jeff Merkley, was running for the U.S. Senate and the Bus Project was in a good position for him to take on another project. He expected to jump into a competitive election for a place in the state's citizen legislature. In a move that had not occurred in over three decades, Smith found himself unopposed for the seat.

Jefferson Smith is not the only Bus Project veteran in the Oregon Legislature, nor is he the only young elected official serving in the legislature. Oregon has seen a growth of young state legislators, helping to transform the state's public life and political culture. While not every young legislator is a Bus Project veteran or was helped by the organization, the group's presence in Oregon public life has helped voters understand the importance of electing younger candidates and helped younger candidates overcome the stigma with some voters of electing a younger person. In addition, more young professionals in Oregon are starting to see public service as a career option, instead of settling into the business world only. "It has a significant impact," state representative Brent Barton, D-Clackamas, said of the growth of young elected officials in the state. "I see it often but I don't know if others do."

Barton is, in many ways, the target individual Smith is trying to get to run for office in Oregon. An alum of Stanford University and Harvard Law School, Barton returned to Oregon to practice law and got involved in the Bus Project. He first made the decision to run for office in 2008, at the age of 28, challenging a Republican incumbent for a seat in the state House representing the Portland suburbs. He had to handle the fact that the district had not elected a Democrat in 25 years and the incumbent was not going to go quietly. While Barton used the Bus Project's resources to his advantage, along with his own energy and enthusiasm, he noted that his opponent fought back hard. The biggest issue he had to overcome was the fact that he looks younger than he is. "All of the attack mail showed a picture on a blog taken in 2004, where I look like I'm 15," he said.

Urban areas are centers of young professionals, be it the city center itself, home to Smith and fellow young elected officials like Ben Cannon and Jules Kopel-Bailey, and the suburbs, home to Barton. It is not surprising that many of the Oregon's current crop of young elected officials hail from Portland, the state's largest city and economic center. Portland also is one of the nation's most progressive cities, home to such ideas as light rails and alternative transportation programs. Ideas considered the norm in Portland are normally seen years later, if ever, in other areas of the country.

Barton is taking a leap as he enters his second year in the House; he has announced his candidacy for an open state senate seat in 2010. An attorney in the Portland office of a large law firm, Barton is sacrificing his House seat in the attempt to become a senator. But he is also positioning himself to move up the ladder of Oregon politics and one day put himself in a position to become a statewide officeholder or possibly a congressional candidate.

Interesting, during Blumenauer's time with the Democracy Forum, Portland was not the center of the young elected universe in Oregon. While Blumenauer started his career in the Oregon House of Representatives alongside other twentysomethings, only a percentage came from Portland. Others came from Medford, Salem, and Astoria. The group was mainly between 23 and 28, with Portland holding the plurality of the membership.

Blumenauer is not surprised about the rise of young elected officials in his state, either today or when he was a part of the Democracy Forum back in the 1970s. He said many things have come together to allow for the rise on both occasions. Some have been the culture of the times. The early 1970s was a time of change and a new generation came to power following the Vietnam War and the turmoil of the 1960s and today with President Obama encouraging a new generation to look at public service and the aftermath of September 11 and the Iraq War is causing more young professionals to look at careers in public service.

The national time culture played a huge role in the rise of Democracy Forum participants into elective office, just as it has today. Blumenauer came into politics following work as a college student on a campaign to lower the voting age to 18. Having briefly involved himself in political life in order to get a public policy issue change on one of the less glamorous issues, that of voting rights, but one that had captured the hearts and minds of many young people of his generation, he felt he could go into the arena of running for public office himself. The entire time captivated him and the voters, he said. "It was a time of high energy and there was a lot of activism that helped," Blumenauer said. "I was a local face of what we were seeing nationally."

Oregon is known as a liberal state and the time period when the Democracy Forum came to light was one of the most liberal periods of the time. While Republican Richard Nixon captured the presidency in 1968, the entire culture of the late 1960s and early 1970s continued to grow liberal policies, with Nixon even establishing the Environmental Protection Agency in the wake of Earth Day. The continued protests against the Vietnam War, the civil rights movement, the women's rights movement and continued campus activism, led to a generational clash nationally with Vice President Spiro Agnew claiming to speak on behalf of what he called the silent majority.

While this was the national climate at the time, Blumenauer said the Democracy Forum lived up to its name bringing together a lively exchange of ideas from across the political spectrum. Some were liberal like him, while others were very conservative, including several who won elective office at a young age in this time period. He said this summarizes the entire Oregon political environment. "It is a lively political tradition that is deeply enriching," Blumenauer said. "People who embrace it are likely to make a successful connection with voters." He noted that the young conservatives in the Democracy Forum who chose to run for office back in the 1970s were a part of the culture of the state's political system, while at the same time sticking to their core political philosophy. "They embraced the personal connection," Blumenauer said of the conservative young elected officials who were a part of the Democracy Forum.

In 2006, the voters of Oregon ended up sending five Democratic candidates under the age of 35 to the state House of Representatives. Meeting up in Salem in 2007 as they started their first legislative session together, the group consisting of Ben Cannon, Brian Clem, Chris Edwards, Sara Gelser, and Tobias Read, started meeting and decided to pool their energy and their age to help plan out ideas for the future of the Beaver State.

Ben Cannon is a humanities teacher in Portland and a Rhodes Scholar who has lived in Oregon since he was five years old. He chose to run for the state House in 2006 at the age of 30. Getting involved in the Bus Project after returning to Oregon from Oxford University in 2003, he began working for other candidates across the state and he was living in the legislative district he grew up in. He quickly found a growing interest in politics and an empty seat in the House in the 2006 election, but it was not something he had seriously thought of running for until others approached them. "I thought they were crazy," Cannon said of the initial overtures he got about running for the state House in 2006. "It was not on my mind to run at all. I thought it would be many years from now when my kids were grown."

Thinking more and more about the idea of running, Cannon grew to find himself liking the idea and asking, why not run for office? He entered the race and immediately launched a grassroots campaign, where he eschewed donations from corporations and political action committees. He limited himself to knocking on doors and talking to voters, even recruiting his students to help campaign for him. He brought a coffee can with him when he was knocking on doors to solicit small-dollar donations. Cannon also said no to hiring the state's permanent political infrastructure, instead hiring friends to run his campaign. He also took a more intellectual approach to his campaign literature, providing details to the voters when he sent literature out instead of filling the pieces with glossy photos of him in action. Cannon said that he wanted the voters to know he was serious about policy issues and trying to think outside the box in how he approached politics.

Getting to Salem, Cannon wanted to harness the same outside the box approach he used in his campaign and to use it in the legislature. Finding four other legislators who were members of his generation helped him out and helped him want to organize the group to do something. Meeting as a group, the five freshmen representatives found that they had many common thoughts and common goals. They wanted to accomplish many of the same things to help the state during their time in Salem. During this time, they talked a lot about different things they wanted to do and how they could channel their presence in the legislature into helping their generation. They wanted to do something for those young professionals in their late 20s and early 30s, but also for the next generation. They were using their youth to impact and change the political arena. These included discussions on issues like better funding for higher education, lowering the student loan debt and promoting renewable energy and the environment.

In their first legislative session in 2007, the group put together a five-point legislative agenda that they wanted to advance for the state. This included advocating for same day voter registration, laws for young families including allowing children with disabilities to stay at home with their families, and stronger domestic violence laws, economic development bills to extend a tax credit to small businesses and promote business development in the areas of renewable energy, sustainable development, and pharmaceutical development, promoting projects for sustainable growth in the state and creating more scholarships for students to seek higher education.

Following their first legislative session, the group of five wanted to continue their momentum and put together a plan for their second legislative session in 2009. One of the first things they did was to put together a tour of college campuses statewide to hear from the next generation of Oregonians about what they wanted from their state government going forward. Cannon said the group was focused on bringing this conversation together in order to allow more people to have their voices heard in state government.

The concept of touring campuses is not a new one nationally. There are many state legislators who hold occasional office hours on campuses in their districts and in North Dakota — the forty-second legislative district is almost entirely the University of North Dakota — where a legislator needs to attend keg parties more often than they attend soirees. At the same time that Cannon and his band of young Democrats were touring Oregon's college campuses, a trio of young Republican legislators in New York State, Jack Quinn III, Marc Molinaro, and Rob Walker, hit the road to tour state college campuses and have a conversation with young professionals statewide.

During their college tours, Cannon and his group heard a lot from the students about issues including the burden of student loans and the need for more state aid for public universities. The group also heard a lot about the economic problems plaguing the country in 2008, with students asking if there would be jobs for them when they graduated and what was being done to create more jobs. Students who were native Oregonians were asking the group if there was going to be a push for more jobs in the state or would they need to move out of the state after graduation, leaving behind their friends and family. Cannon said that the entire college tour continues to remain at the top of his mind as he moves forward in the House of Representatives. "It definitely reminds me how vitally important it is as we engage in significant budget cuts that we find ways to maintain the accessibility of our community colleges and higher education," Cannon said in an interview in early 2009.

Tobias Read was part of the Five Under 35 group and said the group's focus and conversations with Oregonians helped shape him and helped shape a group legislative strategy. He noted that part of what helps Oregon has been a successful group like this and be an incubator for young elected officials is the size of the state and the state government. He noted the legislature is small enough in order to get the relationships together to impact change and that the state government is a big enough entity to have a significant change on the system and the lives of the people of Oregon. Read noted that with almost a third of the residents of the Beaver State being under the age of 35, there is a need for him and his group and the other young elected officials, like Smith and Barton, who entered the House of Representatives in 2008. "A good legislature ought to reflect the people of the state," Read said.

Smith believes the growing group of young elected officials in Oregon has impacted the state's environmental agenda. Across the country young elected officials have made the environment a key issue. Looking long-term 40 to 50 years, when many will be settling into retirement as grandparents and great-grandparents; young elected officials note they want to work on environmental issues in order to protect the planet for themselves and future generations. Smith said that in Oregon they are also using the environmental movement to help grow the economy, making up the sponsors of a package of bills relating to green jobs. "There is a high correlation of the chief co-sponsors of the green jobs bills and the young legislators," Smith said. "This excites me since I see this as one of our biggest challenges."

Smith noted that the group of young elected officials who took office in 2007 and formed the quintet were able to see success on several pieces of legislation which would impact the younger population in Oregon. He cited a bill passed that allows early voter registration for 17-year-olds before they turn 18; he noted this bill was pushed by the Bus Project. "Some of the efforts around voter access is coming from the young elected officials," Smith said.

All of the current crop of young elected officials in Oregon see their presence and the existence of the Bus Project as impacting the people of Oregon. In Barton's case he does not think this group would be sitting in Salem if it were not for Smith's decision to create the Bus Project and the long work that many people put in encouraging people to get on the bus. "It has a significant impact," Barton said of the Bus Project. "I see it often but I don't know if others do."

He said that he and other young professionals who have a desire to run for office need the group to serve as an incubator. They can gain the skills that they need to run a campaign, meet activists who can help them, make contacts with those who can raise money for them and get ready for a run for office. Barton is talking about the creation of a network for up and coming young elected officials in Oregon similar to any other networking group for any other profession. The Bus Project is to politics what young lawyers groups are to bar associations and young accountants groups are to accounting societies.

Smith agrees with Barton's assessment that the Bus Project has had an impact on the future of Oregon's politics and government. He does remain more philosophical about it. "Did the Bus change Oregon or did Oregon make the Bus?" Smith asked. "In 2006 we had nine candidates 35 and younger and a few running against one another. We had five who won and two of those had been board members and four were volunteers. It is hard to divorce what is happening with young candidates in Oregon and what is happening at the Bus."

Barton notes that one of the reasons he chose to run for the legislature in 2008 was because several of his close friends had decided to run for House seats that year. All of them were friends he made during his involvement in the Bus Project. A lunch with a close friend, Jules Kopel-Bailey, who was seeking a House seat in another district helped swing him to be a candidate himself.

Talking in the beginning of 2009 just as he embarked on his career in Salem, Barton said he and his young colleagues were about to confront the state's budget crisis. He was not looking forward to this task, knowing that the declining revenues were going to force many tough decisions to be made. Speaking like a legislator who had won a close and tough election in a swing district, he notes that the decisions facing the legislature on the budget are not easy to make either from a personal perspective or a political perspective. "It makes me physically sick," Barton said. "These choices we are forced to make could be career limiting." Barton also notes that the debate on the budget could hurt the growing number of young elected officials now filling the hallowed halls of power in Salem; decisions that could impact them now or in the future, should they seek higher office and move on from governing the Beaver State. "There is a generation in Oregon of political talent about to have a bad record," Barton said in early 2009 of the impact the budget votes would have on him and his young colleagues.

Oregon is a state that is helped a lot by the culture of the state. It is one of the most progressive and open-minded in the country. It is a state in which community organizing is normal and groups form in order to bring like-minded individuals together. This has been seen in terms of the Democracy Forum and the Bus Project. Oregon is showing signs of having continuing evolution of the state including having more groups form down the line. The two groups formed thirty years apart but in similar times. The Democracy Project formed in the extraordinary time of change of Vietnam and the many struggles and changes of the 1960s. The Bus Project was born following many of the partisan battles that marked the 1990s in a time when change was coming to music and culture and when young professionals were seeing a transformation of the economy. This generation saw a president impeached for actions surrounding an extramarital affair and then the horrific events of September 11, 2001 and the start of wars in Afghanistan and Iraq. This generation found itself lied to about the need to go to war in Iraq because of what was said to be the existence of weapons of mass destruction in the country. With the similarities to the steady growth of the war in Vietnam by the Johnson administration, it is not surprising the two groups formed at the times that they did.

The groups filled voids that young professionals were seeking. A need to impact change. A need to take control over their own destiny and the shared destiny of a country. A time when people were looking to give back in some way. Some would act like Steve Fulop in Jersey City or Eric Garcetti in Los Angeles and join the military, but others wanted to give back and change the political system like Smith and Barton. Many will sit by the sidelines and help out candidates and get involved behind the scenes, not having a desire to run for office themselves. But others want to make that run for office. They want to be a part of the political equation and be a part of the political discussion. They want to have an impact on the future.

The real impact of the rise of young elected officials is being seen in Oregon both now and in the past. The current crop of young elected officials has organized themselves into a group that has put together a shared agenda, with ideas to help the young people of the state. The group is gaining more and more people who came up together politically in the Bus Project and supported each other in the election process and have pre-existing relationships that can help them move a shared agenda forward. Looking at the impact of the Democracy Forum, you are seeing a group that had a long-term impact on Oregon. Many of the people who first became involved in the group when it first started and then chose to run for office became the top political leaders in Oregon. Blumenauer continues to represent Portland in Congress, being one of the nation's leaders on the environment and on transportation alternatives. Vera Katz was the first woman to be speaker of the house in a state government in the nation. She later moved to be the first woman mayor of Portland. Not only did she break ground for woman nationwide, she also showed that her involvement in the Democracy Forum would have a long-lasting impact on the future of the state and the city of Portland.

The group of young elected officials now in power in Oregon has forged close ties through the Bus Project and it will likely have the same impact long term. Many of them will continue to have a role in the Beaver State's politics and government for decades to come. The bonds formed now will be seen in the future and the Bus Project and Five Under 35 will be networks for new young elected officials to come together. Barton said that the Bus Project helps bring young politicians together to overcome the hurdles that they face as young people in the political arena and helps them overcome them.

Oregon is a state that has been helped by its progressive political history by making it more receptive to young elected officials. And it is a state that has been and will likely continue to be shaped by its young elected officials. Blumenauer believes the culture of Oregon has led to the general acceptance of young elected officials in his state. The culture of an open state where new ideas are accepted and thinking outside the box policy wise is a way of life. "I will tell you I have been in politics almost 40 years and I have found that there generally is an interest in and acceptance of young people who are serious in service and have something to say and are interested in engaging people," he said. "Oregon in that period and it has continued to be about a lot of issues and we like to talk about them. It is a more open process; there is not a political machine that controls access to the nomination. Oregon has had a popular tradition dating back more than a century. Oregon gave the nation referendum and recall."

CHAPTER 9

"I need to prove that I was not elected by my frat buddies": North Dakota's Forty-second Legislative District

"I need to prove that I was not elected by my frat buddies," North Dakota state representative Corey Ray Mock said of one of his main focuses in state legislature.

Not exactly the statement you hear from many politicians. In fact it is pretty uncommon. It is a pretty safe assumption that Eric Garcetti on the Los Angeles City Council, Sean Duffy in the Ashland County, Wisconsin, district attorney's office, and Jack Quinn III in the New York State Assembly are not saying the same thing at any point. At the same time it can be said that Heather Hudson in the Greenville, Mississippi, mayor's office is not saying the same thing about a sorority. Actually it has more to do with Mock's district than any desire of a fraternity to flood one district with voters in order to elect one of their brothers to the House of Representatives. In fact, Mock's fraternity has no organized agenda in state government.

Mock represents an incredibly unique district, one that is formed because of North Dakota's small population and the fact that the state's urban communities like Grand Forks and Fargo allow for the small population needed for a legislative district to be concentrated in a small area. In Mock's case, his district is almost tailor-made to elect young people — maybe not Mock specifically, but someone like Mock. A young, clean-cut recent grad who was in a fraternity or sorority.

Mock, 23 when first elected in 2008, represents the University of North Dakota (UND) and that doesn't mean he represents the university along with other parts of the district as well. He literally represents the university along with student and faculty housing surrounding the university. While Garcetti is dealing with community groups in Los Angeles's Hancock Park neighborhood and Tom Kean in the New Jersey Senate is hanging out with the Westfield Neighborhood Council and Speak Up Summit when touring his district, Mock's prime community groups include fraternities, sororities, and hall councils.

Kean's snacking on crudités at a community event in the leafy bedroom community of Madison while Mock is likely to drop by a kegger or pizza night in the dorm to talk to his constituents. While Kean represents two residential colleges in his district, they are a small part of his constituency, while for Mock it is his constituency. It's a different type of district, one that is unique in the country where Mock is more the norm for a legislator rather than the exception.

North Dakota's legislature has multi-member districts consisting of one senator and two members of the state House of Representatives. Elected to four-year terms, half of the legislature is elected in presidential years and half is elected during the mid-term elections. Even numbered districts, like Mock's, are elected in the presidential years. The legislature in North Dakota is a part-time position. The state constitution has the feel of a rural Midwestern state, geared towards having legislators come in, share their knowledge in governing the state for a short period, and then go back to their professional lives. The legislative calendar is geared towards the fact that the state is largely rural, with the session occurring in the winter, when farmers are not likely to be hard at work. The session is roughly 90 days, unless it is extended by the governor. The session is also held once every two years, forcing lawmakers to cover all business during a short period of time. Study committees meet in the interim to research issues and draft potential legislation for the next regular session. North Dakota's legislative rituals can seem quaint in states like New York or California where the legislature is a full-time position, with legislators living half the time in the state capital for most of the year, maintaining full-time offices in the capital and their district. For Mock, his full-time staff is himself; he does not have a state-financed office in his district or a state-financed staff to handle constituent issues, draft legislation, and churn out press releases on whatever subject is bothering him at the moment.

This is not the only part of North Dakota political life, even in the most urban parts of the state, that seems almost quaint to someone from a large more urban state, particularly those in the Northeast and Industrial Midwest. Races for the state legislature cost less than races for Town Council in some towns in the other states, bringing a more grassroots feel to the state legislative races. Using Kean or Quinn, up in the suburbs of Buffalo, New York, as comparisons, both ran in larger districts and spent more money than Mock would even dream of spending. In Kean's case he has always been able to run with two running mates in one of the safest Republican districts in the state — one so safe that the Democrats routinely run sacrificial lambs for the seats. But yet he — and his running mates — spent more than Mock or any of his District 42 counterparts.

North Dakota's forty-second district is a politically split environment. The voters chose to go in this direction during the 2008 election, an election that saw an all Republican delegation replaced with a delegation consisting of two Democrats and one Republican. The 2008 election also saw the district go from having two legislators in their 20s teamed with a legislator in his 50s to a delegation that looked like they were about to be carded at the nearest bar. Both parties chose to go with the model that the district had in place since 2004, two candidates in their 20s and then one more mature candidate, with the Republicans being able to run two incumbent state representatives, including Representative Stacey Dahl, a 27-year-old first elected in 2004. The other young Republican representing the district, state senator Nick Hatcher, announced he was going to retire in the 2008 election, if retirement is the best phrase to use for a twentysomething changing career paths. To fill Hatcher's Senate seat, the Republicans asked a twentysomething to make the race. On the Democratic side, two of the nominations went to candidates under the age of 30. Mac Schneider, a former captain of the UND football team and member of a well-known North Dakota political family, was tapped for the Senate seat. Mock grabbed one of the House nominations.

The election saw Schneider, Dahl, and Mock elected, setting up for several months at least a three-person delegation made up of legislators all in their 20s. Schneider would turn 30 during his first year in the Senate. Mock said the trend to electing such a young delegation in a district where the median age is 22.6 is a recent phenomenon. "It used to be the district that had consistently elected the longest-serving legislators," Mock said, noting that they were not exactly young when they started in public office. It's unique — some would say it's bizarre. Three state legislators in their 20s all representing one district at the same time, but then again the district is unusual and designed to elect and keep a young perspective in government and to keep the UND represented. No other state college has this level of attention from a legislative delegation. Yes, every other public institution of higher education in the country is represented by state legislators and those legislators advocate for the universities and help the university, but no other plays such a dominant role in who can get elected to office.

Consequently, Schneider, Dahl, and Mock place higher education issues at the forefront of their agenda. There is no way they can avoid higher education issues, well, unless they want to write themselves off as one-term wonders who will have no shot at reelection. The three routinely push for increased funding for the university while in Bismarck and make lower tuition and fees a top priority in their legislative agenda. Issues that would not likely be on the agenda for another legislator, even one who represents a public college, are on the agenda for this trio.

The 2009 legislative session in North Dakota was unique for any of the 50 state governments. While most states have been suffering the impact of the Great Recession, with high unemployment and dwindling tax bases and reserves, North Dakota's economy has been stable. Unemployment hasn't risen and the state is operating with something that most governors and state legislators can only dream about — a surplus. Schneider notes that he and Mock immediately looked at the budget surplus as a way to help their district. "We have a state budget surplus and one of the things we campaigned on was to freeze tuition for two years like Montana did two years ago," Schneider said in early 2009. "In a state where we are keeping more young people at home, that's important."

Dahl said three of the issues that have dominated her time since she was first sworn in to the House in 2005 have been university tuition and free and other higher education funding issues. But at the same time, she has had to recognize that there is a small part of the district that is not the UND and is not a student-dominated voting bloc. She needs to keep them in mind along with the students. "We have a mix of students and residents," she said. "It is an older neighborhood with a fair amount of older people and a great mix of younger residents."

Even the backgrounds of the candidates and what they bring to the ticket is something that is different in North Dakota's forty-second district compared with any other district in the country. Schneider is a member of a political family, but one that is centered in Fargo not Grand Forks. He is also a former aide to a congressman and a law school graduate, but that is not one of the top things he brought to the ticket. The fact that he is a former captain of the UND football team gives him more street cred in the district.

Dahl was lobbying the state legislature for the North Dakota Student Association when she was recruited to run for the first time in 2004. A state representative asked her if she was interested in running for a seat in District 42, noting that she had the profile to make a race for the legislature. At the time, she focused her government advocacy on tuition and higher education issues and had a background in Greek Life at UND. She had been in the leadership of her sorority at the school where Greek Life is a dominant aspect of the student life. Dahl does admit to being surprised when she was first asked about running for the House of Representatives. "He asked if I had thought about running for the legislature and I said I thought you had to be 65," she said.

Mock had experience in politics from high school in Minot when he was a moderate Republican and he served in the youth cabinet for Governor John Hoeven. Moving to college, Mock was accepted into the emerging leaders program and joined a fraternity, getting elected to a fraternity seat in the student senate. But at the same time he had an offer to study abroad in Norway and he declined the student senate seat to spend a semester in Norway. Returning to Grand Forks, Mock ended up putting any student government dreams on the backburner. "I decided that my time was best suited in the Greek community," Mock said. "I was secretary and then president of my fraternity. I was president of the interfraternity council."

Mock would also become a volunteer at the Boy's State program, where he would meet others politically active in the small state, including the executive director of the state Democratic Party. With the 2008 elections coming together, the Democrats were looking to fill out the ticket in the forty-second district and believed that the recent graduate Mock was a good candidate. "They were looking for a candidate who was familiar to students," Mock said. "They wanted a candidate under the age of 30."

Running for office in the forty-second district was also interesting and different for the three. As I wrote earlier in this chapter, the makeup of the district makes it a different field. And the three acknowledge that. Mock said he and his running mates made an intense focus to campaign at the Greek houses. Sounding more like a candidate for student government president than a seat in the state House of Representatives when he discusses his campaign strategy, Mock said there was a need to focus closely on the Greek community. He knew that once you got a majority of any Greek house, the entire house would likely follow. With every vote counting in the election of a state legislator in North Dakota, one fraternity and sorority in Grand Forks could sway the entire election.

Mock said the fraternities and sororities had historically gone with the Republican candidates for state legislative seats in the past. In order to overcome this the Democrats put more of a focus on these houses, also knowing that swaying one house would help sway others. Much like Jersey City councilman Steve Fulop would play up his involvement as president of a neighborhood association and Oregon state representative Jefferson Smith would play up his role in founding a civic activism group in their races, Mock's background as the former president of the coordinating council of UND fraternities was played up and given the same treatment.

Schneider said the Greek strategy was a key part of the Democrats strategy for the 2008 race in the forty-second district. "The way it shakes out in District 42, is that the students are the swing vote," he said. "Meeting with student groups and going to Monday night meetings at fraternities and sororities are big. There was one sorority that we hit up four times. It is half running for legislature and half running for student body president."

Mock notes that, while they focused a lot on the Greek community in their campaign, this focus was not exclusive. They campaigned at dorm events on a regular basis and would go door-to-door in the dorms in order to get those voters. At the same time they would knock on doors with the non-students in the district to show that they were not just campaigning to represent the campus.

Dahl said that in both of her races, which cost $12,000 in 2004 and $40,000 in 2008, a similar strategy was used by the Republican ticket. She attributes the more expensive 2008 race on the more competitive nature of the Democratic ticket. "We went to every fraternity, sorority and dorm to talk to students," she said. "We all knocked on each door once."

All three cannot find a district they would rather represent more than the forty-second. While the three do not call the district home from a perspective of having grown up there, they have settled down in Grand Forks and have grown to love the city and the district. When Schneider decided to go to work after working on Capitol Hill and getting his law degree in Washington, he said he could have taken a job in New York or Washington or another big city, but he didn't. He wanted to come back to North Dakota and help to continue to help his home state. Instead of the large law firm in the gleaming glass building overlooking the East River or the Potomac, he instead set up a branch office of the family law firm in Grand Forks.

The energy of the district and the age of the district mean a lot to the three legislators representing the forty-second district. They note that, where else can they represent the needs of their friends from school and the needs of the population that first brought them to Grand Forks and put them in a position to succeed in life? "It's energizing," Schneider said of his district. "You are campaigning where the youngest and brightest in North Dakota call home." North Dakota's forty-second district is an anomaly but one that is of benefit to the people of North Dakota going forward. Public higher education issues are of importance in every state in the country. With dwindling financial resources, many states have chosen to balance the budget on the backs of college students. Tuitions rise, resources are cut, funding is moved around. Student fees, the hidden revenue stream on campuses, are raised, making it harder for students to afford certain public universities.

Public higher education is a way to stimulate the economy of a state and region. Colleges are typically the largest employers in a region and serve multiple fronts on the impact they have in the economy locally. The first front is the sheer amount of jobs a college — particularly a large public university — can create. Jobs that will hire people and bring new people to the region, which will stimulate the real estate and construction industries and raise property values. The second is the side industry that is established: the various service enterprises that pop up around any campus — particularly the large public ones — in order to serve students, faculty, staff, and the occasional parent who wanders by. These restaurants, book stores, malls, hotels, and bars are important to the future of the regions around the college and the economic future of these regions. The third economic impact is the side institutes and research centers that are part of colleges that can also create new jobs.

Having the perspective of the students of North Dakota and the UND in the state legislature is important and it sets an important precedent for the entire country. The team of Schneider, Mock, and Dahl can discuss the student impact of tuition hikes and the impact of student fees. They can promote the public investment in UND and help bring the student perspective out there. For too many years the voice of the students has been missing in the public policy debates over public higher education issues and now, in North Dakota, three recent alums of the UND can bring these issues to the forefront. They serve in a unique position, one that is unlikely to change in the near future from the institutional distinction of the district. In terms of representation, the current team will face voters again in 2012. They can get these issues out there and promote the economic benefits of public higher education in North Dakota.

While there are a lot of interesting benefits in terms of having the forty-second district trio in office, it is impossible to completely recreate them. No other legislative district in the country can have the perfect storm come together of a perfectly sized district with a large state university in the middle of it to provide the voters and the need to have districts of a small amount of voters because of the state's small population. But other districts in other states stay away from this. There is a fear in many places about giving too much power to college students in terms of political power. The political power elite fear the needs of the college students and what they could represent. Will they be more liberal, will they elect more Democrats, will you see a rise of the Green Party? These are all questions asked by those in places of political power who are designing the districts for election. In some places, there is a debate over the issues impacting higher education that are discussed with little regard for students.

The fear of a student-run election and an impact it could have on government, including from an ideological perspective has been seen before. In 2003, the students and young alumni of the State University of New York at New Paltz were able to team up to elect a new mayor and new village trustees in New Paltz putting into place 27-year-old house painter and former student Jason West as the mayor. West and his running mates made up the first Green Party of a town. West and his running mates ran a socially progressive government, in line with the Green platform and also the beliefs of many of the residents of the Village of New Paltz. At the same time, West ended up performing gay weddings in his capacity as mayor and then found himself being criticized for ignoring local issues including infrastructure, which tops the concerns of many residents.

At the same time, the legislators of North Dakota's forty-second district have proven that they do not represent an ideological extreme. In the time since the majority or all of the district has been represented by people under the age of 30, they have not shown a slant one way or the other, and this was with alternating Republican and Democratic majorities. The legislators remain moderate, unless you count a belief in pressing for lower tuition and lower fees and more state investment in public higher education.

North Dakota's forty-second district will continue to be the legislative district that is at the side of the thousands of state legislative districts across the country, but it will also be one that brings a unique perspective to government and is likely to continue to elect young people to office. It will be a district that will have an impact on North Dakota and the future of the state.

CHAPTER 10

The Jersey Collision that Won't Happen: The Story of Steven Fulop and Peter Cammarano

Politics in Hudson County, New Jersey, has never been for the faint of heart. The county's politics have been as bare-knuckled and back-room focused as people would find in the heart of most urban political machines. Think Tammany Hall in New York or Illinois' Cook County or the James Curley's Boston and you get the picture.

Hudson County has been changing though, and the demographic and real estate changes have had some impact on their elected officials. More reformers have come in and the machine-backed candidates have taken on a more yuppie image, hoping to win over the hearts and minds of the young professionals who have packed the Hudson County waterfront in search of affordable apartments and condos near Manhattan.

Hudson County, however, continues to be a county of many contrasts and many divergent areas, with maybe one thing uniting the county politically: the overwhelming enrollment of registered Democrats in the county. Hoboken has transformed from the gritty waterfront home of Frank Sinatra to a gleaming waterfront mecca for young professionals with new and renovated condos dotting the waterfront and other parts of the Mile Square City, along with enough bars and nightlife to rival Manhattan. Jersey City's waterfront and downtown has been transformed with skyscrapers containing new condos and apartments, along with offices for the financial services industry seeking cheaper rents across the Hudson River from Wall Street. But the interior of Jersey City remains the way it has been with Irish and Italian enclaves along with heavy African American and Hispanic areas. The northern part of the county is dotted with small working-class cities, which have been seeing more and more luxury development as developers run out of space in Hoboken and Jersey City and buyers seek more affordable places.

Walking into a meeting room on the second floor of the Columbia University Club of New York in March of 2008, two of Hudson County's then current young elected officials were participating in a panel discussion on the subject of young elected officials. Sitting as almost bookends on the panel, the two look very similar. Both were young, looking younger than their age; both were born within months of each other in 1977; both were dressed in suits, with one preferring to roll up his shirt sleeves; both looked like the rest of the young professionals who have flooded the Hudson County waterfront in the last decade. You could tell both were ambitious and in a hurry politically. Both had the potential to be among New Jersey's next generation of leaders. Looking at this panel you could not help but think that possibly you were looking at future governors or senators from the Garden State. But when you listened to them, you could hear two different career paths and two different approaches to politics; two people who were so much alike on the surface but who were so different; two elected officials who were on a collision course given their ambitions, which had the potential to bring them into conflict as they looked to move up and out of their current communities.

The two are Steven Fulop, the councilman from Jersey City's waterfront and Peter Cammarano III, then a councilman-at-large in Hoboken, who would be elected Hoboken's mayor in 2009. The two of them were elected to their council seats in 2005 and both took the oath of office on July 1 of that year. Both had similar constituencies and similar issues covering their cities. Both were viewed not only as ambitious but as the chance for Hudson County to shed the corruption image that had plagued the county's Democratic machine for decades.

Fulop and Cammarano appeared to be on a collision course with each other. With only so many opportunities for political advancement available, along with the fact that two young white males from Hudson County would never be able to advance simultaneously up the New Jersey political ladder, sooner or later the two would end up in direct competition with each other. The various ethnic factions that make up the Hudson County Democratic Party and the New Jersey Democratic Party would never let the two of them climb the ladder outside of Hoboken and Jersey City at the same time. One would be able to move up and the other would not. With Cammarano having strong support from the venerable Hudson County Democratic machine and Fulop having strong support among good government types for his ethics reform pushes, they brought different bases to any campaign for higher office.

This collision course suddenly and dramatically ended in the early morning hours of July 23, 2009 when FBI agents arrested Cammarano in the largest corruption sting in New Jersey history. Mayor for only 22 days at the time of his arrest, Cammarano was charged with soliciting and accepting $25,000 in cash bribes from a federal informant during his mayoral campaign and in the opening weeks of his administration. The arrest brought Cammarano's promising career to a screeching halt and ended his anticipated battle royal with Fulop. Following a week of protests in front of his home and in front of City Hall, Cammarano announced his resignation on July 31. He had not just been Hoboken's youngest mayor: he had also been its shortest serving mayor.

How did these two get to this position and how could two people who, on paper and at first glance, looked to be the same person be so far apart politically?

Steven Fulop is like many of his constituents in downtown Jersey City. Born in 1977, Fulop grew up the son of Israeli immigrants in Edison, New Jersey, Working in the family deli in Newark, Fulop pursued a passion for soccer while growing up and in fact spent his first year at Binghamton University playing on the school's soccer team. His life did not scream politics while growing up. Fulop started working for Goldman Sachs in Chicago before transferring to Wall Street in 2000. Relocating to the Jersey City waterfront like many of his peers, Fulop seemed to be settling in for the textbook life of a young Wall Street trader: serve a few years with Goldman, get an MBA, move up the career ladder, settle either in an urban or suburban environment, dabble in civic affairs, and then possibly settle into another retirement career after amassing a nest egg.

However, Fulop chose a different path. On September 11, 2001, Fulop was on a conference call at Goldman Sachs' offices across the street from the World Trade Center when the terrorist attack occurred. "We were close enough to feel the building vibrate when the plane hit," Fulop said of the moment American Airlines Flight 11 slammed into the Trade Center's North Tower. Evacuating the building, Fulop could see the burning towers as he fled for his life to a boat on the Hudson River. Just off the shore of Lower Manhattan, Fulop would witness the towers collapse in front of him. He could not even leave the horror when he went home, as his Jersey City condo had a view of the smoke rising from Ground Zero. In the days following the attacks, Fulop made a decision that stunned many of his family, friends, and co-workers: he enlisted in the Marines and was deployed to Iraq, becoming one of the first troops to enter Baghdad in the opening days of the war. "Actually seeing it firsthand as close as I was, was a scary experience," Fulop said of 9/11. "It changed my life and propelled me to public service."

A month and a half after 9/11, Fulop completed the process of enlisting in the Marines and was preparing to ship off to boot camp at Parris Island. Lack of sleep, constant physical activity, being screamed at in his face, and being at the beck and call of a drill sergeant, Fulop experienced a change of pace from the life he had been living. With many marine enlistees being from poorer neighborhoods and families across the country, Fulop's Wall Street background stood out, but he notes that the Parris Island experience is one which brings everyone together, regardless of background, and makes them into marines and that his background or others, never stood out.

Arriving in Kuwait in December of 2002 as a member of the Sixth Engineering Supply Battalion, Fulop was at the front lines of the march into Iraq. Working on water purification projects, bridge building, and fuel farms, Fulop would be at the forefront of danger as the United States headed towards Baghdad to topple Saddam Hussein. During his time in the desert, the threat of death even closer than it had been on 9/11, Fulop would reexamine his priorities and his commitment to public service. He felt prouder of the United States and what his family had gone through to get where they were. He felt prouder of his Jewish heritage and grew closer to it. He found himself another step closer to the decision to run for office. "It was a scary experience," he said. "It was a good experience that made me a better person going on."

Returning home to Jersey City following the war, Fulop became more involved in local civic associations in his home neighborhood of Paulus Hook, including taking over as president of the local neighborhood association. He, and other returning veterans, was honored by Jersey City mayor Glenn Cunningham, who paused when he read the proclamation based on Fulop's unique personal story. Cunningham, a former marine, made an effort to get to know Fulop and would cross paths with the young trader at Paulus Hook-related functions over the coming months in 2003. At the time, Cunningham was locked in a blood feud with then congressman Bob Menendez, D-Hudson County, for control of the Hudson County Democratic Party. As a part of this, Cunningham chose to run candidates for a slate of offices in the 2004 Democratic primary including county clerk, county surrogate, and against Menendez for Congress.

One day in the spring of 2004, Fulop was leaving work and got a cell phone call with a 201 — Jersey City — area code. With many of his friends living in the 212 — Manhattan — area code, he was surprised by the call and even more surprised when it was Cunningham's chief of staff inviting him to see the mayor in the morning. When he arrived at the meeting with Cunningham, the mayor explained his primary plan to Fulop and then asked him to run for Congress. Fulop, who had been in student government in college, had hesitations of running what would likely be a losing race for a county government office, but jumped at the chance to challenge the entrenched Menendez. Leaving the mayor's office, Fulop jumped feetfirst into the race, recruiting a close friend, politically active attorney Steven Newmark, to run his campaign, along with assembling a campaign team made up of friends and some Cunningham allies. Campaigning over two months that spring, Fulop had to deal with an effort to toss him off the ballot and other tricks from the veteran Hudson County politicos who were leery of the young upstart. A week before primary, Cunningham suddenly died after a bike tour with Fulop, leaving him without the mentor who brought him to the game. After losing, as expected, to Menendez in the primary, Fulop started to think of what to do next. He decided to seek a city council seat in the May 2005 city elections.

With close support from the remnants of the Cunningham organization, Fulop challenged an incumbent backed by the party machine, Junior Maldonado, by appealing to the young professionals who were making up more and more of the downtown constituency at the heart of the district. Edging out Maldonado, Fulop became the only council member not aligned with the new mayor, Jerry Healy, or the Hudson County Democratic Organization (HCDO). He made reform issues central to his campaign — foreshadowing what he intended to do in office. "Absolute power corrupts absolutely," Fulop said, recounting Lord Acton's famous nineteenth-century quote as the main theme behind his 2005 campaign.

Unlike many outsiders elected to office, Fulop made no effort to become close to Healy or the HCDO. Fulop made ethics reform and good government his signature issues. In a county like Hudson, where indicted public officials could be considered a demographic, the issue was bound to make Fulop a known entity. He opposed the HCDO during the 2006 congressional primary and the 2007 state legislative primary, where in the end he even had to oppose Cunningham's widow, Sandy, in her bid for a state senate seat. During this time, Fulop's push to end dual public office holding and establish an anti pay-to-play law did more than just establish himself as a thorn in Healy and the HCDO's side, it gave him a large public following in his district, making him more and more of a threat to Healy's future — and a force to be reckoned with. Fulop was no longer the outsider to be dealt with: he was a serious player in Jersey City politics. He even managed to become a fundraising force, amassing a good war chest for a ward council seat.

Fulop appears the least likely person to either be a former marine or to challenge a hard-nosed political machine and establish himself as a powerful force in Jersey City. Built like a runner, a quick look at him would stereotype him as a yuppie, which is true. But talking with him shows a deep interest in politics and in the issues surrounding the political situation in New Jersey. Intensely curious, he is quick to ask questions to gather as much information as possible. He shows a deep passion in reform issues and in trying to change the culture of Jersey City politics and government. Fulop has been able to inspire many in his ward to rally to his side on reform issues. Entering a restaurant in downtown Jersey City one evening, the scene looked no different than many parties held at restaurants throughout the New York metropolitan area. But on this night it was different. The party was geared to Fulop announcing his reform initiatives to ban dual office holding and pay-to-play through citizen referendum. The bar was packed with the people gathered inside listening intently and cheering Fulop on. One could feel electricity in the air and the crowd gathered held Fulop at a level not seen for politicians in local government.

The referendums failed when the petitions were given to the city clerk for validation. The city's chief attorney advised the clerk that the signatures had come up short, with Fulop saying he had been given a lower number when the process started. Defeated in his attempt to get reform measures on the ballot, Fulop would instead work other methods to get some ethics reforms passed in Jersey City.

Fulop was suddenly one of the names people were mentioning to challenge Healy for the mayor's seat in 2009, giving more urgency to any move to get him out of local politics. There was talk of the HCDO moving Congressman Albio Sires out of Congress in order to offer Fulop the seat, an offer Fulop said he would not consider. When Fulop started pushing his good government efforts to a citywide referendum, launching them at a rally jammed with cheering loyalists, Healy and company started finding legal loopholes to block his petitions. While Fulop turned up on the wrong side of the presidential election, backing Hillary Clinton while Healy backed Barack Obama, he managed to turn lemons into lemonade by bringing more fundraising clout to his side. Fulop began to look more and more like a threat to Healy and the HCDO for the powerful mayor's office.

Then the one thing that Healy and company could not have developed as a reason to move Fulop out of the mayor's race came up — the economy tanked. A trader by profession, Fulop took a personal hit from the economic downturn in the fall of 2008 and with the city council being a part-time job, he announced he would seek reelection in 2009, instead of the mayor's office. With Healy's stock on the rise with high approval ratings and being a close ally of the new president, it seemed like a wise decision. Fulop didn't publicly back a mayoral candidate and while Healy put forward a challenger to Fulop, it was a half-hearted challenge that seemed to shout that Healy realized that Fulop was unbeatable in the downtown. When the May election rolled around, Fulop stopped being the one-term-wonder people had thought back in 2005, elected on a wave of Cunningham sympathy, patriotism, and good government support, he won with the largest percentage of any ward council member, easily trouncing his opponents with 61 percent of the vote. While Fulop remains the only non-Healy ally on the council, his power has increased and everyone is pointing to him as a mayoral candidate in 2013, more so than they were in his first term.

Just to the north of Fulop's ward sits the Mile Square City of Hoboken. As young professionals packed the New Jersey waterfront looking for cheaper apartments close to Manhattan, this city was the center of this movement. Hoboken lost one of the largest percentages of residents out of any metropolitan area on September 11. Born just under five months after Fulop in 1977, Peter Cammarano had a different path to power than Fulop. Raised by a single mother and his grandparents, Cammarano's father left him and his sister when they were young and was a deadbeat father. The grandson of a Passaic County politico, Cammarano had been exposed to politics from an early age. Cammarano has harbored political ambitions since he was 11 years old. He has patterned his life to be able to run for elective office. Quiet and soft-spoken he does not look like, or act like, the typical Hudson County politician. His law office — he was one of New Jersey's top election lawyers before being elected mayor — was decorated with World War II memorabilia and tributes to his love of Abraham Lincoln. He has a deep passion for the space program and confesses to reading physics books for fun. Cammarano has read many books on Lincoln and the Civil War and lists books on the subject as among his favorite. Cammarano's lifestyle screams political and history geek; in fact he majored in political science and minored in history at Boston University.

"I grew up in a family where we spoke around the dinner table about politics, government, economics and history," Cammarano said in 2006.

He remembers his intense interest in politics came around his eleventh birthday in 1988 when he was with his family vacationing at the Jersey Shore. The inspiration was former Texas governor Ann Richards and the line in her Democratic keynote address about George Bush "being born with a silver foot in his mouth." "We were watching the national conventions of both parties," he said. "We were watching the Democratic National Convention and Ann Richards was giving the keynote and she was this nice silver-haired old lady and she gave that great line and I remember thinking that was a great line. Here was a nice old lady attacking the vice president of the United States."

Cammarano got more interested during the first Bush administration, reading *The New York Times* daily and following the Gulf War. He decided to run for student government in high school and lost. When he made it to college, he ran for student government again and lost. In law school he ran in his first year and lost, finally winning a student government race in his second year of law school and again in his third. Moving back to New Jersey after graduation, Cammarano enrolled in Seton Hall Law School. If his desire to go to Boston for college screams looking for a change of pace from New Jersey, his choice of a law school screams New Jersey politics. Seton Hall's law school in Newark is almost a training ground for New Jersey politics, graduating more than its fair share of future mayors, county leaders, state legislators, judges and other members of the Garden State's political elite. There are only three law schools in New Jersey, Rutgers has campuses in Newark and Camden and there is Seton Hall. While many people in the state go to one of these three because of their status in New Jersey, others may choose a campus in Manhattan or Philadelphia based on where they lived in New Jersey. Many end up choosing Seton Hall solely because of its reputation within New Jersey as a place to easily gain connections to the state's business, legal, and political elite and a tie-in to the school's alumni network, which reaches far into the state's political culture. It is likely Cammarano chose the law school for these reasons.

In a school that has more than its fair share of students who were looking at potential political careers in New Jersey, Cammarano's desire to run for office one day came through loud and clear to his classmates. His wife, Marita, relates a story that sums up the thoughts of their classmates of his future. "I told one of my friends that I was dating Peter and he said 'so you want to be first lady,'" she said in 2006. Marita Cammarano would end up a first lady. But no one would have guessed that her tenure as First Lady of Hoboken[1] would last 30 days and the chaos involved in the final days of her tenure as the wife of the youngest mayor of the state's demographically youngest city. During his time in law school, Cammarano showed he was destined for a career involving politics. He worked as an aide to a state senator and wrote a law review article on the McCain–Feingold campaign finance law, which would accurately predict the eventual decision of the Supreme Court in this historic case. Others who went to law school with Cammarano said it was clear he was looking toward a political career one day.

Moving to Hoboken seemed like a no-brainer for Cammarano given the ease of transit into Newark and the high amount of members of his generation moving to the city. Cammarano didn't jump immediately, first moving to Newark to be closer to the law school and then back to Passaic County where he lived with his grandparents, who had helped raise him. During law school, Cammarano had been active in politics, volunteering for campaigns and making contacts in New Jersey's political world, aiming to possibly practice election law following graduation. He moved to Hoboken in late 2001. "Starting in high school, I went to Hoboken to have fun," Cammarano said. "I had a daydream that I would live in Hoboken and work in the World Trade Center. I read the story in the *Times* about Hoboken losing 53 people to 9/11. I wanted to repopulate what was lost in Hoboken. I was looking for an apartment a week after I read the article.

Following graduation in 2002, Cammarano settled in to what he describes as a good job, but one that caused what he described as the toughest year of his life: he became a law clerk to a state judge. During this year, Cammarano had to refrain from political involvement, which is something equivalent to shutting off his oxygen supply. "My then girlfriend said I went into withdrawal," Cammarano later recalled, citing his future wife, Marita. Moving through the year, Cammarano did indeed survive. After his clerkship ended, he took a job with the law firm of Angelo Genova, the state's top Democratic election attorney. Cammarano had indeed arrived in state Democratic circles.

At the same time, Cammarano got involved in the 2004 presidential campaign, helping to collect signatures for John Kerry. He was spotted by Hoboken political leaders, who saw him as a potential future candidate, during this time and was quite literally approached on a street corner about becoming involved with then mayor David Roberts. At the time Roberts and other Hoboken Democrats were looking for a candidate who could appeal to the city's young professionals and young families and the born-and-raised old-time residents. "I was on a street corner in Hoboken getting signatures and the political organization in Hoboken knows if someone is on a street corner," he said. "The mayor noticed I was there and he had his friend, Freeholder Maurice Fitzgibbons, ask me what I was doing. It made these guys aware of this kid who was doing this."

With both sides becoming more and more competitive in trying to control city politics, this was a necessity to win in the future. With Cammarano's youthful looks but background that screamed old-timer, including his now fiancée's grandfather being a former Hoboken comptroller, he was the perfect fit. Cammarano was soon recruited to run with Roberts for an at-large city council seat in 2005, which he easily won.

Cammarano's path to the city council wasn't smooth. In fact, he had to deal with a personal issue, one that could be unique to young elected officials: his upcoming wedding. It was scheduled for the Saturday before the June runoff election. Given the dynamics of his race, it was very likely a runoff would occur, and also likely that Cammarano would be a part of it. Doing so would put the runoff election at the same time as he was going to be on his honeymoon in Hawaii. Rather than making the decision about their honeymoon, he and his fiancée chose to wait until after the first-round election in May, where he did in fact make the runoff. "The wedding was planned in advance. My wife had scheduled the honeymoon before I was asked to run, two weeks in Hawaii," he said. "It was lucky we got travel insurance because we had to cancel. We did a week and a half in St. Johns and left the day after the election. My wife is a saint. I sat her down and said 'if I'm sitting on a beach in Hawaii and find out I lost by a small vote, I won't forgive myself.'"

On the city council, Cammarano took a vastly different approach than Fulop. Where Fulop is the outsider looking to set a legislative agenda opposite of the mayor, Cammarano was a key mayoral ally on the council. Pushing his own initiatives, along with working as a part of Roberts' council majority, Cammarano was seen by many as being groomed for the mayor's office in the 2009 election. Cammarano was coy in 2006 about whether or not he was being groomed for the mayoralty. "Am I being groomed? I don't know," he said in 2006. "From what I hear, it sounds that I am on a short list to become mayor at some point. That is very humbling and fulfilling. It is gratifying to know it's on anyone's lips.

He made land use one of his key issues, serving as the council's representative to the city planning board for most of his term. With development being a key issue in a city that is only one square mile but has many developers clamoring to build new condos and apartments, especially in the first years of the twenty-first century, this would put Cammarano front and center with the city's top issue. It would also introduce him to many developers, a ready-made source of campaign contributions for a future race. In fact this could foresee what would eventually happen. Outside of development, he also fought to build a World War II memorial, honoring his family's service in the Marine Corps.

During his council term, Cammarano gained more and more exposure in state Democratic circles, serving as Menendez' 2006 campaign attorney for the U.S. Senate race and in the same role for Hillary Clinton in the 2008 New Jersey presidential primary. The presidential race would be one of the few times he and Fulop would be publicly working on the same side of things politically. In 2007, he managed the race for HCDO candidates running for ward seats in Hoboken. Cammarano was seen more and more as a rising star in the HCDO and in statewide Democratic circles as someone who would likely be running for higher office with strong institutional support in the Democratic Party.

During 2008, he was Roberts' staunchest ally on the council during a protracted budget battle which resulted in the state placing a monitor to oversee city finances and a large increase in property taxes. The battle, while putting Cammarano on the side of lower property taxes, also placed him firmly in the camp of the established political culture of Hoboken. While to some the 2008 battle was a battle over low taxes versus high taxes, to others it was a battle over reform versus status quo.

Entering the 2009 mayor's race, Cammarano found himself in third place. Councilwomen Beth Mason and Dawn Zimmer were seen as the frontrunners, working off the same reformist zeal that Fulop had tapped into in Jersey City. Cammarano focused on the 2008 budget battle and his position in trying to keep taxes down, while Mason and Zimmer had been on the opposite side of the issue. Both had been stressing reformist credentials during the mayor's race and said the tax hike was needed to deal with what they said was mismanagement of city finances during the Roberts administration. Mason had ties to Fulop in the realm of both being considered top reformists in their cities pushing many of the same issues. Zimmer straddled multiple sides of the reform effort in Hudson County but was part of a separate cause from where Mason and Fulop were approaching the issue.

Cammarano focused on being a representative of new and old Hoboken. He stressed he could bridge the gap between both communities. Mason also tried this tactic trying to recruit council running mates representing the old Hoboken and tying herself to old-timers in city politics. Zimmer stayed firmly planted it the new Hoboken camp.

During this time, he started to move up in the polls, possibly into forcing frontrunner Mason into a runoff, then a near disaster struck. A local website reported that Cammarano had been keeping a secret from voters for years: his teenage daughter. While he had listed his wife and their young daughter in his official biography, and had so since his daughter's 2007 birth, he had kept secret that his high school girlfriend gave birth to his other daughter in 1995. In the article, Cammarano was also accused of being a deadbeat father who had ignored his daughter for years. Cammarano held an angry press conference where he denounced the accusations, saying the Peter Cammarano who was the deadbeat father was his own father who had not been a part of his life since he was a small child. In addition he said he had kept his older daughter's name out of his official biography for her own privacy.

Cammarano finished second in the first round of voting, just behind Zimmer and went into the June runoff. Reshuffling his council team because most of his original running mates lost the first round, the mayor's race got more competitive when Mason rallied her supporters around Zimmer in hopes of ending Cammarano's career in elective office. The machine tally on Election Day showed a win for Zimmer, the absentee and provisional ballots gave Cammarano a narrow win. While he ended up the new mayor in 2009, Cammarano ended up in a position of weakened power as Zimmer's allies won three council seats. Combined with Mason and Zimmer, they controlled a bare majority of the council, with other council members joining forces against the new mayor. With Zimmer as the new city council president, Cammarano suddenly had to govern the city with a council aligned with the woman he narrowly beat. While Fulop found himself in a power position following the 2009 election, Cammarano found himself the chief executive but with a legislative branch which would love nothing more than to see him fail.

While the city council would have loved nothing more than to see Cammarano fail, none expected what would happen just 22 days after he took the oath of office. During the spring mayoral campaign and during the first weeks of his administration, Cammarano had several meetings with an FBI informant at the Malibu Diner in Hoboken. During these meetings the informant, who was wearing a wire, discussed a potential development with Cammarano and offered him cash bribes in order to obtain favorable land-use decisions. In the end, Cammarano is accused of accepting $25,000 in cash from the informant, much of which is said to have been earmarked for his campaign, something a veteran election attorney would know was illegal.

Buried in the federal complaint against Cammarano are quotes taken from conversations he had with the informant at the Malibu Diner which on the face of things are not helpful to the mayor. During one meeting, Cammarano is blunt in how he views the world should he make it to the mayor's office. "In this election, hopefully, we, we, we, you know, we get to the point where I'm sworn in on July 1, and we're breaking down the world into three categories at that point. There's the people who were with us, and that's you guys. There's the people who climbed on board in the runoff. They can get in line . . . And then there are the people who were against us the whole way. They get ground . . . They get ground into powder," Cammarano is quoted as saying in the federal complaint.

In the same conversation, the informant told Cammarano that they'd meet again several days after the June 9 runoff election and he'd hand over another $5,000 in cash. Cammarano who was about to leave the diner responded by saying, "Definitely." According to the complaint, Mayor-Elect Cammarano held a meeting with the informant on June 23, after the runoff election. During the meeting, Cammarano talked about how his campaign had overwritten the bank account by $19,000 to pay out street money checks for the runoff. Street money is a common New Jersey practice where checks are given to those who "volunteer" on election day. It is usually given to many union members and others who take a day off of work to help a candidate. During the meeting, Cammarano is quoted as saying his campaign had taken out a bridge loan of $20,000 to cover the costs of the checks but he needed to pay the loan back. This was after the informant asked how much money Cammarano would need. During the meeting the informant said he'd provide cash and told the mayor-elect that he hoped he did not forget to fast track the proposed development project once he took office. "[W]e're going to be friends for a good long time," Cammarano is quoted as saying in the complaint.

The images from July 23 were shocking even by the standards of New Jersey, where politicians being hauled off in handcuffs on corruption charges is so common the scene should be placed on the license plate as the state image. Dressed in a powder-blue shirt and khakis, Cammarano looked ready for a dinner party or business casual day at the office, not a typical criminal defendant. The youngest of the 44 arrested that day, the most unlikely looking criminal and the highest ranking of those arrested, Cammarano would find his picture plastered in papers and television programs nationwide. Instead of being a rising star in politics with the limitless future, he found himself the national "poster boy for political corruption." The morning after the arrests, I exchanged e-mails with a former mayor of Westfield, New Jersey, a suburban community of 29,000. This conversation was in my role as editor of *Westfield Patch* and for a follow-up article seeking local reaction to the corruption arrests. In the conversation the former mayor, Tom Jardim, the only Democrat to be elected to lead Westfield in a century, and a former young elected official himself, not only said he knew Cammarano casually but also said something that summed up the feelings of many in the state: "The sheer stupidity of these people is mind-boggling."

On April 20, 2010, Cammarano pled guilty in federal court to extortion charges as part of a plea agreement he negotiated with the U.S. Attorney's office. In the plea agreement, Cammarano admitted to willingly accepting illegal cash campaign contributions and conspiring to delay and effect interstate commerce. As part of the plea deal, he will be sentenced to 24–30 months in federal prison.[2]

Cammarano was seen as a new vision for Hoboken. As the city shakes its reputation as a longshoreman's town and into a yuppie paradise, there continues to be a tension between born-and-raised residents and newcomers. Resembling many of the yuppies, he was seen as someone who would guide Hoboken into the twenty-first century. His arrest shocked many people, who did not think someone who looked like them could be arrested for such a crime.

While July 23, 2009 was the worst day ever for Cammarano, in some ways it was one of the best days Fulop has ever had in politics. Many of the others arrested alongside Cammarano were from Jersey City, including city council president Mariano Vega, Assemblyman L. Harvey Smith, former assemblyman Louis Manzo, and political consultant Joseph Cardwell. Top aides to Mayor Jerry Healy were arrested, including a deputy mayor. With the arrest of many top aides and close allies, there was speculation that Healy was somehow involved in what is the alleged to have occurred.

Vega had been considered a potential mayoral candidate. Smith, a former acting mayor, was looking to possibly run for the office again. Manzo had run and lost five times before for mayor but also had a following in the community. Healy was likely to want to keep his hold on the office for as long as possible. Cardwell's biggest client is state senator Sandra Cunningham, who is seen by many as wanting to occupy the mayor's chair her late husband had held. With the careers of this group deeply wounded or destroyed by the actions of July 23, suddenly Fulop found himself one of the last men standing for the 2013 mayor's race.

In fact, Fulop's consistent calls for government and ethics reform, including campaign finance reform, made him stand out even more. He could go back to the issues he had been stressing for four years and stand out as a reformer in a sea of corruption. In the aftermath of the arrests, Fulop was up front in calling for suspensions of the city employees who were arrested in the probe and for the resignation of Vega from the city council. Fulop's star continued to rise. Fulop would continue his reform quest in the days and weeks following the arrest. While Healy suspended the full-time city employees who were arrested, Fulop wanted more. Vega was not forced to do anything with his role as city council president, which is the second-highest in city government. Fulop wanted him to resign or be suspended from the presidency. Tapping into the large and enthusiastic group of supporters that have followed him like a pied piper for government reform, Fulop held a rally on the steps of city hall calling for resignations and more reform. He used the aftermath as a way to continue to push the ethics reform measures he had made a hallmark of his career and that he wanted to see adopted.

Fulop started putting together fundraisers for his campaign treasury as a part of the never-ending campaign cycle that American politics has become — even at the municipal level. He didn't deny that the funds he was raising were for a future citywide race, noting he had no desire to run for an at-large council seat, which leaves only the mayor's office. There has even been speculation that Fulop could end up running for mayor sooner than 2013, in the event that Healy leaves office early and a special election is held. But that remains a long shot.

Fulop continues as 2010 begins to push new reform proposals for Jersey City. In the last days of the 2008–2010 state legislative session, lawmakers passed a bill allowing New Jersey cities with non-partisan elections to change the date of the election from May to November, the same day as the regular general election. The local governments would need to adopt this as well. Just as acting governor Stephen Sweeney[3] signed the bill into law, Fulop was advocating for its passage in Jersey City, saying it will save money for city government and allow more people to be aware of the municipal election. This will also be beneficial to Fulop politically, allowing more voters to come to the polls for a municipal race, which will make it easier for a non-machine-backed politician to run citywide. In addition, there is a chance this would put the 2013 mayor's race on the same ballot as the 2013 governor's race, where there is a good chance that Newark mayor Cory Booker will be running for governor. Many likely Booker supporters in Jersey City would likely also back Fulop for mayor. While others in city government showed no support for the chance of the mayor's election date, Fulop has pledged to look at a citywide referendum to adopt the change.

Looking long term, Cammarano's arrest suddenly ended the long-awaited collision course between the two, who could be found as likely candidates for Congress or U.S. Senate one day, possibly the governorship. With Hudson County a Democratic stronghold it was not outside the realm of possibility to see one of them tapped for lieutenant governor one day. With Cammarano taking the mayor's office, he suddenly outranked Fulop in the county and state political hierarchy and was labeled a rising star statewide. He was appearing alongside the state's political brass and gaining more political power, even if his power within Hoboken was limited by the city council. With Hudson County Democratic politics being dominated by the local mayors, Cammarano now held a seat at the table. A future mayoral win by Fulop could place the consummate outsider on the inside and allow him to eclipse Cammarano since Jersey City far outweighs Hoboken in population. All of these scenarios have ended.

Cammarano was groomed for the mayoralty and for a career in politics, with his mentors hoping to see him advance to the statewide stage one day. He worked closely with the Democratic elite in Hudson County and around the state, and, upon his election as mayor, was welcomed into the fold by statewide officials and rising stars like Newark mayor Cory Booker. He fell into circumstances beyond his control in an environment where federal law enforcement is looking to prosecute New Jersey politicians, and had an ill-timed relationship with a wired government informant.

Fulop is on a path to a mayoralty and possibly higher offices, but has not been groomed for the job. While one could say Glenn Cunningham brought him to the dance — and Fulop continues to speak highly of Cunningham — Fulop has worked hard to become his own man and to distance himself from Cunningham and some of the unsavory characters surrounding the late mayor. He didn't endorse Mrs. Cunningham in her bid for the state senate and worked to establish a reputation separate from any of the tarnished politicos in his county. Even in 2004, his congressional campaign may have been supported and promoted by Cunningham, but his inner campaign circle consisted of close friends who had no ties to Hudson County politics and all of whom lived in Manhattan. His campaign manager's sole connection to Hudson County was Fulop and occasionally crashing on Fulop's couch. Since then Fulop has brought more Jersey City and New Jersey political types to join him and has made inroads with the reformist wing of the political sphere in Hudson County, there is still a distinctly outside feel to the Fulop operation. His 2009 reelection campaign manager is a fundraiser for a local charter school active in reform politics. He also continued to bring in friends from Manhattan and other parts of New Jersey to help him in his campaigns.

Fulop now has the bright future while Cammarano is trying to salvage what remains of his political and legal careers. Fulop can look forward to 2013 and what could likely be an easy race for mayor of what should then be the state's largest city. He can look forward to a future race for governor or the Senate, possibly setting himself up to be the nation's first Jewish president.

While Fulop is looking forward to a future with endless possibilities, Cammarano is facing a stay in a federal prison, as well as salvaging his law license. Even if he had been acquitted of the charges, being the "poster boy for corruption," and generating headlines from New Jersey to Alaska for his arrest does not help cement a long-standing political career. The days following the arrest saw groups picketing his house and office demanding he resign from office. The governor, a Hoboken resident, called for his resignation, and long-time Democratic Party allies kept jumping on the resignation bandwagon.

Eight days after his arrest, Cammarano finally gave in to the unforgiving pressure and announced his resignation, noting that he did not want to subject the city to the distractions coming from his case. His mayoralty lasted 30 days and saw little in terms of accomplishments. He launched his kids' nutrition program, made several public appearances, and conducted at least one wedding. He even named a cabinet, but the city council had yet to confirm them before his arrest. Cammarano even had a chance to attend a rally with President Obama while mayor.

Two young elected officials —the same age, similar cities, similar lives, similar ambitions. Two who had been on a collision course. Two who will now be forever linked for being on that panel on that March day in 2008, and, on that July day in 2009, for being on opposite ends of anyone putting together a list of winners and losers from the corruption bust.

Notes

1   Peter and Marita Cammarano separated in the summer of 2009 and subsequently divorced.
2   On August 5, 2010, Cammarano was sentenced to up to 24 months in a federal prison camp.
3   Stephen Sweeney was elected president of the New Jersey Senate on January 12, 2010. In this office, under the provisions of the state constitution in effect until noon on January 19, 2010, the senate president is first in the line of succession to the governorship and serves as acting governor when the governor is outside of the state. Shortly after Sweeney took office as senate president, Governor Jon Corzine left for Switzerland and Sweeney assumed the duties of acting governor for most of Corzine's last week in office. Under the new provisions of the state constitution taking effect at noon on January 19, 2010, the role of first in line of succession transfers to the newly created office of lieutenant governor. Following the inauguration of Lieutenant Governor Kim Guadagno, the senate president moved behind the lieutenant governor in the line of succession, including serving as the acting governor in the event the governor leaves the state.

CHAPTER 11

Does the Mayor Have to Listen When the Principal Calls Him to the Office? Young Mayors in America

When people have visions of a mayor, there are common perceptions that come to mind. Most mayors are thought to be in their 40s, 50s, or 60s; pillars of the community, who have been involved in a long list of community activities and have contributed to the life of the community. Many have served on city councils in the past, while others come to the mayor's office after having served in county government or in state legislators. In some large cities, it is not uncommon to even see former members of Congress becoming mayors.

These are the perceptions of what a mayor is and what a mayor should look like. The title itself gives a certain stature to the holder. Just the title elevates the holder the way any singular political office does: a mayor, a governor, the president are all elevated because of this.

At the same time there are occasional cases when the mayor is not who you expect him or her to be. The mayor looks young, almost not old enough to shave. The mayor looks barely old enough to drive, let alone command a police force and declare states of emergency. The mayor looks like he should be writing college term papers, studying for finals, and hanging out on the quad, not cutting ribbons, signing ordinances, and riding in parades. The only thing the mayor looks like he should be presiding over is a student government meeting, not a city council meeting. But there are exceptions to the rule and there are young mayors elected to office, some in their teens. It is easy to dismiss the teenage mayors as being from small towns or being flukes of the election; that they declared a candidacy and were able to slide in on a variety of circumstances. You could argue they win because they have a well-known name in a small town, or there was sudden voter anger towards the older candidate and the voters went with the young candidate, or that the voters thought the teenage candidate was older when they were first voting.

People will dismiss the young mayors, thinking they ran as a joke and will treat the office as a joke; that they ran for whatever reason and just wanted the title; that they do not want the duties of the office, and will not perform the duties of the office. It is easy to say they ran, won, and will coast through their term, looking to impress their friends but not be serious about being a mayor, even a part-time mayor.

Michael Sessions started 2005 as a 17-year-old high school junior in Hillsdale, Michigan. By all rights he should have been focused on several things: taking his SATs, applying to colleges, enjoying his up-coming senior year of high school, and spending time with his friends. He should have been doing homework and writing papers and just being a high school student. By all rights, he should have ended the year in the final weeks of the first semester of his senior year in high school, finishing up college applications and getting ready for his last semester of high school. He should have been planning to spend those final weeks of 2005 focused on applications and the prom and graduation and just preparing to become a college student in the fall of 2006. That's not how it turned out. Sessions spent the final weeks of 2005 as a senior in high school but worried about city budgets, property taxes, police overtime, potholes, land use, recreation issues and the other issues that face municipal governments from coast to coast.

As a junior in high school, Sessions decided he was going to run for the mayor's office in the city of just over 8,000 people, challenging a sitting incumbent. It was, on the face of it, an unconventional decision: a high school student challenging the mayor. Sessions had a challenge to overcome as he started up a bid for the top spot in city government. The petition to run for mayor was due on May 10 and his eighteenth birthday was on September 22 of 2005. Under Michigan law he needed to be 18 to be elected mayor and while he would be 18 on the day of the non-partisan election in November and legally eligible to be elected mayor, he was not legally eligible to be on the ballot to run for mayor, since he was under the age of 18 on the day the petition was due. He would have to run as a write-in candidate.

Sessions said he had thought of seeking an appointment to a city board instead, seeking to implement his goals that way, instead of making the race for the mayor's seat. But he was concerned he would not be able to accomplish anything in that way of service. "I said hey look and said I could get myself on a board but chances are they will overlook me," Sessions said in a 2006 interview. A lifelong resident of Hillsdale, Sessions said he wanted to run for the mayor's seat in order to work on economic development issues. An old line auto community, Hillsdale was dealing with many of the same issues cities in the Industrial Midwest were dealing with in the aftermath of the decline of the manufacturing industry. Sessions believed that as an outsider to the city's political establishment he would be able to bring new ideas to the economic development debate. He also believed that as an 18-year-old he would be able to think more outside the box in terms of being a mayor of an aging industrial city.

As a write-in candidate, Sessions was the only opponent of the sitting mayor. Under normal circumstances, the mayor should not have worried, given that the challenge is on the write-in candidate, since a voter has to do more for them. Even long-shot candidates on the ballot have it easier than Sessions did in that they are convincing people to push a button, pull a lever, check off a box or do something similarly easy to cast a vote for that candidate. Sessions had to convince people to actually write-in his name and spell it right in order to get the votes he needed.

Sessions plunged himself into a door-to-door campaign talking about economic development and his commitment to the city and improving the economy. He talked about reducing city regulations in order to promote economic development and in a nod to the fact that he was at the time a high school student, he talked about the need to get new people and a new generation involved in city government. He said he would not necessarily reappoint the same people to city boards and commissions. Sessions said at the same time he was not seeing much of the incumbent on the campaign trail.

While he campaigned, his age and being a high school student did come up. "People would ask me my age and I would say it should not be a factor," Sessions said. "The factors should be enthusiasm and my ideas." Still Sessions found himself talking voters into why they should vote for him and why they should give him a chance to be the mayor. During the race, Sessions was able to pick up the endorsement of the firefighters because he supported bringing another fire company to Hillsdale. At the end of the day, Sessions ended up shocking the world and unseating the incumbent. The 18-year-old high school student running a write-in campaign unseated a sitting mayor in a Michigan city.

Sessions' election immediately placed Hillsdale on the national map. The high school student mayor — while not the youngest ever in American history — was national news and a national curiosity. He gained notice from national publications and television shows. People wanted to know how he could have been elected. But at the same time he saw the coverage as being a benefit to his town because he was bringing national attention to Hillsdale, which normally did not receive the type of attention that he was receiving in the days and weeks following the election. Other mayors from the country were reaching out to him, offering advice and inviting him to visit their towns. He struck up a friendship early on with Joe Vas, the then mayor of Perth Amboy, New Jersey. Sessions was able to discuss ways that the two cities could work together and Vas would invite him to make an official visit to Perth Amboy. Sessions would make the trip and in addition to touring Vas' city and studying how Perth Amboy overcame the decline of the manufacturing industry. Sessions would also get a tour of Rutgers University in nearby New Brunswick and struck up a friendship with Greg Schiano, the Rutgers football coach. As Vas was also a state assemblyman at the time, Sessions found himself being honored on the floor of New Jersey's assembly within months of taking office.

In Hillsdale, Sessions started his term trying to work with a city council made up largely of people who were aligned with the former mayor. Under

Hillsdale's form of government, the city administrator handled the day-to-day running of the city's government with the mayor presiding over the city council, making appointments, serving as the city's spokesman, setting agendas, performing ceremonial activities and communicating with officials at other layers of government. Sessions quickly had to start working a city council made up of people aligned with the mayor he had ousted. Sessions had to deal with many of his colleagues asking how an 18-year-old with no life experience was even qualified to be the city's mayor. He would respond by noting that many of the issues facing city government were not issues that anyone faced in the world. He would question if his predecessors had much experience in dealing with issues like water main breaks and aging sewers. Sessions noted that, in the first days of his term, he would ask: "[D]id the last person know about these things? When you get on a job it is the on the job experience that makes it great," he said.

Sessions said the toughest part of being mayor while a high school student was the time issue. He was in school for six hours a day during his first eight months in office. While the mayor's office is part-time and he was not needed for routine decisions and the city council meetings were in the evening, Sessions said the time he was in school took time away from various mayoral duties. He would not be able to attend certain daytime meetings or events that he was invited to. Sessions, interviewed while still a high school student in 2006, said he was looking forward to college and the flexibility a college schedule would bring in order to be able to focus time during the day on the mayor's office and the ability to work on economic development issues in his role as mayor.

Sessions would only end up limiting his involvement in city government to one term. Like Derrick Seaver, the Ohio state representative elected at the age of 18 who decided to leave before term limits kicked in, Sessions would do the same thing. He would end up not seeking reelection to a second term in 2009 and moved into the private sector. Under city law, Sessions could have held the mayor's office for two consecutive terms. Sessions' term at the helm of Hillsdale was not without controversy and ups and downs. In 2007 he pled no contest in a court case of sending false and malicious e-mails to the mother of his former campaign manager. During his mayoralty, Sessions would also suffer from testicular cancer. He would recover from the cancer and go into remission.

John Tyler Hammons of Muskogee, Oklahoma had similar thoughts to Sessions in early 2008. During this time, Hammons saw how his hometown of 40,000 could reinvent itself and start thinking in a new time period. Hammons at the time was 19 years old and always interested in government and saw that the incumbent mayor was not seeking reelection after one two-year term in the May 2008 election. After speaking with mentors, Hammons decided to throw himself in the mayor's race opposing a former mayor and four other candidates in a non-partisan election. Hammons did not enter the mayor's race lightly. He gave it a lot of thought and asked himself if he was the right person to think about new ways to grow the economy and lead the third largest industrial base in Oklahoma. During this time he sat down with his campaign's spiritual advisor in order to decide if he should make the race. "I felt led to it after thought and prayer," Hammons said. "That's where I could make the biggest impact."

Hammons would focus his campaign on a door-to-door grassroots race, like Sessions. During this time, he did not get much immediate age discrimination but people would ask him what he could bring to the race having never served on a volunteer board or commission in the city. People would quiz him about the issues and ask him what he could do as Muskogee's mayor. Hammons would talk about his platform and answer detailed questions about the city's economy and how he would promote economic development. Like many young elected officials who focus on being as knowledgeable about policy in order to overcome any questions about their age, Hammons became a policy wonk on many issues. "For a long time people here thought government and industry were separate," Hammons said in a 2009 interview about his platform. "We need to work together, that's reinventing ourselves."

Coming into the part-time mayor's office, Hammons found himself working closely with people who were old enough to be his parents and grandparents. His own secretary in the mayor's office was twice his age. He quickly went about working to build relationships with the city council members, department heads and other staffers he would be working closely with during his time in the mayor's chair. In addition to overcoming what he termed as a generation gap with many of the people he was closely working with, he had another issue to overcome: having become mayor of a large Oklahoma city of 40,000, some questioned whether Hammons was his own man or whether he was a front for someone else. "Someone is not spoon-feeding me," he said.

Outside of economic development, Hammons found two initiatives to put forward quickly upon taking office. He launched a healthy eating initiative early on and he also launched a reading challenge for school children in Muskogee. Hammons starting promoting city programs to assist residential housing redevelopment and a Cherokee Nation program to help Cherokee citizens buy a home. He also gained inroads with the Chamber of Commerce types and the city business community where he showed them that he was energetic and committed to working on their issues. Gaining a national profile because of his age, he waned to utilize that in order to help build more of a stature for his city, including promoting tourism.

Hammons's first months in office were not all smooth. Using a state law that allows charter cities in Oklahoma to propose their own laws, Hammons proposed that Muskogee create its own campaign finance reporting laws, saying the city needed them. He found that it wasn't that easy. "I proposed them and it was shot down," he said. "We never had it before and the Council voted it down 6–3." Prior to being elected mayor, Hammons had set out to become a delegate to the 2008 Republican National Convention. Lobbying the Oklahoma Republican Party for a delegate spot, Hammons used his youth to his advantage, saying it would be good for the party to have him in its delegation. He was given the spot and then he found himself in a unique position with the high profile of being the country's youngest sitting mayor.

Hammons enjoyed the time in Minneapolis where he helped nominate John McCain and Sarah Palin. While he did not meet either of the pair, he did get a chance to meet the first President Bush, and his personal hero, Rudy Giuliani. "It was a wonderful time and it was an opportunity to meet people I had read about and saw on TV," Hammons said in early 2009. "I got to meet my hero, Rudy Giuliani. I turned 20 on September 4, 2008 and that's the day I got to meet him. America's youngest mayor got to meet America's mayor. He knew who I was. I would have loved to meet John McCain and Sarah Palin, they are great Americans."

Hammons demures a bit on his political ambitions noting that he is still young and at the time only in his first two-year term as mayor. He will be up for reelection in May of 2010. He still is in college and then he hopes to go to law school. Hammons wants to concentrate on his job as mayor and helping Muskogee move forward. But with law school in the future, he said there are two jobs that do interest him in the future. "I would like to be the Muskogee County district attorney one day. I want to be a lawyer and I would love to serve the county as district attorney. I would like to be the governor of Oklahoma. Oklahoma is my home, it's the greatest state in the union."

It is not surprising that the cities that took a chance on these teenage mayors were the way they were. Yes there is a size difference and Muskogee is a lot larger than many communities that go with teenaged or early-20s mayors. Many are even smaller than Hillsdale. Many are small rural communities where it almost makes sense — in some cases there are not that many people who want to take on the role of mayor. Harry Zikas being elected mayor of Alpha, New Jersey, in 1999 at the age of 19 is a case in point. Zikas did face a competitive election to lead the town, but it is smaller than either Hillsdale or Muskogee. Alpha is a small rural community near Pennsylvania that at the time of Zikas' election did not have a stop light. Zikas would install one during his eight years as mayor. But size doesn't matter, rather the circumstances in the cities do. Both communities were old line manufacturing communities. The American manufacturing sector has declined in the last 20–30 years and the communities that relied on manufacturing as the main economic base have seen declines. People have left, home values have declined, people question if there are jobs. The question of youth leaving the community and going to other cities, states, and regions in order to find a job becomes the issue.

Electing a mayor who is young and thinks outside the box shows that a community like this wants to bring in someone who is not part of the old guard and someone who will be innovative. They are looking for something new and something different. They are looking for new leadership and that is what a young elected official can bring. Many young elected officials can think outside the box and have thought outside the box and a teenage mayor is no different. In addition the novelty of electing a teenage mayor is bound to bring national publicity and a national spotlight to a community. It will bring a spotlight that can help bring publicity and business to the town, which will help the community in the future. The concept of a young mayor, even a teen mayor, does make sense in certain communities, especially those that are looking for a change and looking for a difference in how things are done.

CHAPTER 12

Conclusion

Young elected officials form a complex subject, one with long-term impact on the American political landscape. It takes a special type of person to enter into the political game at a young age. To give up the normal lifestyle of a young professional — to give up certain liberties and time in order to run for, and hold, elective office — it also takes a person who is likely to think outside the box.

Why do I say a special individual who is willing to give up liberties? As was mentioned in Chapter 7, young elected officials do not end up living normal lives while they are in office. And for those who plan to hold office one day, they do not live normal lives even before they enter elective office. They are constantly on the go and worried about what they will do in public and what their public profile is. Granted, that is something a lot of people worry about, even if they do not have the high public profile of an elected official, young elected officials are in another category entirely. The new realm of media, where anything can be news very quickly, where one slip-up can end up as a YouTube video or a picture on Facebook, leads to even more caution among young elected officials than there may have been in an earlier time.

They have to give up more and more of their time for campaign activities and to further their career. The rise of the constant campaign has young elected officials spending more of their time attending political party and community events. They need to attend events for community groups that expect — rightly so — their community leaders on a regular basis. With many holding full-time professional jobs and holding elective office on a part-time basis, they end up giving up their personal interests and personal lives. Taking time away from friends, family, and fun in order to serve the public and to attempt to build a career in politics.

Simultaneously, the current technology has made it an even greater time sacrifice for a young elected official in the twenty-first century, as so much of politics consist of contact, conversation, and the sharing of information. You need to know what other people know and to also share what you know. Politics can at times be a profession of paranoia, and the need to share information is at times needed to cure any paranoia that may exist in a politician. A young elected official 20 or 30 years ago did not need to be in constant contact, with cell phones and BlackBerries being non existent. Today they can easily be reached — or reach others — by phone, text message, or e-mail. The technology gives rise to having more contact and more exchange of information. Young elected officials need to talk to others in politics even more often and cannot *not* be in constant contact.

This ends up leading many of them to give up more and more of their personal lives to spend it on the phone and answering e-mails. They are sacrificing more time for the sake of gaining political power and prestige and attempting to move up the ladder of politics.

The question is, what type of sacrifice this will be, and how it will shape young elected officials now and in the future? To an extent, the same modern technology actually makes it easier for young elected officials to have that work/life balance that eluded previous generations. They are able to be at home while using a computer, BlackBerry, or phone. They do not need to be meeting in-person as much or to be glued to their desks waiting to talk to others and exchange information. So while they may have to give more time because they are in constant contact, they can also be at home more often because of the modern technology. This is, of course, if the young elected official chooses to spend more time at home and actually wants to spend time with family, rather than using the traditional political smoke screens.

The social media that is making it tougher for young elected officials to live normal lives is also helping more young professionals run for office without having to break down the traditional barriers of party machines. Through social media they are able to reach out to more people and build coalitions and raise money more easily than young elected officials of before. Looking at young elected officials over the years, you are seeing more break-in at higher levels now than in past years. There are several reasons, including more acceptance of young people in positions of power and the ability to run for office more easily because of modern technology.

Young professionals choosing to be candidates for elective office are able to raise funds and put together connections more easily because of the existing social media. They can use their networks on Facebook and LinkedIn to help put together initial fundraising lists and what they need to move forward politically, at least to start. They are able to gain the seed money and support in order to run for office. They can also use sites like Facebook to help market their candidacies. They can use fan pages in order to put out information to others in their constituency in an easier way than in past generations. Social media like Twitter can also help get information out there to the voters. Young professionals will also have easier access to alumni networks and larger aspects of alumni networks because of social media than past generations, giving another spot to gain early support for a race.

By having access to this social media and the ability to build networks and fundraising bases outside of the traditional party structures, young elected officials will be able to help gain more support outside of the party structure. Look at Steve Fulop in Jersey City for example. While he came into office as a young reformer with some help from a former mayor and a compelling life story of enlisting in the Marines after witnessing the September 11 terrorist attacks, he has been using social media and his website and e-mails blasts to put together larger groups to advance his position and put together the coalition he'll need for the next step up the political ladder and future steps. He will not need to use the traditional party machine to help move him forward.

Now this is not to say that a politician at an older age can't use social media to help break into politics outside the party structure — but it is different. While more and more Facebook users are 50 years and older, the popular social networking site also continues to be the province of young professionals and those in college, making it easier for someone who is young to build a bigger social media network quicker. In addition, an older prospective politician will have more likely built up a base in community groups like the Rotary Club and the Optimist Club, along with being part of a political party group to gain the support they need. Especially for local office, they will have served on volunteer boards in town, gaining the experience needed for the local race. They will not need to be quickly appointed to a planning board seat like a Phil Morin in order to gain some experience before a party boss places them on the ballot for local office. Consequently they will be the frontrunners for the party backing. It is rarer to find young elected officials who have the connections to run for office early on, especially the younger they are. They may have been involved in party politics from an early age, but they are balancing other college student activities and may at times be kept at the outskirts of the party and not involved enough to gain the support. Young elected officials will need to gain the support from those outside the party structure in order to get themselves into office. This continued and growing use of social media by young elected officials is chang-ing the way politics is played. But this is the case of many politicians and the growing use of social media for political campaigns.

But one area where young elected officials are changing the world and the world of campaigns is in thinking outside the box. It could be Jason Kander and his unusual campaign ideas and taking photos with people he met when he went door-to-door. Or it could be thinking outside the box in the realm of public policy like Roz Wyman opening up the West to baseball and bringing the Dodgers to Los Angeles. Young elected officials will continue to think outside the box and bring new ideas to the table and do things differently. They are not wedded to the way things have always been done: they want to try new things. They are willing to take that risk.

Many of them took risks in order to run for office in the first place. Some of them, like Pam Iorio in Tampa had to quit their jobs in order to run for office and took that risk. Or in other cases they are taking time away from their full-time jobs in order to hold a part-time elective office, which is a big risk as their full-time employer may end up laying them off in the end. Or they will have to take time away from their personal lives and risk personal relationships.

The risk-taking that the young elected officials embrace when they decide to run for office continues to go into the work they do when the get into office. They are willing to think outside the box and do new things, consequently risking their careers in elective office and potentially alienating their colleagues with the result that nothing gets done. But this risk-taking is something that is needed in modern politics. Far too often politicians are too cautious, looking to do things that will get them reelected, not looking to take that chance and take that risk. In terms of campaigns, they will continue to follow the traditional safe method of how to run for office and not look to take a risk in how to run a political campaign. And the risks while in office will be tackling issues that are not normally tackled or making a proposal that is different.

Now this is not to say that all young elected officials are risk-takers. There is a percentage that is more risk averse and wants to set themselves up to run for higher office in the future and make politics into a long-term career. Because of this, they will avoid such risks and differ from many of their brethren as young elected officials. But by and large, some in large ways and some in small ways, young elected officials are willing to take risks. The willingness to take risks comes from their age. Many noted that if they quit their job to run for office, it was because being in their 20s and single put them in a position in life where they could take that risk, which they may not have taken at another point in time. In terms of taking a risk while in office, many of them have full-time jobs and careers outside of politics. While many have some thought of a long-term political career and no one wants to lose, they also have fallback careers. They do not need politics in order to be in their full-time job, by and large.

Age also impacts young elected officials in other ways. Many are more likely to take a new approach to policy. Their age may affect education policy, in that they are closer to having been students and thus have a different perspective with what needs to be done in terms of the schools. In the area of fiscal policy, they talked a lot about needing to not borrow more and more, knowing they will be around to have to pay off that public debt. Another area where young elected officials are leading is the environment, since they will likely live to see the long-term effects of today's environmental policies.

Young elected officials will try other types of things based on their age. While there will be issues where a young elected official will not think any differently than other elected officials, partially because there are no ways to do things differently, the difference in generation will continue to evolve the positions of young elected officials to be different and to propose different solutions. Young elected officials are showing a desire to work on ethics reform issues. They are like Fulop in pushing pay-to-play bans or Kander who has made ethics reform a major concern of his in Missouri. This is logical for them and for other young elected officials as one way to think outside the box is to change the way government runs and to make government more ethical. Young elected officials have grown up in an age of cynicism towards government and have seen the long-term impact of unethical behavior in past years. They want to change the way things are done and bring about a new approach. Yes, there are examples of young elected officials engaging in unethical behavior, but it is more likely that they will want to change ethics laws.

In 2008, young people looked to Barack Obama for change. While there were debates at the beginning of 2010 over what type of change President Obama had brought, it is clear that one of the demographics that supported him strongly did it on the promise of change and you see that carried over to how young elected officials behave while in office. Obama's election helped win races for office in 2008, since many voters were looking for change in that election and what group to reflect change better than someone under the age of 35? Young elected officials are the future of the American political process. Those in office under the age of 35 today are the leaders of tomorrow. It is, perhaps, a clichéd statement, but a true one. There are many examples of young elected officials rising to higher offices moving forward. This includes presidents, governors, and senators. Young elected officials are ambitious people by nature. You cannot run for elective office under the age of 35 without an ounce of ambition, but they are ambitious for the future in a variety of ways.

There are some who will never run for a higher office because they prefer where they are or choose to be in politics only for a short period of time before moving on, like Derrick Seaver in Ohio. But others are vastly different. Some will keep their ambitions in check, like Eric Garcetti in California, where he admits ambitions but remains mute on where he wants to go and expresses interest in two different elective career paths. Then there are those who do not express any ambition and say they are happy where they are. While some are genuine, many are playing the time-tested political game of playing down ambition in order not to tip their hat too early or not to offend their current constituents if they do not have a final plan in mind. And then there are those like Anthony Sytko of New Jersey who pretty much decided his future in politics and ran for office at an early age in order to put himself on that career path and is looking for what steps he can take as he attempts to move up the political ladder towards his stated goal.

Young elected officials will continue to change the American political landscape and will continue government. Many of them will be around for many years and will be changing politics and government. With young elected officials showing over the course of many decades the common threads of thinking outside the box and taking risks, it is pretty clear that people who are the young elected officials of the future will likely think and act the same way as their predecessors. Many of them will work very hard and make personal sacrifices in order to be in politics. Many of them will look to give back and look to change things.

Young elected officials will continue to be elected because people will continue to look for change. They will see no better example of change than someone who is young and looks young. It is not a coincidence that Michael Sessions and John Tyler Hammons were elected mayors as teenagers in older industrial cities. It is because the voters saw them as change and were looking for someone new and not tied to the city's old guard to govern them with the hope they would move the city in a new direction and in the direction of economic development. This does not mean that young elected officials will only be seen in small rural towns or areas in need of economic development. While in some of these places the political system makes it easier for a young person to run since the party structure is not as powerful, young elected officials will be seen everywhere. Whether a Jessica Lappin, Josh Svaty, or Alex Padilla, young elected officials will continue to be part of the landscape of American politics. Young elected officials have had an impact on government today and in the past. They will continue to have an impact in the future.

Appendix

YOUNG ELECTED OFFICIALS

Name	Office	Year	State	Notes	2010 Higher Office Campaign	Unsuccessful Previous Runs for Higher Office
Jeff Anderson	Duluth City Council	2007	Minnesota			
	President of the Duluth City Council	2009	Minnesota	Elected by city council		
Kyle Andrews	Niagara County Legislature	2001	New York			
	Niagara county treasurer	2010	New York	Appointed by Gov. David Paterson in March 2010 to fill unexpired term through Dec. 31, 2010. Seeking election to a full four-year term in 2010		
Brent Barton	State House of Representatives	2008	Oregon		Running for state senate	
Andre Bauer	State House of Representatives	1995	South Carolina		Running for governor	
	State senate	1998	South Carolina			
	Lieutenant governor	2002	South Carolina			
Jennifer Beck	Red Bank Borough Council	1998	New Jersey			
	General Assembly	2005	New Jersey			
	State senate	2007	New Jersey			
Earl Blumenauer	State House of Representatives	1972	Oregon			
	Multnomah County Commission	1978	Oregon			
	Portland City Council	1986	Oregon			
	U.S. House of Representatives	1996	Oregon			
Jon Bramnick	Plainfield City Council	1983	New Jersey			
	General Assembly	2003	New Jersey	Appointed to an unexpired term in 2003, then elected to a full term in November of that year		

(continued)

Name	Office	Year	State	Notes	2010 Higher Office Campaign	Unsuccessful Previous Runs for Higher Office
	Minority whip General Assembly	2007	New Jersey			
	Republican conference leader, General Assembly	2009	New Jersey			
Shane Brinton	No. Humboldt Union H.S. Dist. Bd. Mem.	2005	California			
	Arcata City Council	2008	California			
Frank Brogan	Martin county superintendent of schools	1988	Florida	County schools superintendents are elected in Florida		
	State commissioner of education	1994	Florida			
	Lieutenant governor	1998	Florida	Resigned in 2003 after three months in his second term as lieutenant governor to become president of Florida Atlantic University in 2009. Appointed chancellor of the State University System of Florida		
Don Calloway	State House of Representatives	2008	Missouri			
Peter Cammarano III	Hoboken City Council	2005	New Jersey			
	Mayor of Hoboken	2009	New Jersey	Resigned after one month in office after arrest on federal corruption charges		
Ben Cannon	State House of Representatives	2006	Oregon			
Chris Carter	State House of Representatives	2008	Missouri			
Jun Choi	Mayor of Edison	2005	New Jersey	Defeated for reelection in 2009		
Jennifer Credidio	Guttenberg City Council	2002	New Jersey	Did not seek reelection in 2006		
Eric Croft	State House of Representatives	1996	Alaska	Served four terms in the House		Unsuccessfully ran in the Democratic gubernatorial primary in 2006. Unsuccessful candidate for mayor of Anchorage in 2009

(continued)

Name	Office	Year	State	Notes	2010 Higher Office Campaign	Unsuccessful Previous Runs for Higher Office
Tony Cuneo	Duluth City Council	2007	Minnesota			
Stacy Dahl	State House of Representatives	2004	North Dakota			
Brett Davis	State assembly	2004	Wisconsin		Running for lieutenant governor	
Sean Duffy	District attorney of Ashland County	2002	Wisconsin		Running for Congress	
Michael Dukakis	Brookline Town Meeting		Massachusetts			
	State House of Representatives	1962	Massachusetts			
	Governor	1974	Massachusetts			
	Governor	1982	Massachusetts	Defeated for reelection in 1978. Reelected to a non-consecutive term in 1982		Unsuccessful Democratic candidate for president in 1988
Bob Franks	General Assembly	1979	New Jersey			Unsuccessful candidate for U.S. Senate in 2000 and governor in 2001
	Republican state chairman	1987	New Jersey			
	Republican state chairman	1990	New Jersey	Left the state chairman's post in June 1989. Regained the position in January 1990		
	U.S. House of Representatives	1992	New Jersey			
Michael Frerichs	Champaign County Board	2000	Illinois			Unsuccessful candidate for state House of Representatives in 1998
	Champaign County auditor	2002	Illinois			
	State senate	2006	Illinois			

(continued)

Name	Office	Year	State	Notes	2010 Higher Office Campaign	Unsuccessful Previous Runs for Higher Office
David Fried	Rockland County Legislature	2003	New York	Did not seek reelection in 2007		Unsuccessful candidate for state assembly in 2006
	Spring Valley Village Justice	2009	New York			
Steven Fulop	Jersey City Council	2005	New Jersey			Unsuccessful candidate for Congress in 2004
Eric Garcetti	Los Angeles City Council	2001	California			
	President of the Los Angeles City Council	2006	California	Elected by City Council		
Sean Gatewood	State House of Representatives	2008	Kansas			
Mike Gerber	State House of Representatives	2004	Pennsylvania			
Andrew Gillum	Tallahassee City Commission	2003	Florida			
	Mayor pro tem of Tallahassee	2004	Florida			
Eric Gioia	New York City Council	2001	New York	Term-limited out of office in 2009		Unsuccessful candidate for New York City public advocate in 2005
Raj Goyle	State House of Representatives	2006	Kansas		Candidate for Congress	
Jeffrey Graham	Mayor of Camden	2007	South Carolina			
Trey Grayson	Secretary of State	2003	Kentucky		Running for U.S. Senate	
John Tyler Hammons	Mayor of Muskogee	2008	Oklahoma			
Kevin Hardwick	Susquehanna Valley Board of Education	1974	New York			Unsuccessful candidate for Erie County Legislature in 2001 and 2003
	Binghamton Town Board	1985	New York			
	Tonawanda City Council	1996	New York			
	Erie County Legislature	2009	New York			

(*continued*)

Name	Office	Year	State	Notes	2010 Higher Office Campaign	Unsuccessful Previous Runs for Higher Office
Andrew Hevesi	State assembly	2005	New York			
Walker Hines	State House of Representatives	2007	Louisiana			
Elizabeth Holtzman	U.S. House of Representatives	1972	New York	Member of House Judiciary Committee during Watergate		Unsuccessful candidate for U.S. Senate in 1980 and 1992
	District attorney of Kings County	1981	New York			
	New York City comptroller	1989	New York	Defeated in 1993 for reelection		
Sam Hoyt	State assembly	1992	New York	Succeeded his father, William Hoyt, to the assembly seat		
Heather McTeer Hudson	Mayor of Greenville	2003	Mississippi			
Pam Iorio	Hillsborough County Commission	1985	Florida	Term-limited out of office after two terms		
	Hillsborough County supervisor of elections	1993	Florida	Resigned to run for mayor in 2003 under the Florida "resign to run" law		
	Mayor of Tampa	2003	Florida			
Tom Jardim	Mayor of Westfield	1996	New Jersey	Did not seek reelection 2000. Ran for mayor in 2005; defeated by Republican Andy Skibitsky. First Democrat in 90 years to have been elected mayor in Westfield		Unsuccessful candidate for General Assembly in 2001
Shane Jett	State House of Representatives	2004	Oklahoma		Candidate for Congress	
Connie Johnson	State House of Representatives	2000	Missouri			
Jason Kander	State House of Representatives	2008	Missouri			
Mary Kapsner Nelson	State House of Representatives	1998	Alaska	Did not seek reelection in 2008		
Marc Keahey	State senate	2009	Alabama			
	State House of Representatives	2005	Alabama			
Thomas Kean Jr.	General Assembly	2001	New Jersey	Appointed to an unexpired term in 2001 and then elected to a full term in November of that year		Unsuccessful candidate for Congress in 2000 and U.S. Senate in 2006

(*continued*)

Name	Office	Year	State	Notes	2010 Higher Office Campaign	Unsuccessful Previous Runs for Higher Office
	State senate	2003	New Jersey	Appointed to an unexpired term in 2003 and then elected to a full term in November of that year		
	Minority leader of the state senate	2008	New Jersey			
Jules Kopel-Bailey	State House of Representatives	2008	Oregon			
Jessica Lappin	New York City Council	2005	New York			
Chris Lee	State House of Representatives		Hawaii			
Marko Liias	Mukilteo City Council	2005	Washington			
	State House of Representatives	2007	Washington			
Keith Loughlin	Westfield Town Council	2009	New Jersey			
Eddie Lucio III	State House of Representatives	2006	Texas			
John McGee	State senate	2006	Idaho			
Andy Meisner	State House of Representatives	2002	Michigan			
	Oakland County Treasurer	2008	Michigan			
Robert Menendez	Union City Board of Education	1974	New Jersey			
	Mayor of Union City	1986	New Jersey			
	General Assembly	1986	New Jersey			
	State senate	1991	New Jersey			
	U.S. House of Representatives	1992	New Jersey			
	U.S. Senate	2006	New Jersey	Appointed by Gov. Jon Corzine to fill a vacant Senate seat in January 2006. Then elected to a full term in November of that year		
Gifford Miller	New York City Council	1996	New York			Unsuccessful candidate for mayor of New York in 2005
	Speaker of the New York City Council	2002	New York	Elected by city council. Term-limited out of office in 2006		

(continued)

Name	Office	Year	State	Notes	2010 Higher Office Campaign	Unsuccessful Previous Runs for Higher Office
Corey Ray Mock	State House of Representatives	2008	North Dakota		Running for secretary of state	
Philip Morin III	Cranford Township Committee	1996	New Jersey			Unsuccessful candidate in special election convention for General Assembly in 2003
	Deputy mayor of Cranford	1999	New Jersey	One-year position appointed by Township Committee		
	Mayor of Cranford	2000	New Jersey	One-year position appointed by Township Committee		
	Deputy mayor of Cranford	2002	New Jersey	One-year position appointed by Township Committee		
	Union county Republican chairman	2004	New Jersey			
Don Ness	Duluth City Council	1999	Minnesota			
	President, Duluth City Council	2001	Minnesota	Elected by city council		
	President, Duluth City Council	2004	Minnesota	Elected by city council		
Blake Oshiro	State House of Representatives	2000	Hawaii			
Alex Padilla	Los Angeles City Council	1999	California			
	President of the Los Angeles City Council	2001	California	Elected by city council		
	State senate	2006	California	Sought Senate seat after being term-limited off the city council		
Josh Penry	State House of Representatives	2004	Colorado		Briefly ran for GOP nomination for governor	
	State senate	2006	Colorado	Not seeking reelection in 2010		
	Minority leader, state senate	2008	Colorado			
Dan Quayle	U.S. House of Representatives	1976	Indiana			Unsuccessful candidate for Republican presidential nomination in 2000

(*continued*)

Name	Office	Year	State	Notes	2010 Higher Office Campaign	Unsuccessful Previous Runs for Higher Office
	U.S. Senate	1980	Indiana			
	Vice president of the United States	1988	National	Defeated for reelection in 1992		
Jack Quinn III	State assembly	2004	New York		Running for state senate	
Tobias Read	State House of Representatives	2006	Oregon			
Aaron Reardon	State House of Representatives	1998	Washington			
	State senate	2002	Washington	Served one year before resigning to take office as county executive		
	Snohomish county executive	2003	Washington			
Andrew Romanoff	State House of Representatives	1999	Colorado	Term-limited out of office in 2008	Running for U.S. Senate	
	Minority leader of the state House	2003	Colorado			
	Speaker of the House	2005	Colorado			
Patrick Rose	State House of Representatives	2002	Texas			
Michael Ross	Boston City Council	1999	Massachusetts			
	President, Boston City Council	2009	Massachusetts	Elected by city council		
Jasper Schneider	State House of Representatives	2006	North Dakota			Unsuccessful candidate for state insurance commissioner in 2008
	State director, USDA Rural Development	2009	North Dakota	Appointive office in the administration of President Barack Obama		
Mac Schneider	State House of Representatives	2008	North Dakota			
Bret Schundler	Mayor of Jersey City	1992	New Jersey			Unsuccessful candidate for governor in 2001 and 2005. Unsuccessful candidate for state senate in 1991
	State commissioner of Education	2010	New Jersey	Appointive office in the cabinet of Gov. Chris Christie		
Derrick Seaver	State House of Representatives	2000	Ohio	Did not run for reelection in 2006. Convicted of drunk driving in 2007		

(*continued*)

Name	Office	Year	State	Notes	2010 Higher Office Campaign	Unsuccessful Previous Runs for Higher Office
Bakari Sellers	State House of Representatives	2006	South Carolina			
Michael Sessions	Mayor of Hillsdale	2005	Michigan	Did not seek reelection in 2009		
Jessica Sferrazza	Reno City Council	2000	Nevada		Running for lieutenant governor	
Josh Shapiro	State House of Representatives	2004	Pennsylvania			
	Deputy Speaker, state House of Representatives	2007	Pennsylvania			
Jefferson Smith	State House of Representatives	2008	Oregon			
Stephen Solarz	State assembly	1968	New York			
	U.S. House of Representatives	1974	New York	In 1990, ran against Nydia Velasquez in a heavily Hispanic district carved from his old district and was defeated		
Josh Svaty	State House of Representatives	2003	Kansas			
	Secretary of agriculture	2009	Kansas	Appointive office in the cabinet of Gov. Mark Parkinson		
Jane Swift	State senate	1990	Massachusetts			
	Secretary of Consumer Affairs	1997	Massachusetts	Appointive office in the cabinet of Gov. William Weld		
	Lieutenant governor	1998	Massachusetts			
	Acting governor	2001	Massachusetts	Under the Massachusetts Constitution, served as acting governor following the resignation of Gov. Paul Cellucci in 2001 until the end of the term in January 2003. Declined to run for election in 2002		
Anthony Syrko	Garwood Board of Education	2005	New Jersey	Appointed to a three-month interim term. Chose not to seek election to the remaining two years left on term		Unsuccessful candidate for Union county freeholder in 2009
	Garwood Borough Council	2007	New Jersey	Did not seek reelection in 2010		
John Tobin	Boston City Council	2001	Massachusetts			
Ben Vig	State House of Representatives	2006	North Dakota			
Stephen Webber	State House of Representatives	2008	Missouri			

(*continued*)

Name	Office	Year	State	Notes	2010 Higher Office Campaign	Unsuccessful Previous Runs for Higher Office
Jason West	Mayor of New Paltz	2003	New York	Defeated for reelection in 2007		
Henry Wojtaszek	North Tonawanda city attorney	1997	New York	Elected to two-year terms and then the first four-year term in the city attorney's office		Unsuccessful candidate for Congress in 2002
	Niagara county Republican chairman	2000	New York			
	Niagara county Republican chairman	2002	New York	Following the elections successor resigned the chairmanship and Wojtaszek was reelected		Resigned in June 2002 to run for Congress unsuccessfully
	N.Y.S. Republican Party vice chairman	2006	New York	Defeated in 2009 in bid for Chairman of the N.Y.S. Republican Party		
Roz Wyman	Los Angeles City Council	1953	California	Defeated for reelection in 1965		
Alex Zikas	Alpha Borough Council	2005	New Jersey			
Harry Zikas	Alpha Board of Education	1998	New Jersey			
	Mayor of Alpha	1999	New Jersey	Declined to seek a third term as mayor in 2007 to run for a seat on the Borough Council instead		
	Alpha Borough Council	2007	New Jersey			
Dan Zwonitzer	State House of Representatives	2004	Wyoming			Unsuccessful candidate for Congress in 2008
Terry Bellamy	Mayor of Ashville	2007	North Carolina			
Rosalind Jones	State House of Representatives	2003	Louisiana			
Cam Ward	State House of Representatives	2001	Alabama			

Index